BROKEN BY RELIGION

HEALED BY GOD

Other books by Gordon Dalbey

Healing the Masculine Soul
How God Restores Men to Real Manhood

Sons of the Father
Healing the Father-Wound in Men Today

Fight like a Man
A New Warrior for a New Warfare

No Small Snakes
A Journey into Spiritual Warfare

Do Pirates Wear Pajamas?
and other Mysteries in the Adventure of Fathering

Religion vs. Reality
Facing the Home Front in Spiritual Warfare

Pure Sex
The Spirituality of Desire

Loving to Fight or Fighting to Love
Winning the Spiritual Battle for Your Marriage

Gordon Dalbey may be contacted
for speaking engagements and other resources at
Box 61042, Santa Barbara, CA 93160
www.abbafather.com

BROKEN BY RELIGION, HEALED BY GOD

Restoring the

Evangelical, Sacramental,

Pentecostal, Social Justice

Church

By

Gordon Dalbey

CivitasPress

Publishing inspiring and redemptive ideas.[sm]

Copyright Notice

Religion is the tree of the knowledge of good and evil,
a badge of lost innocence.

Division in the Church distracts us
from the true and raging war against God's rule.

"WWJD" speculates about a dead Jesus.
WIJD--What Is Jesus Doing?—that's the question.

A lifeless church has cut itself off from Jesus,
the Source of its life.

Safety is not the absence of threat
but the presence of Jesus.

Too many Christians are trying to be good
without confessing they can't.

God's antidote to religion is neither secularism nor piety.
It's Jesus.

You're not ready to know the Savior
until you know you need to be saved.

Communion is not a time to reminisce about a god named I was,
but to welcome the God named I Am.

Religion promotes a virtual relationship with God.

All human division arises from
the common impulse to hide our shame.

Religion commands us to control our lives;
Jesus invites us to trust God's control.

Youth dismiss church not because they're so immature,
but because the church is often so immature.

Christians are outsiders because God created us
to transform the world, not adapt to it.

Material comfort is good as the undeserved gift of God;
evil when it blinds us to the suffering of others.

This book is dedicated to Francis MacNutt,
whose pioneering courage, upending truth, and persevering grace
blazed the trail for my journey.

Contents

Holy Father! Keep them safe by the power of your name, the name you gave me, so that they may be one just as you and I are one. (John 17:11)

Foreword

"Too hot to handle."

"Something here to offend everyone."

When I began writing this book in 1985, many editors praised it and a prominent agent in Colorado Springs excitedly pronounced it "a sure thing." None of us, however, anticipated the resistance from publishers—as the above sample quotes.

"I don't get it," the agent fumed. "This is a message of life to churches!"

You can't see a lifeboat as helpful until you see you're drowning.

Today, decades later, it hardly needs documenting that the church is not widely respected in modern culture. Amid increasing hostility between races, nations, religions, social classes, and political parties, Christianity is too often seen as a force which sustains, if not fosters enmity and division. To others, the followers of Jesus seem more anxious to squabble among ourselves than to follow Him together into a broken world, united in His power to heal it.

The evidence against us is clear and indisputable, namely, the epidemic, largely unchallenged division between Christian denominations and movements. We preach love and harmony, yet our practice betrays our values so brazenly that often the world cites us only to ridicule our hypocrisy.

Meanwhile, the Good News is that even now, as always, Jesus intercedes for us with the Father "that they may be one, just as you and I are one" (John 17:11).

In fact, the world is still open to our witness. I know that, because its awful brokenness today testifies that the human heart still longs for what Jesus came to give us. It's what the world can never give us, namely, God's power to overcome the shame that divides us and to enable the caring community we long for.

What's more, His Spirit sustains that vision today in Jesus' Body, the Church, and empowers us to fulfill it. I know that, too, because I've experienced it.

That's what this book is about.

RELIGION AS VIRTUAL RELATIONSHIP

This is my personal story of division in my own church and a search for real and engaging relationship with Jesus to overcome it. It's about an upending season of both pain and renewal, in which I was forced to leave the church as I knew it in order to discover the church as Jesus knows it.

But it's also about the crippling brokenness in His Body today, which that journey revealed.

In fact, the scandalous separation among us Christians today—most often justified by each faction as an attempt to be more godly—simply reflects our separation from God.

Historically, that is, religion has too often promoted an intermediary, virtual relationship with God—substituting performance standards, rituals, supernatural gifting, theologies, and ideologies for the tears and joys, fears and hopes of genuine relationship. Insofar as an email "protects" you from the discomfort and risk of face-to-face encounter, religion can protect you from God. To that extent, it proceeds from a discomfort with, if not a distrust of God, and betrays a fear of His presence and activity.

Thus, the Pharisees feared Jesus.

Religion's most recognized agenda is to render its followers "right with God," and in that sense, "righteous." Yet the biblical faith itself understands that this is not something human beings can do. Insofar as religion is animated by human effort to win God's favor, it's patently unholy—because it's unreal. The God of the Bible is simply not impressed by our efforts to be good, because He knows all too well what our shame conspires to hide, namely, that we can't be good. "I know that good does not live in me—that is, in my human nature," as the Apostle Paul put it, "for even though the desire to do good is in me, I am not able to do it." (Rom. 7:18).

Even Jesus balked when addressed as "Good Teacher":

Why do you call me good? No one is good except
God alone (Mark 10:18).

Indeed, "It is not the healthy who need a doctor, but the sick," Jesus declared, citing the ancient prophet Hosea:

> But go and learn what this means: "I desire mercy, not sacrifice." For I have not come to call the righteous, but sinners. (Matt. 9:12,13NIV).

Like the two trees in Eden, religion thrives on the knowledge of good and evil, while the human heart thrives on the freedom of life in Jesus. American Revolutionary Thomas Paine wrote that **"Government, like dress, is a badge of lost innocence."[1] The same might be said today of religion.**

Rather than draw us closer to God, religion can distance us, as it seeks—like a well-crafted email--to cover the shame of our human inadequacy and its consequent fear of intimacy (see Gen. 3:8ff.). On the Cross, however, Jesus did not simply cover our shame; he deleted it, and proclaimed, "It is finished!" (John 19:30).

Too often, religion implies that human effort can overcome the separation between us and God. That's simply a lie. In fact, it's plain foolishness. As Paul scoffed, "Only crazy people would think they could complete by their own efforts what was begun by God" (Galat. 3:3TMB).

Religion is a crutch; Jesus is new legs.

When we distrust God's ability to complete His work in us and instead seize control, we not only separate from Him, but from our authentic, needy selves. Thus divided within our hearts and unwilling to embrace our own broken selves, we can't witness to the Father's heart to embrace a broken world. Instead of a Church united in our heartfelt longing for Jesus— and thereby, empowered as agents of His reconciliation—we Christians become infected with the world's brokenness, host its enmity, and disable each other.

A LARGER EXPERIENCE

As a young man, I saw this dynamic of distrust and control destroying myself and other men. In 1987, when most churches had forgotten men, I sensed a move of God underfoot that would one day free us to recognize and receive the Father's heart for His sons. In that year, I wrote my first of four men's books, *Healing the Masculine Soul*, aimed at reconciling us to God, to our manhood, and to women. The rest, as they say, is history--even yet unfolding in the ongoing Christian men's movement.

Today, as clearly as then, I sense the God of reconciliation is again shaking His Church. This time, it's a movement with both an ancient and modern flavor. It calls the followers of Christ from every tradition--as members of His One Body--to respect, embrace, and express each other's distinct but complementary visions as affirmed in the Bible.

It's a move toward vibrant unity, not humdrum uniformity. The holy banquet is being prepared, and it's no bland melting pot of one flavor and consistency. Rather, it's a spicy stew of several ingredients, which simmers today as Christians yearn for a larger experience of God than our separate traditions have allowed us.

Yet God's movement to unite His church in these times is no mere religious housekeeping. Rather, it's a preparation for battle that promises to shake the foundations of life on this planet.

On September 11, 2001, the world was stunned by terrorist attacks upon the World Trade Center in New York and the Pentagon in Washington, DC, killing over 3000 people. This evil was perpetrated by a particular religious faction whose self-proclaimed righteousness drove them not only to separate from others, but indeed, to destroy those who disagree with them.

In response to the growing terrorist threat, many churches donated money, prayed for the victims, and preached understanding. Helpful as those efforts can be, Christians cannot hope to overcome this demonic sectarian spirit in the terrorists and their ilk as long as we allow and even foster it among ourselves.

As Jesus declared, "How can Satan cast out Satan?" (Mark 2:23).

In fact, the word "di-abolic," or "of the devil," comes from a compound root "di," meaning "to split" as in "di-vide," and "abol" as in "abol-ish." Jesus, however, has come not to divide and abolish, but rather, to unite and mobilize the sons and daughters of God. Thus, he cried out in our behalf,

Holy Father! *Keep them safe* by the power of your
name, the name you gave me, *so that they may be one,*
just as you and I are one. (John 17:11b, italics mine)

COMFORTABLE WESTERN CHURCH

The name Jesus is a transliteration of the name Joshua, which in Hebrew means "God Saves." The power of this name lies in its affirmation of

God's most significant character trait, namely, a Father's will to rescue and save His children. At its best, Christianity witnesses to the present, saving power of God as revealed in Jesus. Those who don't face their need for Jesus to save them can't know either His power to do so or the value of uniting together in His name.

Hard as it's been for the comfortable Western Church to acknowledge, the Body of Christ has been at war with the world since Jesus was born and King Herod sought to kill him. Significantly, the religious establishment engineered His death. **Unto today, God has therefore been moving to unite His Church not after the shame and fear of religion, but rather, after the trusting intimacy of His Father-Son relationship with Jesus.**

That's why God's men's movement preceded and now undergirds this message, in revealing Himself as Father to a fatherless generation—who cannot know His heart for His Church until we confess our own unmet longing for a father and seek Father God to fulfill it. Until we know God as our Father, we can't recognize each other as brothers and sisters.

9/11 signaled that the enemy of God will meet any initiative of such Kingdom significance with vicious counterattack.

This book, therefore, is not simply about tolerance for or fellowship with people who are different from you. It's about together living out Jesus' determination to unite His Church. Like God's perfect vision for this broken world, His hope for the Church remains as yet unfulfilled. In fact, since being ordained in 1977, I haven't found any church that manifests it fully. Our inability to grasp God's goal, however, does not invalidate it. Ideals, it's been said, are like stars—we never reach them, but we set our course by them.

In this post-9/11 world, Christians must realize that we have no choice but to stand together. Indeed, Jesus prayed for His people to "be one" in order to "keep them safe." The unholy division among us is not only immature folly, but complicity with the *di-abolic* enemy of God and thereby, suicide as His Body.

Significantly, we shall see herein that this enemy is not simply one particular religion, but rather, a deeper human impulse which fuels all human division and which manifests most graphically in religion itself. This book portrays not only that destructive impulse, but the saving work of Jesus that overcomes it.

Divided, we fall. When Christians turn away from Jesus' call to unite His Church, we become isolated in our separate villages and unable to lead others into God's larger, universal purposes. The problem is not that other religions are too strong, but that our divided Christian witness is too weak—not only to save the world, but the Church itself.

Jesus did not come from the selfish heart of a tyrant, to intimidate and subjugate humanity. He came from the loving heart of a Father, to free and empower His children to their destiny. Neither, therefore, is this book about condemning other perspectives, but about restoring Christians to the fullness of our faith—which alone can secure our distinctiveness and revitalize our witness to God's saving power.

Jesus' Body has suffered division for centuries, which has beckoned scoffers and seekers alike to dismiss Christians as more focused on squabbling among ourselves than on working together to restore a broken world. "We have grown old in our sin," as author Francis MacNutt has declared. "The division has been with us so long, we are familiar, even comfortable with it…. (T)his division is an absolute scandal. We are living in sin, but not too much bothered by it."[2]

The same sectarian, shame-based religion that fueled the 9/11 terrorists infects the Body of Christ today. Like towers of human construction, a Church divided today will fall tomorrow, and with it the world Jesus died to save.

As His Kingdom advance comes under increasing attack, surely God is exasperated by this unholy "Christian" charade, this virtual battle among ourselves which distracts us from the true and raging war against His rule. He has already shown us, over 2000 years ago, what victory in this eternal war requires, namely, that we humbly follow Jesus to the cross. There, we must beg for His upending truth and persevering grace to turn us from competing against each other to cooperating with God.

That's what the Father sent Jesus to fight for in our hearts.

That's what I hope this book will stir in your heart—and in your church.

Broken by Religion:

The Dismembered Body of Christ

At the center of all this, Christ rules the church. The church, you see, is not peripheral to the world; the world is peripheral to the church. The church is Christ's body, in which he speaks and acts, by which he fills everything with his presence. (Ephes. 1:22,23TMB)

Introduction

A Broken Church

> Christ cannot be divided into groups! (1 Corinth. 1:13)

An uneasy but refreshing vitality has been stirring in churches for decades now. You've likely seen signs of it yourself, maybe even in your own congregation:

Evangelicals determinedly promoting racial reconciliation and world peace.

Catholics and Episcopalians deliberately studying the Bible and being born again.

Pentecostals joyfully celebrating the sacrament of communion.

Presbyterians, Lutherans, Methodists, and other Oldline Reform congregations excitedly laying on hands and praying for physical healing.

"What's wrong with this picture?" you might ask.

"Nothing at all!" any first-century Believer would declare. In fact, our biblical ancestors would challenge us today, "Why do any of these common biblical practices of the early Church seem so strange to you—and why aren't all of them practiced in your own congregations?"

What, indeed, has so fractured the modern Church, and what is the Living, Risen Christ doing to heal His Body?

The cry for unity today is embodied by a growing youth culture often generations removed from any church experience. Alienated by broken families and increasingly isolated by media technology that can only fabricate relationships, young men and women are now longing for a whole and genuine experience of God—even as for caring, secure community. Their cry for wholeness and centeredness in a fragmented, anything-goes world calls the Body of Christ to decide which is more important: clinging to a truncated identity in your own church's particular practice, or letting God bring us all into a full biblical expression of Christian faith, and thereby save the next generation for His future.

Why, indeed, have we Christians withdrawn from this larger experience of the biblical faith, and how can we let God express it fully among us all?

Certainly, the journey to that unity and its larger perspective must pass through particular circumstances if individual human beings are to grasp it. God's timeless and universal Story, that is, must be told through specific people in particular times--even as through a first-century carpenter from Nazareth.

Other books have appropriately featured a particular facet of the biblical faith, such as evangelism or healing. Some have criticized denominationalism and called for Christian unity. The larger vision which this book urges, however, grows not out of a larger theology, but rather, out of my own personal longing for a fuller experience of God—a longing which I see growing today both locally where I live and among Christians around the world where I minister.

ENTHUSIASM VS. TOLERANCE?

The preface to this larger vision therefore opens some years ago over tuna fish sandwiches at lunch with a then-fellow Oldine Reform pastor. After noting that all our church programs were going well enough, eventually we both confessed a frustration over the lack of enthusiasm both in ourselves and in our congregations.

Dismayed, confused, we fell silent. Finally, my friend set down his sandwich and knit his brow. "How can we who are so tolerant of differences," he asked, "ever get that enthusiastic zeal of the others who are so particular in the way they see things?"

After experiencing a wide variety of churches over the years, I'm seized even today by that frustration.

I've battled the lifelessness in churches whose major goal is universal tolerance. On the other hand, I've also battled the isolation and condemnation in "enthusiastic" congregations who felt threatened by differences, and therefore, were unwilling to meet others at their genuine point of need.

Does a church have to be intolerant in order to be enthusiastic? Does a church have to be lifeless in order to accept and engage people where they are?

"I believe that the most nettlesome dilemma hindering interreligious dialog," as Harvard Divinity School Professor Harvey Cox declared,[3] "is the very ancient one of how to balance the universal and the particular." Counting himself as "one of the universalists," he decries the "radical particularists" who insist that theirs is the only true vision.

Yet Cox confesses that during the often boring "dialog" exercise among different faith perspectives, he has "secretly wished to bring some of those enthusiasts in":

> Deprived of the energy such particularists embody, a dialog-among-the-urbane can, and sometimes does, deteriorate into a repetitious exchange of vacuities. It could end with a whimper.

With a statement frightfully prescient since the 9/11 terrorist attacks, Cox--writing over a decade prior in 1988--adds,

> At the same time, I fully believe that without the large-hearted vision of the universal that the interfaith conversation incarnates, particularism can deteriorate into fanaticism. And in our present overarmed world, zealotry can easily hasten the moment when everything ends with a bang.

We are left, he concludes, "with a paradox":

> Without the universal pole, there would be no dialog at all. But without the particular, the dialog dissipates its source of primal energy.

Certainly, today's divided and unbalanced Church frustrates God, as it keeps us Christians from engaging Him fully as individuals and from uniting corporately to bring His Kingdom rule on earth as it is in heaven.

How, indeed, did this brokenness begin? How is God present and working among us today to overcome it, and how can we cooperate with Him?

Our search for the roots of that brokenness and the healing hand of God at work in it must begin with the ancient Biblical witness and the light that it sheds on our own experience today. And here, like its prophets, we must proclaim a warning as well as a promise.

The Good News is that God is still at work in and among us, saving us from our self-centered nature and drawing us to Himself, healing and empowering us to do His Kingdom work. Our task is to recognize what God is doing and join Him.

Major temptations, however, threaten to short-circuit this task.

Overwhelmed, you can dismiss God's Story as too grand for an individual like yourself, and therefore, as remote and irrelevant. *Uniting God's Church is just too much for me,* you can sigh—and be in good company. As the Psalmist marveled,

> When I look at the sky, which you have made, at the moon and the stars, which you set in their places—what is man, that you think of him, mere man, that you care for him? (Ps. 8: 3,4)

Indeed, in an effort to avoid the shame of your own inadequacy, you can dismiss your individual story as too small, and thereby, insignificant. Too quickly, you can seize upon God's Story instead and leap to heady religious pronouncements, divorced from the truth of genuine experience and the personal grace of the Father's saving hand: *I'll just exhort others to shape up and achieve God's higher standard,* you can rationalize; *That way, they'll be preoccupied with their own shortcomings and never see that I'm not measuring up myself.*

BALANCING TRUTH AND GRACE

Thus, the seduction of legalistic religion. "God gave the Law through Moses," as John counters, "but grace and truth He gave through Jesus Christ" (John 1:17). **The healing God seeks in us today is not about doing the right thing, but about being a real person, so that His Spirit can empower us to do right** (see Ezekiel 36:26ff). In this present media age of deceptive appearances, discerning the truth is essential. But amid the universal shame of our sinful human condition, we can't walk in truth without the grace that restores us when inevitably we fall short (see Rom. 7:24,25).

We can't get where God wants us to go, that is, unless we start where we are. That's often uncomfortable, because most of us who live in this broken world are not where we'd like to be. In our hearts, we know that only the truth can set us free from our shame—but we wonder if there's enough grace to face it safely.

It's dangerous being real in a world literally hell-bent to cover its brokenness.

You could get crucified.

Yet only those who can confess their smallness are ready to discover God's largeness--and that's something to get excited about. Thus, after noting his relative insignificance, the star-gazing Psalmist concludes, "O Lord, our Lord, your greatness is seen in all the world!" (Ps. 8:9). Confessing God's greatness amid our smallness gives the Psalmist—as even us today—courage to press on after his divine destiny.

This book will stir you to a faith both passionate about its truth and compassionate in its grace. You'll discover here freedom from the world's trap between universal tolerance on the one hand and narrow condemnation on the other. You'll find freedom to confess the truth of God's Word and to experience the uplifting grace of the Father who speaks it.

I invite you here to allow God's work in my life to awaken you to telltale marks of His work in your own life—and thereby, begin to discover God's eternal Story being told even now in your story. That's how He draws us together as One Body into the great adventure story He's telling among us all in these troubled but promising times.

TAKEAWAY

Something new is happening in churches these days: Evangelicals battling racism and social injustice, Pentecostals celebrating the sacrament of communion, Sacramentalists reading the bible and being born again, Oldline Reform churches laying on hands and praying for healing. The Lord is restoring His fragmented Body to the Original Church which He founded.

Why do you think churches divide? How do you see God working now to unite us all under His leadership? Are you part of the solution, or part of the problem?

1

"Are You a Christian?"

Toward a Spiritual Ecumenism

Christ is the head of his body, the church; he is the
source of the body's life. (Col. 1:18)

Shortly after coming to the Southern California coast to pastor my
first church, I received an onsite theology lesson while jogging on the
beachfront bike path. Excited about living on the ocean and buoyed by my
Harvard seminary degree and new clergy status, I had decided energetically
to do as the natives and take up running.

About a mile after setting out, with the sea breeze uplifting me from
behind, I reached the pier triumphantly and slowed among the bathers
and shoppers. As I drew up to gather my breath amid the crowd, I spotted
a young man striding toward me casually dressed in Levis, T-shirt and
sandals, brandishing a large black book in one hand. At once, my inner
theological monitor leapt to "warning" status.

Oh, no! I thought, determined to forego my jogging break and turn
back immediately.

Too late.

"Excuse me," the young man offered, stepping in front of me. "Are you
a Christian?"

Startled by his question, my escape momentarily foiled, I stopped.
Panting, I debated whether to say anything--then decided to let him have

it.

"In fact," I puffed, "I just finished three years of seminary and am pastor of a church near here!" Assuming that this revelation would end our conversation decisively, I turned civilly to go. "Excuse me, now, but I..."

"That's great," he noted matter-of-factly. "But do you know Jesus?"

"WHAT?" I exclaimed--and then caught myself as a mixture of anger and confusion arose within me. For an uncomfortable second I stood there, poised on my take-off foot. "Of course!" I huffed at last.

For a strange moment, I hesitated—then turned quickly and ran away.

The winds pushed against me as I jogged home, and I pushed back, anxious to distance myself from the scene. As the crowd thinned and finally disappeared, my pace slowed. Genuinely puzzled, I reflected on my encounter with the street evangelist.

I had expected from him something more "churchy," like, "Are you born again?" Then, I could have replied confidently, if not smugly, "Yes, every day is new for me!" That was always good for confusing the buttonholers.

But what did he mean, "Are you a Christian?"

Certainly, I thought, panting and wiping sweat from my brow, I'm not a Buddhist, a Moslem, a Jew, or anything else! I'd gone to church as a boy; now, as an adult, after three long and expensive years of seminary training I had chosen a denomination, which had confirmed my qualifications for Christian ministry by ordaining me.

I looked up and saw my starting point ahead. *Do you know Jesus?* The question leapt into my mind again.

The audacity of that kid! I scoffed, then leaned into the wind and sprinted home.

FAITH GAP

Today, I realize that I fled from my beachfront inquisitor because we both knew I should have been able to answer his questions sincerely, if not confidently. My proud attempt to discount them with my church credentials simply revealed the emptiness of my faith. I really didn't know what it means to be a Christian beyond religious affiliation.

In fact, I did *not* know Jesus. The pier evangelist had opened the door to a dark secret, a hidden insecurity, a fearful gap in my faith that I had hoped my ordination would officially cover. Even as I later scoffed at his "simplistic thinking" and "overbearing style," in my heart I knew that all my intelligent indignation was just a smokescreen for a lifelong sense of incompleteness and inadequacy in my faith.

Growing up, I knew that Christians "believe in God." I had heard of some people, called "atheists," who didn't believe in God, and therefore were not Christians. But so far as I knew, as long as you believed in God, that made you a Christian.

Eventually, I discovered that people called "Jews" believe in God, but were not Christians, because they didn't "believe in Jesus." Since I was not a Jew, I concluded that I must therefore believe in Jesus. That was easy enough, because for me it meant simply to accept the fact that the man named Jesus in the Bible really did live at one time.

The notion that this Jesus, who lived thousands of miles away and thousands of years ago, could intervene to affect my life now in any real way, never occurred to me--largely, I suspect, because it had never occurred to the adults I met in churches, or even in seminary. In fact, I was over thirty and well into my first pastorate before I ever met an adult who knew the founding Person of my religion on a first-name basis.

MR. CHRIST

Indeed, the only time I'd seen adults' talking about Jesus in any personal way--calling Him "Jesus" instead of "Jesus Christ"--was with children. Only little kids sang "Jesus Loves Me." The message was clear: Any sense of personal relationship with a living, active God was basically childish, and nothing for mature adults. "Mr. Christ" would do just fine, thank you.

Furthermore, I knew absolutely nothing about any Holy Spirit beyond singing the ancient "Gloria Patri" and "Doxology" hymns on Sunday morning. From the former's refrain, "Glory be to the Father/And to the Son/And to the Holy Ghost" to the latter's "Praise Father, Son, and Holy Ghost," I determined to know no more about some kind of "Ghost," no matter how "Holy." A quick song once a week was plenty enough.

As I grew up and left home for college, I continued to visit a variety of churches among the Oldline Reformation denominations of my youth. I went to chapel at my Methodist-related university, enjoyed a retreat at the Episcopal student center, shared the pulpit on Youth Sunday at a

Presbyterian church, worked with a Lutheran ministry to apartment singles, and greatly admired the United Church of Christ Dean of the Chapel at my graduate school. In addition, I taught at Catholic high schools both in the Peace Corps and later in suburban Chicago.

Through all these experiences, however, my basic childhood perspective was never challenged. That is, **everyone was quite comfortable and free talking about a generic "God," but seemed to assume that only simple-minded folk talk personally about "Jesus."**

I did, however, hear church people talk about "the spirit." I use the lower case, because they rarely used the term "Holy Spirit." Try as I might, I couldn't figure out just what this "spirit" was. It seemed vaguely related to a sense of spontaneous human impulse, as "I just went with the spirit and did it." Or maybe it was like "school spirit" at football games, that is, a generally good feeling—as, "there was a good spirit at the meeting last night!"

I derived no sense, however, that this "spirit" so casually acknowledged was related in any way either to God or to Jesus, nor—in spite of many clear biblical references--that "it" had any specific origin, focus, personality, or power. Catholics introduced Mary as an apparent corollary to the Trinity, but they seemed just as comfortable talking about "God," as uncomfortable talking about "Jesus," and equally vague about "Holy Spirit."

During my college years in the early 1960's, I shared a desire among the various Oldline denominations to unite not only with one another, but with Catholics and Jews as well. This "Ecumenical Movement" emanated from the civil rights and peace movements, which were based on universal "brotherhood," as it was termed in those pre-inclusive days. Accordingly, it seemed appropriate when Martin Luther King, Jr., expanded his civil rights agenda to stopping the Vietnam War. If we're really all God's children, that is, we should no more be killing each other in Southeast Asia than in Mississippi.

Many Catholics and Jews shared in this desire for unity—if only to avoid the pain of being discriminated against for their particularity—and themselves favored civil rights and ending the Vietnam War. In time, Protestants, Catholics, and Jews did indeed draw together across the country, in local and regional "Ecumenical Councils," "Interfaith Fellowships," and the like. Most often, their agenda focused on promoting interracial understanding, world peace, ecology, women's rights, and other issues which followed upon a shared ideology of universalism.

POLITICAL OR RELIGIOUS UNITY?

Clearly, however, the coalition which emerged from this Ecumenical Movement reflected a political, rather than a religious unity, generated by ideology and not spirituality. Not all Protestants, Catholics, and Jews joined hands, but rather, only political liberals among them. At any gathering advertised as "ecumenical," I rarely found a Southern Baptist, a pre-Vatican II Catholic, Orthodox Jew, or Pentecostal.

In fact, I soon found that even city "ministerial associations" rarely embraced a cross-section. Local pastors saw their city's organization either as "all fundies"--the liberal slur for Fundamentalists--in which case, the Oldline pastors boycotted; or "all liberals," in which case, the conservatives boycotted. Eventually, I was startled to discover that the conservatives had even separated themselves quite deliberately into two warring camps, as Evangelical and Pentecostal.

I rarely heard any in these various groups pray for God to show them their own sin or expand their vision to see others with God's eyes. Rather, it seemed, the problem always lay in one or more of the other camps. In fact, the issue of larger disunity often seemed framed by a bumper sticker I once saw, "Let's unite--do it my way!"

Ultimately, a cavalier attitude toward Jesus served as the theological license for the Ecumenical Movement, and thereby fostered the false foundation upon which it was based. All of us who supported the Movement, that is, could say "I believe in God." But the Protestant Evangelicals and Pentecostals who affirmed "Jesus" largely repudiated its social justice agenda. The ecumenists, in turn, abdicated Jesus to them--assuming that in order to affirm "Jesus," you have to be narrow-minded, exclusive, and "intolerant" of differences.

Regardless of theological views, Christians both Left and Right assumed that you can't affirm Jesus as the Messiah and unite with Jews in mutual respect. Evangelicals and Pentecostals welcomed Jesus but often excluded Jews, even from city-wide Thanksgiving services. The liberals welcomed Jews but excluded Jesus--as if it were patently anti-Semitic to affirm Jesus.

In fact, Jesus was the only Jew permitted at Evangelical gatherings, and the only Jew not permitted in the Ecumenical Movement.

NEW ECUMENISM

Today, I believe God is calling us to a new and authentic ecumenism, one which beckons the very unity upon which the Church itself was originally founded: not a humanly-created unity of political agreements, but rather, a God-created unity of spiritual re-centering. This vision is not politically liberal Catholics, Protestants, and Jews coming together at a civic Thanksgiving Eve service because "we're all Americans." Rather, it's Catholics and Protestant Evangelicals, Pentecostals, and Oldline Reformers surrendering together at the cross to worship Jesus--who has overcome the fearful pride which divides and weakens His Body.

I submit that we Gentiles are not ready for any inclusive religious event with Jews until we have committed ourselves to that vision. Authentic followers of Jesus know that anti-Semitism is utterly repugnant to God. Not affirming Jesus for fear of appearing anti-Semitic is therefore a tragic deception. We fear and persecute Jews not because we have embraced Jesus, but precisely insofar as we have rejected Him and thereby, eschewed His saving power to heal the shame which fuels our bigotry.

Those of us who have dared to face ourselves honestly know that the same anti-Semitism which has infected humanity for thousands of years yet lurks in the most liberal, educated, enlightened, and indeed, religious Gentile hearts. Those of us who have tried hard to exorcise it know that no human power--certainly not our own--can break its hold upon us (see Romans 11:20).

Only the deep conviction of this sin through humble surrender to Jesus, His cleansing forgiveness, deliverance from the evil which fosters it, and Holy Spirit's renewing of our minds can save us from our anti-Semitism. To become wholly surrendered to Jesus is thereby the finest hope we can offer Jews as they struggle to overcome the wounding of our prejudice.

Meanwhile, anyone who's read the Bible knows that God is quite capable of dealing with the Jews Himself. As Gentiles, our primary job is to let Him deal with us—if only to be prepared as He calls us to be part of His work among His chosen people.

FEAR OF JESUS

The Ecumenical Movement, in any case, suffered from a dogmatic fear of being identified with Jesus. It drew churches together not in mutual affirmation of and surrender to Jesus, but indeed, mutual ignorance and fear of Jesus. So blinded by universalist ideology, we withdrew from our very spiritual identity for fear that to be seen as anything specific at all was tantamount to judging others who were not like us.

After all, we reasoned, wasn't that the very basis of white racism, namely, to affirm your white race and thereby judge people of color as inferior? Somehow we forgot that God made each one of us a specific race, and declared that creation to be good. To God, in fact, the white race is good. What's more, in His sight, black is good, brown is good, yellow is good, and red is good—because we're all created in His image.

God's love is not a zero-sum game. There's plenty to go around. You don't have to condemn someone different in order to affirm who you are. You just have to know how much God loves you. As you do, you simply won't need to condemn anyone else for their God-created race. In fact, you'll be too busy expressing His good in you and receiving it from others—no matter what their color.

For liberal white Christians, therefore, the most embarrassing aspect of the civil rights movement was not racism among conservative churches, but rather, the avowedly evangelical flavor of the African-American church, which birthed so many of the movement's leaders. We could link arms enthusiastically with our black brothers and sisters to sing, "We shall overcome." We could even enjoy "Go Down, Moses," which affirmed our "liberation" agenda in its freedom refrain, "Let my people go." But we could only squirm before a chorus of "Nobody knows the trouble I've seen/ Nobody knows but Jesus."

We just accepted quietly, if not condescendingly, that these were poor people, denied the benefits of culture and education like ours. Thus, we included African-American spirituals in our hymnals not for their witness to the saving power of God in Jesus, but to present ourselves as "inclusive," that is, to cover the shame of our racial prejudice. Marking them as "irregular" beside the title, we cataloged them as songs about a curious race, not about a God who hears our human cries and has come in Jesus to rescue all of us from our sinful nature.

In fact, few whites working in the civil rights movement of the 1960's realized that its signature song "We Shall Overcome," which we regarded as simply a "freedom song," was directly adapted from the powerfully stirring hymn, "I'll Overcome Some Day," by African-American Rev. Charles

Albert Tindley:

> This world is one great battlefield/ With forces all arrayed; If in my heart I do not yield/ I'll overcome some day...

> Both seen and unseen powers join/ To drive my soul astray; But with God's Word a sword of mine/ I'll overcome some day...

> A thousand snares are set for me/ And mountains in my way; If Jesus will my leader be/ I'll overcome some day...

> I fail so often when I try/ My Savior to obey; It pains my heart and then I cry/ Lord, make me strong some day...

> Tho many a time no signs appear/ Or answer when I pray; My Jesus says I need not fear/ He'll make it plain some day...[4]

I recall one fellow demonstrator's telling me during a civil rights rally that "We Shall Overcome" had originated with the labor movement of the 1930s. He may have been right about the tune, but we both would've been upended to know that the words and theme stem from a song which proclaims that Jesus saves those who turn to Him in their deepest need.

Black Christians, that is, unlike us white liberals, did not limit Jesus to revelation solely by social justice--perhaps simply because they had seen so little of it.

W.I.J.D.

My personal knowledge of Jesus, therefore, was decidedly flimsy. So far as I could determine, He was the ultimate model of how God wants us human beings to live. He was the perfect man, and His teachings, recorded clearly in the Bible, were therefore the basis of all right human decision and action. He didn't spell out specific directions for every dilemma, but anyone with enough intelligence and education could study His teachings and come up with the right solution.

Certainly, I reasoned, you don't need a personal relationship with Jesus. Anyone can read His principles for themselves, and common sense compensates for whatever is either confusing or apparently missing from the Bible.

Thus ignorant of my Christian spiritual roots, I could only defer to a political ecumenism in my desire for church unity. This is religion at its worst, limiting all permissible revelation of Jesus to our rational human capacity.

Thus, "WWJD," the popular, seductive invitation to speculate "What Would Jesus Do?"—that is, *IF* He were real, present, powerful, caring, and active. The WWJD paraphernalia, from bracelets to T-shirts, in fact broadcast a profoundly anti-Christian message. It spoke for self-sufficient folks, who preferred to keep Jesus dead and his truth-telling at a safe distance—**who dared not ask, "What Is Jesus Doing?" and thereby, allow Him actively to enter their lives and challenge their controlled worldview.**

I'm still waiting for my WIJD T-shirt.

Meanwhile, regardless of political or theological differences, all Christians, by virtue of the name itself, affirm a common link. We're not all "conservatives" or all "liberals." We're not all Sacramentalists, or Evangelicals, or Pentecostals, or Oldline social activists. But we *are* all "Christ"-ians. Our common unity, therefore, lies in the person Jesus, the Christ--and takes shape in our willingness to participate in what God has done in us through Him and is doing now among us through His Spirit.

How genuinely we desire unity in the larger Church will therefore be reflected precisely in how diligently we seek to know and surrender to Jesus.

Those who do not seek to know and surrender to Jesus are not interested in Christian unity. As Evangelicals, they may be interested in doctrinal unity; as Sacramentalists, in ecclesiastical unity; as Pentecostals, in ecstatic unity; as Oldline activists, in political unity--but not in Christian unity. In fact, the more we know and surrender to Jesus, the more we will desire unity in the Church, for as His Body we will experience His own longing for His people to become one.

Ironically, no less a universalist than Harvey Cox affirms this, offering two ways to restore "the indispensable element of particularity" to inter-religious dialogue: 1) "personal testimony," and 2) *not* "soft-pedaling the figure of Jesus himself."

Indeed, he declares, "Jesus is not merely a background figure. He is central to Christian faith." Furthermore, in dialoging with persons of other religions, when Cox "tried to avoid talking about Jesus too quickly," he discovered that "they did not believe they were really engaged in a brasstacks conversation with a Christian until that happened."[5]

Disunity in the Church, therefore, can be traced to an across-the-board resistance to knowing and surrendering to Jesus.

The Oldine Reform churches, for example, are afraid that Jesus will make them evangelical and pentecostal and sacramental. And indeed, He will, even as He strengthens their commitment to peace and social justice.

The Bible states clearly Jesus' desire that His followers be evangelical enough to be "born again" (John 3:3) witnesses for Him "to the ends of the earth" (Acts 1:8); pentecostal enough to be baptized with the Holy Spirit and exercise His supernatural giftings (Matt. 3:11), and sacramental enough to celebrate the bread and cup as His empowering body and blood (Luke 22:17-20). Furthermore, Jesus desires His people to "work for peace" (Matt. 5:9) and minister to Himself in the hungry, thirsty, outcast, naked, sick, and imprisoned (Matt. 25:35-40).

SHAME-COVERING AGENDAS

Likewise, Sacramentalists, Evangelicals, and Pentecostals each fear that Jesus will make them whatever in that list is not their own major emphasis. Regardless of orientation, all of us Christians are frightened unto death of what Jesus will do with us if we place ourselves wholly in His hands.

And well we might tremble, for in Jesus' nail-scarred hands we'll all go with deliberate speed to the cross. There, by His fierce grace, all truth about us shall be revealed until we die to our shame-covering agendas, cry out for God's mercy--and at last confess with the Apostle Paul,

I have been put to death with Christ on his cross, so
that it is no longer I who live, but Christ who lives in me.
This life I live now, I live by faith in the Son of God, who
loved me and gave his life for me. (Gal. 2:19b-20)

The same myopic fear which has kept us from knowing Jesus has blocked unity among the churches. For indeed, "Christ is the head of his body, the church; he is the source of the body's life" (Col. 1:18).

Not only has this truth been lost today in churches of all stripes, but often this intended role of the living, risen Christ has been supplanted by the democratic political model of American culture.

CONGREGATIONAL IDOLATRY

When I began pastoring, for example, a middle-aged lady with deep roots in the denomination was anxious to "explain the basis of our Congregational heritage" and thereby direct my ministry appropriately. Drawing a large triangle on a piece of paper as a model of church organization, she noted that "many other denominations" put the pastor and other officials, such as bishops or elders, at the top, while consigning the congregation to the lower base.

She wrote the word "Pastor" at the top, and "Congregation" across the base, then turned the paper upside down. "In our heritage," she declared, "authority lies in the congregation, not in the pastor."

Certainly, this parishoner's mini-lesson in church polity bore a thinly-veiled warning that I as pastor was not to assert myself too forcefully. Nevertheless, her model captured my imagination.

"Wonderful!" I said, nodding in genuine approval. Didn't that broadly-based model provide the finest safeguard against rigid, narrow, authoritarian leadership? In fact, it seemed to me then, a church run by democratic principles would demand greater participation by individuals and thereby, enjoy a more securely based unity via majority agreement on decisions.

Not until some years later, when our church was languishing and frightened to move in any direction for fear of upsetting anyone, did I begin to see the terrible limitations of our "wonderful" democratic church. As pastor, I readily acknowledged that I was not head of the church--partly, I later realized, from my own insecurities and inability to distinguish between authoritarian and authoritative leadership. But in elevating the congregation as head of the church we had only eliminated Jesus yet again and merely substituted idolatry of the people for idolatry of the pastor.

Congregational idolatry takes shape as an abiding fear that any new program or focus of activity might upset some church members. Its outward symptom is a sense eventually that "things are blah at church"--no matter how much busy-ness may be going on. For **a church becomes lifeless precisely insofar as its members cut themselves off from Jesus, its life source.**

Having suffered egotistic pastors and autocratic church leaders—indeed, having at times qualified as such myself--I believe that all members of the Body should be heard and respected when decisions are made which affect them. All too often, however, we just don't want to take any chances that the risen, living Jesus might want to do something in and through His church that would upset our control. We want our church, not Jesus' church; we want a god who serves our plans, not the One who calls us to die to ourselves in order to serve His plans.

FREEDOM TO HEAR JESUS

Indeed, as Congregational Church historian Rev. Arthur Rouner declared of its founding Pilgrim members, who fled the English king's church for America,

> The reason they wanted to be free was so that no canon laws, no disciplines, nor any state edicts could ever take the place of Christ--ever keep Him away from His Church. They were not anarchists. They did not want freedom for its own sake. It was so they could be free to obey only Christ that they sought freedom.

How tragically removed this attitude seems from present-day American thinking! Indeed, in a passionate cry, this church historian drives powerfully to the heart of the issue:

> The polity and structural organization in itself meant little to the Pilgrims. The Gospel meant everything. I believe it is at this point that we American Congregationalists have betrayed our heritage. For too many of us, our concern for church liberty has become a political concern. We have stood for freedom not so that Christ could tell us what to do, but so that no one could tell us what to do. **When spiritual and evangelical liberty become substituted by this rational and political liberty, then the driving force, the enthusiasm and motivation of free churches soon dies.**[6]

Certainly, members' opinions are appropriately to be considered in church decisions--but are not to be confused with the Word of God. An open forum can be an excellent opportunity for God's will to emerge or become clarified. For Christians, however, any majority vote is credible only insofar as the people voting are themselves surrendered to Jesus, the Head of all churches.

The consequences of not yielding to Jesus become painfully clear when differences arise in a congregation. God is not divided. If everyone has surrendered themselves to Jesus, then a difference of opinion simply means that His word to us has not yet become clear, that our self-centered human desires are clouding His larger purposes among us.

If we sincerely desire to serve God, we then confess our agendas and lay our differences at His feet as a holy occasion to draw closer to the Living Christ and seek His truth. We who have been on our knees individually now fall on our knees together, and humbly beg God to crucify our own agendas and reveal His.

If we refuse thus to "Submit yourselves to one another out of reverence for Christ" (Ephes. 5:21), our differences become an occasion not to surrender to God but rather, to separate from Him and one another. Thus, we fear our differences and water down our life together to avoid disagreements--until we lose our godly spark of "saltiness" (Luke 14:34) and become lukewarm and bland.

Un-sacrificed, we become unsanctified. Determined to establish our life, we die for lack of God's life. To paraphrase Jesus, The church that would gain its life must lose it; the church which loses its life for Christ's sake, will gain it (see Luke 17:33).

REPUBLIC OF BELIEVERS?

God did not submit the Ten Commandments to the people for majority approval. Democracy may well be the very finest governmental form of which this broken world is capable. As Christians, however, we do not proclaim the Republic of Believers, but rather, the Kingdom of God. I'm not saying that any one person or group in a church should command others, nor that all should abdicate and none should exercise authority. Rather, in surrendering to Jesus and wrestling honestly and openly together for God's will, we become His Church and not our own.

In that process, **we recognize that authority comes not from office but from gifting.** As we welcome the Giver, we celebrate His provision by encouraging church members to exercise their gift among us.

Those who have tried this know it's hard work. Often, however, you don't try it until you've found the factional "democratic" route harder in its eventual wounding. The potential of decision-making-by-vote to destroy church community should be obvious: when a proposal "passes" by a majority, what about the minority? Are their opinions thereafter simply to be dismissed and summarily discounted? Who knows how many have left a church with such wounds of disrespect.

God is not divided, and when His Body is divided, it's broken, sick, and in need of healing. You don't just deny it or dismember every wounded limb—or else the infection will spread, the body will die.

Certainly, in this as-yet-unredeemed world, even the most sincere and godly means of resolving differences can fail, and to avoid a debilitating deadlock, church leaders may need to exercise a prayerful decision. Amid the "winners'" temptation to celebrate, however, such an occasion should prompt the Body rather to an appropriate penance and grief at their collective failure to surrender fully to God.

Ultimately, therefore, the simple question, "Do you know Jesus?" frames the only true hope for overcoming disunity in the Church today. To know Jesus is to know the One Who restores us personally by truth and grace, and empowers us corporately as His Church to bring God's rule on earth as it is in heaven.

To know Jesus, however, is first to recognize him in the function of His Hebrew name Y'Shua, that is, "God Saves." Knowing Jesus means confessing your need for saving power--that is, confronting and surrendering your own self-centered, ungodly, unmanageable sinful nature to Him.

That's why we Christians in all churches still shun and crucify Jesus. We're just proud. That's how the Snake suckered us in the first place.

Historically, the variety of Protestant denominations itself reflects the disunity in the Body of Christ unto today. Certainly, the pre-Reformation Catholic Church was not perfect, nor was the post-reformation Protestant movement perfect. Nor should any church, whether Catholic or Protestant, comprise the whole of Christendom, any more than a part of the body comprise the whole (see 1 Corinth. 12:12ff.).

Insofar as the Catholic Church held that role for over 1500 years, however, we may look to it today for a vision of unity more deeply rooted than others'. Thus, Pope John XXIII addressed all Christians at the historic Vatican II Council, in his "Decree of Ecumenism":[7]

> If the churches go back to their roots and seek to
> recover the spotless and seamless robe which the Church
> was as Christ founded it, they will converge into that one

Church.

Such a movement, Pope John asserted, would grow out of forgiveness between Catholics and Protestants for mistakes on both sides which led to the Reformation:

> This change of heart and holiness of life, along with the public and private prayer for the unity of Christians, should be regarded as the soul of the whole ecumenical movement and can rightly be called "spiritual ecumenism."

Significantly, Pope John realized that a spiritually-based unity is beyond mere human power to achieve, and therefore requires us first to seek the mercy and power of God:

> The holy task of reconciling all Christians in the unity of the one and only church of Christ transcends human energies and abilities. It therefore places its hope entirely in the prayer of Christ for the church, in the love of the Father for us, and in the power of the Holy Spirit.

Years ago, when I was still running scared from the beachside evangelists, I used to mock their motto, "Jesus is the answer." Smirking, I would scoff, "What is the question?"

I propose that The Question for today's Church is this: How can our proud and destructive compulsion to separate from one another be overcome, and the Church be thereby restored as one Body?

To answer that question, I turn now to my own personal story.

TAKEAWAY

Jogging on the beach shortly after graduating from seminary, I am accosted by a Bible-wielding evangelist who asks if I am a Christian. Offended, I scoff--but am later convicted. Not all Christians are Sacramentalists, Pentecostals, Evangelicals, or social justice activists. But we're all **Christ**-ians. Christ is therefore the source of our unity.

Do you want to be part of God's move to unite His churches? How badly do you want to know and serve Jesus? Enough to respect other Christians of different churches and learn from them?

2

Platypus Christian:

A Strange but Holy Mixture

> Christ is like a single body, which has many parts; it
> is still one body, even though it is made up of different
> parts... All of you are Christ's body, and each one is a part
> of it. (1 Corinth. 12:12, 27)

After the 1950's sock hops and "happy days" of high school, in 1964 I graduated from college into a cresting wave of social upheaval that broke sharply on the calm shores of my moral conscience. Before the end of the decade, in fact, my most basic loyalties--and thereby, my identity itself--had been upended: my Boy Scout patriotism, by the Vietnam War and peace movement; my European heritage of racial pride, by the civil rights movement, and my very manhood itself, by the women's liberation movement.

As a boy, I had grown up attending the Oldline Protestant Reformation churches that dominated the religious landscape then—such as Presbyterian, Methodist, Lutheran, Episcopalian, Congregationalist. The son of a career Navy officer, I moved often, and our family saw these traditional churches as largely interchangeable.

For some time now, these historic denominations have suffered an increasing decline in membership and influence. Yet they did not always lack vitality. In fact, the accounts of their founders, from John Wesley's

Methodist revivals to founding Quaker George Fox's "quaking," are often charged with passionate sermons and lively, life-changing encounters with God.

Indeed, these churches of my heritage awakened and fueled the exciting, life-changing "social justice revolution" of my young adult years in the 1960s. Wanting to live out a committed faith, I plunged enthusiastically into the "movements" whose banners they waved.

I went to Nigeria in the Peace Corps, returned to live in an African-American community near San Francisco, worked on a civil rights project with American Friends Service Committee near Los Angeles, studied Spanish in Mexico for a summer and taught junior high math in the Latino community of San Jose (CA), joined the March on Washington for peace, and campaigned for women's rights.

SHORT-LIVED VITALITY

Yet by the early 1970s, that season of church vitality was to seem short-lived. The end of the Vietnam War and its immediate personal threat of the draft, coupled with the cry of African-Americans and women to work out their own identity, appeared to cut me as a white male out of my church's radar screen and thus, out of relationship with God. If social justice comprised the authentic Christian agenda—as my Oldline denominations had proclaimed—then I was no longer a Christian.

Through the seventies, including seminary and my first years as a pastor, I struggled to stay involved with the "peace and social justice" movement. Though I did so as an act of faith, nevertheless I found myself slipping further away from the vitality and commitment of past demonstrations, rallies, and campaigns. **Lacking any apparent personal stake in my "cause," I could only cling desperately to its ideology.**

I particularly remember the battle in my conscience when it came time to renew my subscription to an eminent liberal journal to which I'd subscribed faithfully since 1968, when my first published article appeared in it. I didn't want to lose touch with the church community which had helped me embrace the larger world beyond myself. Yet I couldn't remember when I'd last read any article in the magazine that had engaged me enough to save it. A pang of guilt struck me as I tossed the subscription renewal form into the trashcan.

Similarly, I think of my many white Oldline clergy friends who adopted African-American babies in the 1960's and 1970's, in an attempt to model a God who loves the universal human family. Fifteen years later, however, those same couples were seeking a God who could heal their particular family, who could help them deal with a teenager embroiled in normal adolescent rebellion, magnified by root rejections from both the natural parents and the surrounding culture. Their energies which once focused on civil rights demonstrations and political campaigns were now painfully revealed as insufficient to walk in truth and grace with an angry black teenager at the dinner table each night.

Ideology excites a crowd of young idealists, but it doesn't often account for individual, personal needs—which experience and maturity inspire us to respect. Thus the late African-American theologian Cornish Rogers noted,

> One black woman once told me that the reason she left her black Baptist church to attend a Religious Science church was because she was tired of hearing diatribes about liberation and wanted some practical advice about how to survive emotionally in a middle-class milieu.[8]

Undoubtedly, racism still lurks in the dark corners of our hearts, and we continue to need models of God's reconciling love for the whole human family. But if God's true gains in a "peace and social justice" movement are to take root in human hearts, we need tools for living out that universalistic vision amid the demands of our individual, everyday lives.

When 2000 years ago the Creator God of the universe became a single individual from the town of Nazareth, the message was clear: the Universal requires a personal dimension in order for individuals to grasp it. Jesus is thereby a "step-down transformer,"[9] who renders the cosmic power and personality of God present to each individual today.

As a pastor therefore, I began to realize that I could no longer engage the larger social justice dimension of the Gospel without a personal faith renewal.

PROTEST LICENSE EXPIRED

Years earlier, the military draft had provided such a link for me, joining me to the struggle of African-Americans as it arbitrarily took away my freedom and forced upon me a task I judged to be misled and harmful. Yet the end of the Vietnam War had eliminated the draft threat--and with it, the urgency among us white males to challenge the warmakers. Free from the draft, I could no longer claim ready identification with "oppressed" people. My "protest license" had expired.

By 1977, when I began pastoring, I could only bring to my local church the same "peace and social justice" agendas which had brought the faith alive for me years earlier--even as those agendas were becoming more remote, and therefore, uninspiring to me. Struggling as a pastor to stir a vital faith in the only way I knew how, I soon found myself burned out trying to defend a position that was becoming harder for me to grasp myself.

My marriage, meanwhile, was no less a conflict. I had campaigned politically for women's rights, but was struggling to translate those concerns into one-on-one personal relationship issues at home.

By the early eighties, amid growing crises in both my professional and domestic lives, I was forced to accept the fact that neither my personal well-being nor my local church ministry could survive on a diet of heady "peace and social justice" concerns. I knew I needed to focus closer to home, on individual and pastoral needs, but didn't want to become nearsighted and self-centered in doing so.

I realized that our political system based on self-interest voting might allow my concern for larger societal needs, but could not nurture it--yet, neither, apparently, could my traditional church which had prompted it. At the same time, my human nature as a privileged white male simply couldn't be trusted to nurture it out of my own natural impulses. My only hope for sustaining a concern for social justice, therefore, became clear: through a renewal of my faith.

Yet where in the world, my spirit cried out, was I to gain such a rejuvenating personal faith experience?

Certainly, I saw that the Evangelical and Pentecostal churches, so foreign to me then, were bursting with the vitality I longed for. Yet it had become hard enough to maintain my "social action" commitment in my own Oldline church, and I didn't want to risk losing it altogether in a church that seemed to ignore such issues. Furthermore, the "conservative" churches appeared narrow and rigid, and thereby, too ready to affirm all the old loyalties of the flesh--nation, race, gender--which I was still determined to outgrow.

Where, I wondered, could I find a church which affirmed a faith based on both personal spiritual vitality and larger social responsibility? The "liberal" churches seemed so broad and universal as to be personally disengaged; the "conservative" churches seemed so narrow and particular as to be self-centered. The Catholic churches, meanwhile, whose parking lots locally overflowed for each of many Sunday services, did not escape my notice--yet still seemed to me so rooted in their own tradition as to be exclusive.

BEYOND MY COMFORT ZONE

I had myself preached that judging other persons can simply be a way of closing off to some unsettling truth they bear. In spite of my judgment against other churches, therefore, I knew that I'd have to venture beyond my own comfort zone and visit those very churches in order to renew my faith.

In a word, I did just that, and it worked. But the "folks back home" could not affirm what I was discovering in the world beyond our village.

I went to a Catholic mass and found myself surprisingly uplifted. Before long, I was going to 6 a.m. mass daily, kneeling and celebrating the power in the sacrament. I preached excitedly about communion at my church, and at one point, suggested that we install kneelers in a few front pews for those who wanted to kneel for prayer.

"Are you trying to make Catholics out of us?" a deacon demanded.

I attended an Evangelical church and listened fascinated to preaching from the Bible about Jesus' call to be born again and thereby be saved from self-centered pride. I surrendered to Him, was convicted and born again at last. Freed and rejoicing, I preached the Good News at home, urging people to confess we can't do in our own strength what God has called us to do, and to receive new life in Jesus as the One come to save us from this sinful condition.

"Are you trying to make fundamentalists out of us?" several leaders protested.

I visited a Pentecostal church, and experienced the astonishing supernatural power of Holy Spirit to bring words from God to specific needs, to touch people with physical and emotional healing. I began preaching about the supernatural gifts of the Spirit, brought my guitar into

Sunday worship, and started a healing prayer group.

"Are you trying to make holy rollers out of us?" others scoffed.

Stung from all sides, I drew back in confusion.

My own faith was being wonderfully revitalized, as I had hoped. Yet, as I preached out of these new experiences, my congregation became confused. Indeed, those who had been upset with my social justice emphasis were now equally upset with my spiritual renewal emphasis. "You keep going off on different tangents," as one deacon complained; "we just don't know what direction you're going to try and take us next."

If the truth be told--as I was afraid to allow then--in my own heart I sensed that same frustration. **Uplifting as my new faith experiences had been, nevertheless I had discovered quickly that "other" churches were no more accepting of my entire journey than my own.**

Evangelicals and Pentecostals seethed as I praised the Catholic mass and talked about social justice, even as Catholics excluded me from the mass itself as a Protestant. My liberal Oldline churches, in spite of their claim to celebrate differences, had lumped together in one camp all others besides themselves. I was stung, therefore, when Evangelicals scorned my Pentecostal experience of the Holy Spirit.

In time, I found myself sneaking from camp to camp, learning from Evangelicals, Catholics, Pentecostals, and Oldline social activists, yet being careful not to reveal in any one church my sympathies for the others. Amid my new and exiting journey of faith, I learned to hold my visitor's tongue.

As my excitement grew, therefore, I became increasingly frustrated with this travesty and the prejudice in each church that fostered it.

Through it all, I began to wonder--as my own congregation--Where is all this leading? Are these experiences in other churches truly valid avenues to God, or just shallow flashes in the pan? The more I worried, the more insecure and defensive I became.

Certainly, my faith had been stretched, intensified, and renewed. Indeed, I was enthusiastic once again. Yet still I lacked the essential link to connect these various personal experiences with a deeper, common faith within the larger Body of Christ.

For several painful years, my congregation and I struggled with each other. Often, I thought of turning back and forgetting the whole venture. And then I would attend a denominational gathering, find myself weighted down by the lifelessness there, and know again it was too late. I could no more abandon my journey of spiritual renewal than abandon my life itself.

Indeed, I had been too long in the desert. Though I couldn't see clearly the Promised Land ahead, I had nevertheless seen God's fire by night and cloud by day leading me, and tasted manna for the journey. In fact, I'd met not only thirst—in often longing for support--but scorpions as well, in being bitten painfully by criticism. I'd even stopped at times in my self-centered fear and built golden idols of my experience, to judge those who criticized me.

SEE IT, YOU'RE HEALED

Yet I could not turn back. Unsettling as it was for both myself and my congregation, God had lured me into His vision of new life--vast, authentic, exciting--and I was hooked.

Then, in the fall of 1984, I received a flyer announcing a four-day "Healing Prayer" conference led by former Catholic priest Francis MacNutt.[10] At the risk of stirring yet more confusion, I mentioned the event to my deacons—who, to my pleasant surprise, encouraged me to go. Humbled and appreciative, I took that as a "green light" from God to expect something special.

I was not disappointed. But first, I had to be tried.

During the first day's conference teaching, I felt so overwhelmed by conflict both in my church and in my home that after dinner I put my suitcase back in the car and left. When I saw the freeway entrance sign ahead, I hesitated, then pulled into a corner gas station and parked. *Father, I prayed, if there's something in this conference that can help me and the church, turn me around; if not, give me a safe drive home.* After a moment, a distinct peace settled over me—and I returned to the conference.

I still recall sitting excitedly in the host church sanctuary that first night as some 300 of us there anticipated a new teaching on how to pray for healing physical illness.

MacNutt's opening remarks were greeted warmly. And then, a strange, electric hush fell as he declared that, after praying earlier, he had decided to focus that evening **not on healing illness in individual bodies, but rather, on "healing one very special body--the Body of Christ."**

"The more I see what God is doing today," MacNutt began, "it's very clear that He has in mind something more than just healing this and that individual":

> Important as that is, there's a basic sickness in need of healing right within the Christian Body that we all recognize to some extent. But it's a lot bigger than most of us realize, and it's not in the dimensions that most of us think. The healing that's needed is something much deeper than what's needed between Episcopalians and Roman Catholics and Presbyterians, between Presbyterians and Baptists.

Amazing! I thought. *I come here thinking I'll have to set aside my worries over the brokenness in my congregation--and he opens right up speaking about the need for healing in churches!*

I drew to the edge of my seat.

"As I look around at churches today," MacNutt continued, "I see the dimensions of the tragedy, and what God wants to do with us." Struggling to control his frustration amid the urgency of his message, he then made a bold, compelling statement: **"I want you all just to see this. Because if you can see it, you've been healed."**

FOUR DIVISIONS

Portraying "four major divisions among Christians that are tearing the Body apart," he declared that "the most tragic part of it" is that "they all depend on the way we've met God, ...on how people find Jesus."

Catholics, that is, meet Jesus primarily in the sacrament; Evangelicals, in the "born again" confession; Pentecostals, in the "baptism of the Holy Spirit," and Oldline Reformers, in social justice ministries. All of these encounters, MacNutt noted, are rooted in the Scriptures. Why, then, does each group grasp its own way of meeting God as if it were the only way, and scorn the others?

At once, I was startled by how sharply this message portrayed my own, apparently disjointed faith journey and its unsettling effects in my church. As MacNutt declared,

> There are many people in the United States who have found (Jesus) in one way, sometimes in two ways, but I seldom find somebody who seems really to sense all four of these dimensions.

Here, at last, was the link between division in the larger Church and fragmentation of faith in individuals, even in myself. I couldn't believe it; this was my story!

"The major thing that keeps us apart, the practical heresy," MacNutt continued,

> is that every group believes that they have all Christian truth that's really important.... (It's) this prejudice that no other group has anything important to say to me....
>
> There's something in us that wants to narrow things down and block ourselves off. Then, we believe we have all the truth and don't go outside to discover anything. All we see outside is error, and we don't want those other people in proselytizing, because if they get in there, they'll take our people away.

MAJOR DIFFERENCES

Significantly, MacNutt emphasized that these four divisions in the Church today are "major, not minor differences." **Downplaying these differences, that is, only preserves a dishonest, fragile unity, and serves ultimately to dodge the prophetic truth which each bears to the other.** Rather, we must see each as major, even essential parts of the fuller Christian life which, when faithfully integrated, beckon the true personal and corporate harmony which the Body of Christ longs for today as always.

Four days later, I left the conference bearing home the word of reconciliation our church needed--a word that would require no more than our traditional "tolerance of differences" to allow. Indeed, when I presented it to the church Council, in MacNutt's words, they saw it and were healed.

"Oh, so that's what you've been doing with all your different ideas these past years!" as one exclaimed. Unanimously, they urged me to preach throughout the upcoming pre-Christmas Advent season what I'd learned.

After my sermons, the church was at last able to say, "Now we understand and can respect what God is doing in you." As we talked further, however, they decided not to walk with me in that vision themselves. Eventually, in a spirit of mutual respect, I resigned. (see my book *No Small*

Snakes for more of that story).

Today, I'm convinced that indeed, to see this vision--portrayed herein with Francis MacNutt's encouragement--is to be healed. But in order to fulfill that healing, to celebrate the whole and vital faith which God intends for His Church, we have to walk it out.

And there, for all of us, lies the rub.

God may heal your broken leg, but if you never get up from your hospital bed, you won't fulfill the purpose for which you've been healed.

Even now, I see myself as a platypus Christian--that is, a strange bonding of several theological members evolving into union, but not quite there yet. Since my own seeing the vision--and, at least in that sense, being healed--I've met more and more Christians like myself. We sense that we're walking the path to wholeness in our faith, yet are painfully aware of the dismembering forces, both within us and in the larger Church, which so far have not allowed us to affirm that vision as one Body.

And so the original question of how to revitalize one particular church yields to deeper, universal questions: What, in fact, is "that something in us that wants to narrow things down and block ourselves off" from others? How has God provided for us to overcome it?

That is, will Evangelicals, Sacramentalists, Pentecostals, and Oldline activists confess and celebrate the major witness of each other in its authentic, biblical basis? And at last, will we dare walk out that fullness of our Christian faith together, so God can restore His Kingdom on earth as it is in heaven?

As we shall now see, the vitality of the Body of Christ today hinges upon our answer.

TAKEAWAY

The liberal "peace and social justice" agenda of the 1960's loses vitality as I seek a faith which can also address personal needs. I meet Jesus as I am born again among Evangelicals, receive the sacrament among Catholics and the supernatural baptism of the Holy Spirit among Pentecostals. Yet I'm rebuffed by churches in all four camps--who each contend that "Our way of meeting Jesus is the only way." **This division mocks Christ, separates us from God and each other, saps our vitality, and sabotages our larger witness**. Where does this division come from? Have you participated in it yourself? How can we overcome it together?

3

From Blah to "Aha!"

Rediscovering a Whole Faith

I have come in order that you may have life—life in
all its fullness. (John 10:10)

In the spring of 1980, out of a shared longing for vitality in our churches, I joined several other Oldline pastors to visit a Pentecostal pastor. Uncertain but determined in our quest, we were graciously received at his church.

I smiled uneasily.

Harvard Divinity School had trained me well in rational theology and sober thinking. My denomination, accordingly, had judged me fit to be ordained and minister in its own measured, thoughtful style.

Yet, after three years of applying my training in the local parish, something was clearly wrong. At the close of our church's annual meeting shortly before, our lay Moderator had concluded his year-end report matter-of-factly and paused uncertain.

"We're in good enough shape with nothing really to complain about," he said finally. "But actually, the year's been pretty blah."

And indeed, it had been. In fact, no one--until that moment--had mustered the courage to say so, largely because none of us really had any idea how to bring more vitality into the church. Occasionally, an older member would recall "how everybody got excited and pulled together" when the sanctuary was being built years before. But there it now stood, altogether finished, and quite beautiful at that.

And now the church was blah.

Certainly, as the Moderator's report had noted, the required committee meetings had been held, the worship services conducted, the workdays sweated out. Even a rummage sale and several smaller fundraisers had gone over the mark and left us with a budget surplus.

But still the church was blah.

No one disagreed with the Moderator. Indeed, we all recognized his candor as the first step out of our doldrums. In the fresh air of truth, a reflective pause settled over the gathering, and soon an enthusiastic host of remedies burst forth. What we needed, voices declared, was to pull together and be more committed to the church: more potlucks, stimulating outside speakers, youth programs, adult classes. We could even do two rummage sales if only people would work harder!

"Yes, now if only we had more young families," someone rose and vowed to loud murmurs of agreement. "Young couples and children are what the church needs--they always bring a feeling of liveliness. We could just design some new programs to attract them!"

To my tired pastor's ears, this seemed heavenly music indeed, and I confess that I took some comfort in the renewed determination that sprang forth in that moment.

LEAKY TUBE

Yet, even as I write this, I know Jesus weeps. That's probably why it's painful for me to recall years later. I can see now that **every suggestion offered that day to save our church was at best patchwork, like pumping up the leaky inner tube which we in our human striving had made to fill out and support the church.**

Jesus weeps not because we were lazy people looking for a quick fix, nor stupid people with no knowledge of other life within reach, nor evil people determined to frustrate God's purposes. We were solid, loyal members who had given thousands of hard-earned dollars and as many working hours to the church--willingly taking on untold frustrations, problems, and worries in the process.

And now, we were ready to roll up our sleeves again and try even harder to pump life into our church.

That's why Jesus weeps. Because for two thousand years He has been proclaiming to His people, "I am the way, the truth, and the life, (John 14:6)" and "I have come in order that you might have life--life in all its fullness" (John 10:10). He did not say that hard work is the way, nor that young families are the life.

"What I require of you first and foremost," I now believe Jesus was telling our congregation, "is not that you roll up your sleeves, but that you fall on your knees--not that you be willing to try, but that you be willing to die.

"For it is not new programs you need, but new hearts: humbled, broken hearts open to receive me. It is not new families you need, but a renewed family yourselves. The congregation you have are the ones I have sent. First, be faithful to Me and those I've given you. Face your own brokenness, cry out to Me, see how I respond. Then we can talk about more members and new programs."

Jesus was telling us, "What you need is Me," that is,

I am the vine, and you are the branches. Whoever remains in me, and I in him, will bear much fruit; for you can do nothing without me. (John 15:5)

And yet, when all our human efforts at the church had led us to a "blah" *cul de sac*, when vitality had left us, when we even faced that and cried out "Where do we go for new life at our church?" we knew nowhere to look beyond ourselves for the answer.

Jesus weeps because he has been Head of that and every church since before it was built, and its vitality was thereby designed to flow out of His presence and power. As Paul declared,

By speaking the truth in a spirit of love, we must grow up in every way to Christ, who is the head. *Under his control* all the different parts of the body fit together by every joint with which it is provided. So when each separate part works as it should, the whole body grows and builds itself up through love. (Ephes. 4:15-16, italics mine)

This has always been God's plan for church growth and vitality: Surrender to Jesus.

Even--especially--in prosperity, God's people are called back to their source of life:

> When you have all you want to eat and have built good houses to live in and when your cattle and sheep, you silver and gold, and all your other possessions have increased, be sure that you do not become proud and forget the Lord your God who rescued you from Egypt, where you were slaves. (Deut. 8:12-14)

BLAH WITHOUT JESUS

I could not sense Jesus' weeping back then in the midst of our church struggle. Maybe, if I'd wept myself from the pain of seeing so much effort bear so little fruit, I might have connected with God's heart and seen His deeper lesson at hand.

In fact, my own striving had been as diligent as anybody's. I had led the church into ministry at a local nursing home and teenage half-way house, designed extensive information and action programs to reverse the arms race and combat world hunger.

Yet my struggling to commit others to these ministries never produced the unity and vitality which I had envisioned. We had excellent resources. We worked hard. We supported one another. In fact, I first sensed something was wrong when at one well-planned adult Christian education program the lay teacher/planner invited the dozen present to share why they came. "To support you," nearly all replied.

"Obviously," a voice within me cries even now, "you were turning in on yourselves. That's the time to challenge people instead to reach out, to serve the community and world with action programs!"

Obviously, indeed.

That voice is so compelling, so terribly reasonable, that even now it's an effort to curb it. Remember, I tell myself: Remember the hunger walks, the low-income housing campaign, the refugee program, Native American rights, visits to the inner city soup kitchen, the pastor-choir exchanges with Black and Samoan churches.

Yes, we reached out. And yes, we were serving.

But still we were blah.

And still Jesus weeps. Because He was out there where we were reaching. He's there even now wherever the hungry need food, the thirsty need a drink, the stranger needs welcome, the naked need clothing, the sick need caring, and the imprisoned need visiting (see Matt. 25:35,36). **But we could not recognize Jesus out there, because we had not dared welcome Him in here--at home, in our own church, indeed, in our own hearts.**

I didn't know that Jesus was out there in the needy we sought to help—largely because I wasn't humble enough to see His reaching to me in my own need. I wasn't even sure that Jesus was alive. I only knew our church was not. Furthermore, I knew many pastors who said their churches were as blah as ours, who felt just as powerless to overcome that, and therefore, as reluctant to face it.

Indeed, among the group of pastors which our Pentecostal host ushered into his lounge that day were two Methodists, a Lutheran, an Episcopalian, and three Presbyterians. One of the latter was our leader, and we had based our trust entirely on his gentle reassurances.

As we gathered our chairs in a circle and sat down, however, images of a preacher's falling and screaming leapt into my mind. Mustering my most tolerant and inclusive smile, I pushed them aside—only to remember when, as a Peace Corps Volunteer in rural Nigeria, I had ducked below a narrow thatch awning to enter a local holy man's shrine.

STRANGE TERRITORY

Granted, I was seeking something different from my own tradition, or I would never have come to a Pentecostal church in the first place. But this was strange territory and, so far as I knew from my Harvard training, strange things happened in it. Here, the intellectual theologies that allowed me to feel in control, did not rule. From somewhere in the boyhood corners of my mind, I heard a doctor saying, "Sonny, this is going to make you better, but first it's going to hurt for just a little bit."

My prejudices, however, were shattered at once, as our pastor host turned out to be a friendly, well-informed man and a sincere, articulate spokesman for his tradition. After introducing two of his lay pastors-in-training, he invited them to share openly about "problems" the congregation was having as the staff attempted to introduce "a radically new thing" into their church.

As they talked about their struggle with "resistant members" and the "stress of change" within the congregation, the rest of us puzzled uneasily. For us Oldline pastors, the freewheeling Pentecostal style was quite radical and new enough. What in the world *more* could these men be talking about?

Eventually, one of our group interrupted the speakers. "Uh,...excuse me," he said hesitantly, "but just what is it you're talking about that's so radically new an idea for your church?"

"What we're trying to introduce into our congregation," the pastor noted matter-of-factly, "is the idea of service."

"*Service*?" several of us blurted out at once. Startled, we turned to look at one another. *What was so radical about that?*

"I'm confused," I offered. "In our churches, the idea of service is nothing new at all. In fact, we came to your church today partly because we seem a little overloaded in that department, and were hoping you could give us some help in spiritual renewal."

Almost before I finished speaking, the pastor suddenly leapt off his chair, bent over dramatically and began casting a fiery eye about our circle. Startled, the rest of us sat speechless as he whipped a handkerchief from his back pocket and began whirling it around above his head. All at once, he thrust a forefinger lance-like in my direction, then spun around shouting,

"Brothers! The Holy Spirit, I said the HOOOOOLLLYY SPIIIRRRIT, has come upon you! The power, I said the POWER of Almighty God, brothers, is upon you, one and all!" Whip-cracking his handkerchief, he wheeled about, sweeping his hand across the group. "Do you HEAR me, brothers? I said the HOOOOLLLLLYYYYY SPIIIIIIRRRRIT!"

Breaking as suddenly into a genial grin, he stood up and quietly returned to his chair, pausing for the rest of us to gather ourselves.

"That little demonstration is what you're likely to hear in the old-time Pentecostal tradition," he explained, as we all relaxed at last and smiled with him. "It's a lot of sound and fury, but there's really very little substance to it. What we're trying to do here is take the genuine vitality which the Holy Spirit gives us here and channel that into acts of service among us and out in the world.

"Our problem is that many Pentecostal folks like us are just not ready for that. We're used to the dramatic preaching, the spiritual conversions and the emotional highs, but we haven't learned to put all that toward the real needs in the world."

Warmed and humbled by our host's candor, we shook our heads in wonder. "In our churches," I offered finally, "the problem is the opposite, that we're mostly dead emotionally. We need some real fire to bring our people alive. Though we're really uncomfortable with all the jumping and shouting, we know there just has to be more life to the faith than our rational, structured kind of worship."

GEARS AND GAS

"It's true," another from our group declared. "We have all kinds of programs ready and waiting to move people out into service, but everyone's asleep at the church. You have lots of fire, but no model for putting it to use.

"It's like we know how to grow people up, but don't know how to get them born; you know how to get them born, but don't know how to grow them up."

It occurred to me then that my own church was like a fully equipped car , but without any gas. Our host's church, on the other hand, seemed to have plenty of gas--if not an oil field under their property--but no transmissions in their car.

Before the afternoon ended, we pastors sang out joyfully together, lifting our hands to God in praise like King David (see Psalm 134:2) and praying for one another, laying hands on those with special needs.

This was no "blah" event. Nor did it ignore the broken, the poor, the needy.

I sat awed in the circle of pastors. My memory of that scene today recalls Jesus' intimate aside noted by Luke:

> Then Jesus turned to the disciples and said to them privately, "How fortunate you are to see the things you see! I tell you that many prophets and kings wanted to see what you see, but they could not, and to hear what you hear, but they did not." (Luke 10: 23,24)

To a secular eye, this surprising link between Pentecostal and Oldline pastors seems ironic. But to the eye of faith, it reveals God's power at work, in drawing a hopelessly fragmented people together toward a full and balanced Christian faith.

I believe we were privileged that day to glimpse together God's heart for His Church. For a brief moment in our separate histories, the veil parted, and behold: an experience of unity beyond anything our self-centered minds had previously imagined possible. Certainly, we realized that it might not be seen again for some time, for our Pentecostal host that day was no more typical of his larger affiliation than we were of our own.

Once glimpsed, however, such a vision is not forgotten. Indeed, it must not be forgotten, and the one who sees it must tell the story--for it bears the seeds of new life for the Body of Christ today.

I left our gathering humbled, with both a deep respect for my Pentecostal brothers and a new openness to Holy Spirit's reconciling power today. Furthermore, my humility at once led me beyond my earlier prejudices against Pentecostals to sense a profound responsibility to my own Oldline church. For if this Pentecostal pastor had the courage to challenge his own tradition in seeking a fuller, more authentic faith, **if he were willing to risk being rejected at home by promoting unity in the larger Body of Christ--then surely, I must be willing to do the same.**

PERSECUTION AT HOME

My conviction has since been strengthened as I've researched other prominent "conservatives" who have suffered persecution at home for extending their faith toward the "liberal" churches. David DuPlessis, for example, secretary of the first Pentecostal World Conference in 1947 and known internationally as "Mr. Pentecost," ministered often to the Left-leaning World Council of Churches. In 1962, he was expelled from the Assemblies of God for "hobnobbing with the liberals," as he put it.[11]

In 1985, Baptist author and professor Tony Compolo, a popular speaker on economic and sociological issues, was charged with heresy by Campus Crusade for Christ and summoned to defend himself before a national panel of Evangelical leaders. In his defense, he declared that "a religious McCarthyism" is seeking

> to purify the evangelical community of any of us who believe that social and economic justice are requisites in the Christian lifestyle.... There are those who believe they become spiritually righteous and ready for heaven, and there are those of us who say that to become converted is to become agents through whom God can bring hope to the poor and the oppressed of the world. I

want to be committed to the whole gospel, not just the
part that gets you into heaven.[12]

Campolo was absolved.

In 1989, 350 church leaders convened at "Evangelical Affirmations
'89" to define evangelical belief and practice. The resulting draft statement
urged,

> We must respond to the plight of the destitute,
> hungry, and homeless; of victims of political oppression
> and gender or race discrimination and apartheid; and
> of all others deprived of rightful protection under the
> law. We confess our own persistent sin of racism, which
> ignores the divine image in humankind.

The 1980's birthed Evangelicals for Social Action, and the Sojourners
live-in community in the inner city of Washington, DC. In 1989, editor Jim
Wallis of the magazine *Sojourners* wrote,

> The nuclear danger is becoming an occasion of
> fresh conversion for growing numbers of Christians as
> opposition to nuclear weapons is seen as a matter of
> obedience to Jesus Christ. A "new abolitionist movement"
> is emerging based on prayer, preaching, commitment,
> and sacrifice. This conversion of whole sectors of the
> church to peace is unprecedented and is the most visible
> sign of spiritual renewal in our day.[13]

As early as 1979, *Sojourners* carried an interview with Billy Graham
titled, "A Change of Heart: Billy Graham on the Nuclear Arms Race." As
Graham affirmed,[14]

> If I begin to take the love Christ seriously, then I will
> work toward what is best for my neighbor.... Therefore, I
> believe that the Christian especially has a responsibility
> to work for peace in our world. Christians may well find
> themselves working and agreeing with non-believers on
> an issue like peace. But our motives will not be identical.

COURAGEOUS HUMILITY

In an awesome display of courageous humility, Graham then
confessed,

There have been times in the past when I have, I suppose, confused the kingdom of God with the American way of life. Now I am grateful for the heritage of our country, and I am thankful for many of its institutions and ideals, in spite of its many faults. **But the kingdom of God is not the same as America, and our nation is subject to the judgment of God just as much as any other nation.**

That interview reminded me of the late Black Muslim leader Malcom X's statement that he had come to experience that in fact all white people were not "devils," and he could therefore no longer toe the Black Muslim racist line. His immense courage cost him his life.

I confess that in my rebellious youth, I discounted Rev. Graham for being "narrow minded." Smugly, I used to quote one critic who said, "Billy Graham's biggest problem is that he's never done anything that might get him crucified."

No more. Since reading that interview, I have had the greatest admiration and respect for him--and not simply because he has "come over to my side." Rather, to stand for the whole Gospel against the comfortable, divisive tide of your own tradition, which you yourself once fostered—even as the Apostle Paul when as a Jew he persecuted Jesus-believers--requires a deep courage.

As soon as I read that interview, I began to wonder if indeed, I or any of my fellow Oldline pastors would dare to speak so boldly against any equally cherished dogma of our own liberal tradition, out of a greater loyalty to the kingdom of God?

For some years now, in fact, Oldline (once known as Mainline) churches have been hearing internal calls for change. As early as 1989, a *Time Magazine* feature, "Those Mainline Blues," noted a "back-to-basics mood" among American Christians and the "stunning decline of Mainline-reform churches," which have persisted in "a leaning for liberal politics and low-cal theology."[15]

At the 1985 Presbyterian General Assembly, World Council of Churches Secretary Emilio Castro of Uruguay therefore declared,[16]

> Confronted with the tragic problems of today, the gulf between rich and poor, the ideological gulf and the arms race between East and West, we must recognize

that human forces are not enough.

The W.C.C., he then urged, must go "back to the roots of our faith, to the life of prayer, to get the courage, the spiritual vitamins to go on enduring."

My own personal research confirmed this trend. In 1976, the summer before my final year in seminary, a middle-aged United Church of Christ pastor spoke to our student intern group about motivating parishioners. At the coffee break, I asked her how our faith itself can stir people to action. To my surprise, she nudged me aside and lowered her voice.

"This isn't something you talk about to just anyone," she confided, her eyes a mixture of determination and dismay. "But if we don't get some born-again Christians in our churches pretty soon, we're in real trouble. We've got all kinds of programs to deal with racism, war, poverty, ecology—and though most of them are well and good, we really don't know any more where the power comes from to carry them out."

ROOTED IN JESUS

Glancing around the room quickly, she turned back to me, her eyes bright and intense. **"We've forgotten our roots in Jesus Christ.** Our people in the pews are hungering for that spiritual renewal, and unless we give it to them, we just can't expect them to focus for long on the larger social issues, or even the day-to-day issues of keeping a local church going, for that matter."

Indeed, I had often defended my "social action Gospel" to evangelicals with the text,

Suppose there are brothers or sisters who need clothes and don't have enough to eat. What good is there in your saying to them, "God bless you! Keep warm and eat well!"--if you don't give them the necessities of life? (James 2:15,16)

But what if spiritual nurture and growth is a necessity of life? To paraphrase James, suppose there are brothers and sisters who need closer, healing relationship with God and aren't receiving anything at their churches to help them get that? What good is there in urging them, "Let's go out and serve the poor and oppressed! Keep the faith!"--if in the church we haven't given them a vital faith to keep?

Catholics, Oldliners, and Evangelicals, meanwhile, have in turn begun opening to the Pentecostal witness, through the "charismatic renewal" which broke forth in the early 1960's.

That renewal challenged traditional, divisive doctrine, as for example, on supernatural healing. Pentecostals say, "It happened then and it happens now—among all those surrendered to Jesus and open to receive the fullness of His Holy Spirit." Catholics, however, have traditionally said, "It happened then, and happens now--but only through a very few, uniquely ordained saints or holy shrines." Liberals regard the written accounts as merely figures of speech, and say, "Healing didn't really happen then, and so it doesn't happen now." Evangelical "dispensational theology" counters, "It happened then, as the Bible says—but it doesn't happen now."

Meanwhile, focusing only through their political lens, Oldline Reformers have mistakenly seen "Conservatives" as a monolithic block. But the historic division between Evangelical dispensationalists and Pentecostal enthusiasts has become increasingly bitter as charismatic and other "neo-Pentecostal" fellowships have proliferated, drawing members away from Evangelical churches.

A growing number of Evangelicals have been affirming the present-day workings of the Holy Spirit--though not without risk from within their own fellowship. Pop singer Pat Boone was dismissed from his boyhood Church of Christ for doing so; a clergy friend of mine was fired immediately from his Nazarene pastorate when he said he spoke in tongues.

Similarly, former Professor of Church Growth Peter Wagner of Fuller Theological Seminary has described the "painful" process of accepting the evidence of the Holy Spirit's workings today, and wrestling with the dispensational restrictions of his Evangelical Congregationalist heritage.[17] Today, I know of both Southern Baptists and Nazarenes who welcome the gifts of the Spirit.

Evangelical Wesleyan pastor Robert Girard's early classic *Brethren, Hang Loose* opens with a chapter titled, "The Glorious Evangelical Status Quo," and declares,

> As long as we operate the church or any of its
> agencies as institutions set up to teach the learners how
> to act like Christians, how to conform to the "acceptable
> evangelical norm," how to perform in the Christian
> manner, we shall not experience the fresh life we are

seeking. **Because we will still be "living under the law," intent on teaching the flesh how to look and act like it is living in the Spirit --even when that is not true.**[18]

Pentecostals, meanwhile, have begun to talk about co-ordinating Jesus' free-flow style with Jesus' life of active, loving service. As former Assembly of God pastor Gayle Erwin writes,[19]

> The rediscovery of the gifts of the Spirit by Pentecostals and their outstanding fervor prompted them to believe and teach that their revival was the end-time revival. They felt that there was nothing left to discover in the Scripture, thus their charismatic phenomena represented the ultimate--the revival of revivals.

> (T)he Pentecostals did restore to the church a neglected, even lost, power principle....Despite their Jesus-centered worship and enthusiasm, the major emphasis for which they became known was not this knowledge of Jesus, but instead, their consortium with the Holy Spirit.

DRAWING ATTENTION TO JESUS

Erwin then notes that the job of the Holy Spirit is not to draw attention to Himself, but rather, to Jesus Christ—who declared,

> The Holy Spirit...will teach you all things and will remind you of everything I have said to you.

> When the Counselor comes, whom I will send to you...he will testify about me.

> He will guide you into all truth.

> He will bring glory to me by taking from what is mine and making it known to you. (John 14:26; 15:26; 16:13; 16:14)

Erwin then concludes, affirming his Pentecostal heritage:

> Perhaps the grand scheme is unfolding, that the Holy Spirit, now having achieved the attention of a broader spectrum of the church and world, is preparing to sweep aside mythological entanglements and the

Jesus of nostalgia and fulfill his major predicted function--that of glorifying Christ...

The Holy Spirit will...reveal the nature of Jesus to us and convict the world about him. The revivals of emphasis on the Holy Spirit violated this very principle by focusing on the Holy Spirit rather than letting the Spirit speak to us and the world about the person of Jesus.

I believe the world's final great revival will...center on Jesus himself and his nature. The world has seen no power greater than that of Jesus, and the church exercises no power greater than that of living the loving lifestyle of Jesus.

Catholics, for their part, have in recent decades advanced with unprecedented boldness into both social activism and spiritual growth. The U.S. Bishops have released statements on reversing the arms race, economic justice, and political repression around the world. At the same time, the Pentecostal/charismatic renewal has spread widely among both priests and laity. Catholic evangelists are appearing, and biblically-based spiritual growth programs such as Cursillo, Marriage Encounter, and mid-week parish prayer groups have drawn increasing numbers. Among Episcopalian/Anglicans, the Alpha Course in rediscovering a living faith has spread worldwide from England to all denominations.

The Oldline United Church of Christ, meanwhile, has spawned an evangelical Biblical Witness Fellowship and a charismatic Fellowship Renewal Ministries within its ranks, each strong enough to hold annual conferences and publish regular newsletters.

INTRAMURAL FACTIONS

While all these stirrings within the four camps bear hope for a larger unity, often the groups simply become more clearly defined intramural factions within the Body. Rather than embracing and calling the denomination to God's larger perspective, they become splinter groups, beckoning within the denomination the same spirit of division operating among the denominations. Oldline evangelical and charismatic programs rarely acknowledge social justice issues, any more than larger official denominational programs deal with faith conversion or the supernatural workings of the Holy Spirit.

Liberals distrust these new, "conservative groups"--even as in the 1960's, that same distrust focused on the liberals themselves for their peace and civil rights activism. Letters to the editor of the conservative denominational program newsletters regularly contain statements from those who have decided to leave the denomination altogether and join other, more evangelical or pentecostal churches.

Why have these new movements within the churches often served to fortify the old divisions, rather than to obviate them? As Jonah jealously feared the ungodly Ninevites would in fact repent, and thereby merit God's favor (see Jonah 4:1-3), so each faction seems to fear losing its self-proclaimed, most-favored position.

It's like an emotionally unhealthy family, in which each child has a stake in the other's unhealthiness. As long as Johnny remains "a terror," brother Tommy feels secure in knowing that his own faults are not so prominent by comparison. But when Johnny begins to straighten up, Tommy's need to change is brought forth in relief.

Either Tommy now seeks healing for his own brokenness and the family unites, or he beats up Johnny and the family falls apart.

Similarly, either we various Christian factions begin facing our own sin, and thereby allow Christ to heal us all as His Body--or we hide our own brokenness behind finger-pointing and further divide the Church.

When hikers realize they're lost, a hopeful strategy is to go back to the trailhead, where they began.

And so we turn here to the foundational Evangelical witness, namely, the "born again" experience.

TAKEAWAY

Along with several other Oldline pastors, I visit a Pentecostal pastor in hopes of learning how to infuse some of his enthusiasm into my church in order to strengthen our many service ministries. Surprisingly, he says his church has too much unfocused enthusiasm and needs most to grow in works of service! Today, each of the four camps is beginning to recognize its need for the gifts in the other three. Are you? How could you be more open now to learn from other churches besides your own?

The Evangelical Witness:

Meeting Jesus in Being Born Again

4

A Time to Die, A Time to Be Born

—*Again*

> Jesus answered, "I am telling you the truth; no one can see the Kingdom of God unless he is born again."
>
> "How can a grown man be born again?" Nicodemus asked. "He certainly cannot enter his mother's womb and be born a second time!"
>
> "I am telling you the truth," replied Jesus, "that no one can enter the Kingdom of God unless he is born of water and the Spirit. A person is born physically of human parents, but he is born spiritually of the Spirit."
> (John 3:3-5)

Years ago, I bought my first steel-string guitar from an old, street-wise shop owner. Accustomed to soft nylon strings, I winced as my uncalloused fingertips pressed on the sharp steel. "Could you maybe lower the strings closer to the neck," I asked the owner, "so it wouldn't hurt so much when I push them down?"

Nodding and scratching his white beard, he noted that sure, he could lower the strings--"but they'll buzz on the neck when y'pluck 'em."

Nursing my fingertips, I protested. "But there must be some way to lower the strings so they don't buzz!"

"Son," he declared, smiling thinly, "you wanna go t'heaven

without dyin'!"

That brief sermon from a wise old guitar shop owner helped me understand why I had discounted Jesus' call to be "born again," as voiced today by Evangelicals.

Most of us concede that life improvement or benefit--from playing a musical instrument to buying a home--requires sacrifice or suffering. "No pain, no gain," as the old saying goes. You're free in our political democracy to play violin in any symphony you want. But when a tourist in the old joke asks a savvy New Yorker, "How do you get to the Met?" the answer is, "Practice, practice, practice." Thus, the people of Israel are ready to enter the Promised Land only after suffering their desert ordeal; similarly, Jesus receives the eternal, resurrected body only after suffering death on the cross.

PAIN AS AVENUE

Biblical faith does not see the issue as "gain *versus* pain," but rather, "gain *through* pain." As God demonstrated on the cross, suffering is not a mere nuisance, nor tribute exacted by a heartless god, but often the avenue to relationship with the Father and fulfilling His call on your life.

Indeed, their desert wilderness ordeal crying out to God for food and direction teaches the people of Israel to know God--and thereby, secures their destiny. Graciously, God sends them manna from the sky and water from a rock, even a guiding fire by night and cloud by day. The resulting relationship affords Israel not just material provision, but a faith in God to sustain them later in the Promised Land as a divine "light to the nations" (Isaiah 49:6)—even as those nations would murder them for their efforts.

Throughout her history and the crushing trials which that destiny entails, the prophets exhort Israel to persevere by recalling the story of how God delivered them from Egypt into their ordained homeland (see Deut. 8). In fact, the central ordeal in the Old and New Covenants are both intimately connected; the annual Passover feast, which celebrates the deliverance from Egypt's slavery, parallels the Last Supper and the sacrament of communion, which signals Jesus' delivering us from the grip of sin and death.

No matter how purposeful the pain, however, no one enjoys or seeks it. In fact, **people for whom material "gain" lies easily at hand,**

will naturally discount the "pain," if not try to eliminate it altogether. Affluent American Christians, therefore, are often tempted to highlight the blessings of the faith and downplay the sacrifices which inform it.

We want to go to heaven without dying.

Those accustomed to a "Play Now--Pay Later" lifestyle will pack out churches for Palm Sunday and Easter services, without ever observing Good Friday. As a deceptive salesman touts the benefits of the product in order to decoy attention from its cost, we glide happily from cheers of *Hosanna!* one Sunday to *Aleluia!* the next--comfortably skirting the Friday cry which gives meaning to both: "My God, my God, why have you forsaken me?" (Matt. 27:46).

Until you face your fear of abandonment, you're not ready to celebrate God's deliverance.

COST OF BIRTH

When Jesus declares that the gain in seeing the Kingdom of God requires being born again of the Spirit, he therefore implies that spiritual birth bears a cost. That shouldn't surprise us, since physical birth as entry into natural life is painful. Ask any mother.

But indeed, we might also ask the baby. In the womb, that is, you were quite content to stay securely warm and well-fed without even asking or opening your mouth. Then suddenly, convulsive labor contractions rocked your comfortable haven and shoved you rudely out into the cold world.

Similarly, being brought forth into seeing the Kingdom of God--that is, into recognizing the realm of God's super-natural authority and workings-- disrupts your life profoundly. The major difference between the two births lies in your choice. As a baby, the trauma comes whether you want it or not.

Certainly, God can act sovereignly, but as an adult, most often you must respond to God's question, "Has your life become painful and unmanageable enough yet that you *want* me to disrupt it and take over?"

Inevitably, the weight of the world's brokenness will fall upon every human being, because that brokenness is part of our nature, if only when we die. Either we choose to invite God into that suffering as the Great Physician and trust His purposes, or we bear it ourselves unto death.

A "kingdom" is the territory where the king rules. To "see" and "enter" the Kingdom of God, as Jesus urges, is to recognize and move into the place where God rules. That means leaving behind the place where you and your natural desires rule.

It means coming out of the womb.

Wombs are necessary, but temporary. They're great for staying small, but not for growing up. **When staying inside your comfortably self-centered womb becomes confining unto suffocating; when the deprivation and pain of staying within your comfort zone at last seems more destructive than the pain of breaking out, you're ready to be born again.**

Often, God allows us to reach the dead end of pursuing our own rule--as through addiction, divorce, illness, or other severe loss—to make you cry out to Him to rule you. When you reach the end of your own power convincingly enough, that is, you'll cry out for God's power. The degree of newness and power you receive from God depends on how badly you want to get rid of your old ways and how much of your own power you're willing to give up.

f you just want a new, happy feeling of being OK, for example, you could simply put an extra $10 in the Sunday offering, or maybe loan your neighbor your lawn mower when his breaks. But if you can't stop choosing destructive attitudes and behaviors, no matter how hard you try, you need new life. You're through trying; you're dying. Life as you've known it has to end or it ends you. You don't need to be reminded again or trained again.

You need to be born again.

NO PLASTIC SURGERY

God did not send Jesus simply to change a few things we don't particularly like about ourselves, as a holy face-lift. **Jesus is not a plastic surgeon, but a heart surgeon.** He came to transplant your hardened, self-centered human heart with His own (see Ezekiel 36:26ff.).

Here, then, is the key to understanding spiritual re-birth.

Naturally, life proceeds upon a physical time-line of birth-life-death. If, after physical birth and during life, you are to be "born *again*," logically you must first die, and only *then* be *re*-born. A pattern of birth-life-rebirth makes no sense, but only birth-life-*death*-rebirth. Something akin to our natural human processes must therefore die or end in order for you to move from physical birth of human parents to spiritual birth of God's Spirit.

Hence, the cross.

Like Nicodemus, however, our natural human reasoning wonders: How can a person "die" and yet remain alive in this world, even to serve God's Kingdom?

The answer is as simple as it is compelling: by putting to death your natural, self-centered human desires. Thus, the Apostle Paul declares,

> Sin must no longer rule in your mortal bodies, so that you obey the desires of your natural self. Nor must you surrender any part of yourselves to be used for wicked purposes. Instead, give yourselves to God, as those who have been brought from death to life, and surrender your whole being to him to be used for righteous purposes. (Romans 6:12,13)

The problem is that we're not able to do in our own power what God says we must do in order to live life as He intends:

> To set the mind on the flesh is death, but to set the mind on the Spirit is life and peace. For the mind that is set on the flesh is hostile to God; it does not submit to God's law, *indeed, it cannot;* and those who are in the flesh cannot please God. (Rom. 8:5-8 RSV, italics mine)

Paul often uses the term "flesh" (RSV) not to mean our bodies *per se*, but rather, our "human nature" (TEV)--that is, our sin-fueled animal instinct for self-preservation and self-glorification. That's what must die in order for you to fulfill God's created purpose for you.

As Paul explained (with my interpretation),

> As far as the Law (our natural human attempts at getting right with God) is concerned, you also have died because you are part of the body of Christ, and now you belong to him who was raised from death in order that we might be useful in the service of God.
>
> For when we lived according to our human nature, the sinful desires stirred up by the Law (to discount Jesus and save ourselves by our own efforts) were at work in our bodies, and we were useful in the service of death (wasting our energies trying to save ourselves instead of giving ourselves wholly to serving God and trusting Him for the outcome).

Now, however, we are free from the Law, because we died to that which once held us prisoners (we gave up on saving ourselves and instead, have cried out to God to save us). No longer do we serve in the old way of a written law, but in the new way of the Spirit (that is, by trusting God to do it in and through us by grace alone). (Romans 7:4-6, interpretation in parentheses mine)

PROBLEM WITH HUMAN NATURE

"But what's so bad about human nature, that it has to die?" we might ask. "Sure, there's always a bad apple in the bunch, but most of us are basically good people."

Yet when we say, "It's only human nature to do that," invariably we're talking about a selfish, negative act.

Consider stopping by the supermarket on the way home from work. The aisles are crowded, check-out lines packed, and the air electric with impatience. You're tired, hungry and anxious to get home, and standing in line behind several overflowing carts. Suddenly, from on high, an overhead speaker proclaims, "Checkstand Five is now open!"

Instinctively, you and thirty other harried shoppers mired in long lines fix your gaze on Checkstand Five. Who would say, "It's only human nature to wait kindly and let someone else go there ahead of you"? Rather, it's only human nature to drop your own cart into first gear and beat the others out.

I once read about a therapy program for driven "Type A" personalities, which required the client to exit a supermarket by selecting the longest checkout line. Talk about the death of our natural human desires! That's not therapy. That's slow-drip water torture!

If it were so natural to think first of others, we wouldn't have needed Father God to intervene in Jesus to save us from imposing on each other. You don't need Jesus to tell you to eat when you're hungry, to seek comfort when you're inconvenienced, to fight when someone else resists your desires, to couple sexually when urges arise. We can behave like animals quite *naturally*, all by ourselves.

To become more than animal--in fact, to become authentically human children of God--we need His *super*-natural input. "No one can see his own errors," as the Psalmist declares. "Deliver me, Lord, from hidden faults!" (Ps.

19:12).

We need God's input to fast in order to recognize our deeper emotional and spiritual hungers, to give up our own comfort to serve others, to covenant in faithful marriage with your sexual partner, to forgive and speak the truth with love when we hurt each other.

The flesh purports to bring new life, promising quick vitality as you satisfy your own desires. To God, however, the flesh brings death, because its narrow view seduces us away from the purposes for which He created us—and His Spirit who would sustain us. Sure, the flesh has its pleasures, many of which are God ordained within His protective boundaries. But when those pleasures distract you from Him, they beckon the enemy of God.

Jesus was no masochist. He didn't want to die on the cross. He begged the Father to "take this cup of suffering from me!" (Matt. 26:39). That was His self-preserving human nature speaking, and it's what makes Him credible to flesh-and-blood folks like me. But when He surrendered his physical body and natural impulses to God--"Yet not what I want, but what you want"--then and only then did His destiny break forth according to God's plan (see Phil. 2:6-11). So it is with us.

WILLPOWER NOT ENOUGH

Overcoming the natural desires of "the flesh" requires surrendering to an authority far greater than our common human impulses. You won't invite or seek such a higher authority, however, until you recognize the deadly effect of those impulses and your own inability to overcome them.

The core of New Covenant faith lies in Paul's statement that, left to our natural human desires, we are patently unable to submit to God without His intervention in Jesus:

> I know that good does not live in me--that is, in my human nature. For even though the desire to do good is in me, I am not able to do it....What an unhappy man I am! Who will save me from this body that is taking me to death? Thanks be to God, who does this through our Lord Jesus Christ! (Romans 7:18,24,25)

Our natural human pride balks at such honesty. Only when you recognize at last that not submitting to God is destroying your life and others closest to you--that all your willpower is not sufficient to bring you in line with your life's created purpose—are you ready to leave the kingdom of Me and enter the Kingdom of God.

You're ready to be born again.

Born myself in 1944, I've seen how my self-centered nature sabotages my closest relationships and holy destiny. I'm too old now to play adolescent games. I want Father God to rule my life, because I want to get on with the life He created for me.

Thus, the author of Hebrews calls Christians to leave the womb, to stop childishly sucking on (mother's) milk, but indeed, grow up and take responsibility for our choices. "Anyone who has to drink milk is still a child, without any experience in the matter of right and wrong," he exhorts. "Solid food, on the other hand, is for adults, who through practice are able to distinguish between good and evil" (Heb 5:14).

A major grace in aging is that you no longer have the energy to control your life. That means you're closer to letting God control it.

Too often, churches are filled with people trying to be good—but have never dared confess they can't. You don't enter God's Kingdom by proclaiming your goodness, but by confessing your no-good-ness and trusting His goodness. No effort to demonstrate your goodness can compensate for denying your hopelessly sinful nature and distrusting your Father's readiness to save you from its effects (see I John 1:8-10).

CAN'T BE GOOD

Thus Jesus judged the Pharisees. "Those who are well have no need of a physician, but those who are sick," he declared. "I came not to call the righteous, but sinners" (Mark 2:17 RSV; see also Luke 18:9-14).

Goodness is a quality of God, not human beings. Even Jesus eschewed such praise:

"Why do you call me good?" Jesus asked him. 'No one is good except God alone." (Mark 10:1)

Any goodness which proceeds through us is a reflection of what God has given us. The Good News is this: Relax. You don't have to be good in order to win God's love. In fact, you can only be good insofar as you receive God's love. "We love because God first loved us," as John put it (1 John 4:19).

In fact, we can only recognize God's goodness insofar as we give up on our own (see Phil. 3:6-11). "I live in a high and holy place," God declares, "but I also live with people who are humble and repentant, so that I can restore their confidence and hope" (Isaiah 57:15).

We approach God, therefore, by offering not our accomplishments, but only our brokenness and need. We come not just empty-handed, but gripped unto death by our sinful nature and begging to be released.

We come trusting God—powerless, but not hopeless.

I learned this graphically some years ago, when a fellow pastor to whom I'd often gone for prayer and counsel called and asked if he could visit me to pray about a problem of his own. At first, I was elated, proud to think that this man so widely acknowledged for his spiritual maturity would ask for my help.

Over the next few days before our appointment, I considered a variety of advice to offer him on the basis of the sketchy details he had shared. Yet each time I rehearsed one of my solutions for his problem, I felt strangely flat.

As the day itself approached, a fear began to contend with my pumped-up self-confidence. *What if I blow it?* This esteemed Christian leader had asked for my help--*What if I don't have anything helpful to give him?*

Even worse, *What if I give him the wrong advice?*

By the day of our meeting, my fear had metastasized into an abiding anxiety. An hour before he was to arrive, I went into the church sanctuary and fell down trembling before the altar. "Lord," I cried out, "what in the world am I going to tell this man? Everything I come up with just doesn't sound right at all!"

I decided that I simply needed to submit my list of possible solutions to God to show me which of them would work best. As I went over the list, however, they all sounded not just flat, but potentially harmful.

NOTHING TO GIVE

Desperately, I glanced at my watch. I had twenty minutes to...to what? The question leapt out at me. To dream up the one correct solution to the man's problem? But I had already tried my absolute best to do that and....

Suddenly, in a panic, it struck me: *I have nothing to give this man!*

Nothing at all!

But surely--my flesh protested--with all my education and training and experience and reading, I can come up with something helpful! He must think I've got the answer or he wouldn't have called me!

Yet, in that awful moment, I knew it was true: I had nothing to offer this man in need who had given me so much. I knelt there stunned, waiting for the terrible, deathly fear to fall.

Strangely, however, a quiet peace settled over me.

As my utterly defeated self began to rest in that peace, I sensed as a voice within me saying, "At last! Yes, that's right: you don't have anything of your own to give this man. You have only Me and the things I give you.

"That's all you've ever had with which to do My work, and it's all you'll ever have. **I send you people not to get what you can give them, but for what I give you.** This man respects your openness to Me and is coming to hear what I give you for him."

In a flash, I saw the idol I'd shaped proudly out of my education and expertise. In prayer, I released it all to God and laid it at the foot of the cross.

"Forgive me, Lord," I prayed. "I can only do your work with what you give me. If there's anything out of my past knowledge and experience that you can use to help this man, show me. If not, I trust you to give me supernaturally here and now the wisdom and words you want for him."

In a word, our appointment was glorious. As I listened to my visitor, I prayed quietly; when I responded, he often took notes. "This is really helpful," he said at one point; "I want to be sure and share this with the elders." For our prayer, I invited him to come into the sanctuary and kneel with me before the altar, where I'd knelt alone in desperation shortly before. As we prayed, he scribbled more notes.

We parted with a brotherly embrace, and I went immediately back to the altar to give thanks and praise. A few days later, the man called to tell me that his elders "felt as if the Lord was speaking" through me.

Later, I was overjoyed to read these ancient words:

> When I came to you, brothers, to preach God's secret truth, I did not use big words and great learning. *For while I was with you, I made up my mind to forget everything except Jesus Christ and especially his death on the cross.* So when I came to you, I was weak and trembled all over with fear, and my teaching and message were not

delivered with skillful words of human wisdom, but with convincing proof of the power of God's Spirit. **Your faith, then, does not rest on human wisdom, but on God's power**. (I Corinth. 2:1-5, italics mine)

Haleluia! I'm in the Story!

And I've been born again—this time, by the redeeming grace and power of God's Spirit.

LIMITS OF EDUCATION

Years ago, before ever daring to face my own sin and need for God's saving power, I believed that we human beings are wholly good by nature. Our wrongdoing, therefore, simply reflects negative "environmental influences," which can be overcome through education and right-thinking. This paradigm made it easy for me to believe that "sinners" were other persons, especially those below my level of intelligence or accomplishment.

In those days, I often attempted to console and uplift people with the verse, "And God saw everything that he had made, and behold, it was very good" (Gen. 1:31). "God created you," I would say to anyone feeling badly about themselves, "so you must believe that you are good at your core. You just need more opportunity to learn the truth and uplift yourself."

I didn't dare stand with others in their sin, because I had not dared to face my own sin and beg Jesus to stand with me in it.

I don't disparage education. I'm thankful that my schooling has enabled me to serve God in ways I might otherwise have been unable. I want access to a good education for all who desire it.

But evidence abounds that education does not ensure either the ability to distinguish good from evil, or the integrity to act in the "good" way. Few societies in recent history, for example, can compete with pre-WWII Germany for educational achievement in science, psychology, theology, music, and philosophy. Yet all their unparalleled learning didn't turn the Germans from Hitler's ruthless reign. Again, it was "the best and the brightest" who engineered our own tragic Vietnam War.

Education is a tool, not a license. God can use it for His purposes, but only if you surrender it to Him. In itself, education lacks saving power. It can't overcome the deadly effects of turning from God and denying your own inadequacy. All the learning in the world can't save me from my impulse to forget God and everyone else, and look out for #1. In fact, when not sacrificed to God and thereby, set apart for His purposes and made holy, education can serve as a proud mask to hide our sin and only make us more proficient sinners.

An old joke tells of the young pickpocket's mother who insisted he go to college. "I won't have a son of mine becoming a common thief," she huffed. "With a good education, he can at least become an embezzler!"

Nor do I discount the damage that a destructive physical, emotional, or spiritual environment can cause. These must be addressed pro-actively through healing prayer, political action, and social justice ministries. But no matter how oppressive, painful, or damaging our circumstances, without being born again we remain as in spiritual infants in a womb, trapped by our own self-centered desires and unable to grow into God's purposes.

FREE WILL

Yes, God originally made us "inferior only to the angels" (Psalm 8:5). But we're not holy robots. In order to stir genuine relationship, God gave us free will. And from our Genesis, we have chosen so deliberately and so consistently to seize control, that we have corrupted our original being beyond our own ability to purify and redeem it.

We've jumped into a pit deeper than we're capable of climbing out. "Who can understand the human heart?" as Jeremiah laments. "There is nothing else so deceitful; it is too sick to be healed" (Jer. 17:9).

Any parent knows this. You don't have to teach a child to be selfish. It comes with the package.

"Sin," therefore, is not something we do once in awhile when we "slip up"; rather, it's the state of human nature itself. As theologian Paul Tillich declared,

> Before sin is an act, it is a state. Do we...still realize that sin does not mean an immoral act, that "sin" should never be used in the plural, and that not our sins, but rather our sin is the great, all-pervading problem of our life?[20]

That's why John proclaimed upon seeing Jesus, "There is the Lamb of God, who takes away the sin of the world!" (John 1:29).

Jesus, that is, did not come simply to straighten out a few individual wrongdoings, but rather, to lay the axe "to the root" (Matt. 3:10) and restore human nature itself to God. **He did not say, "You must try again to better yourself," but rather, that you must be "born again"--and then went to the cross to demonstrate what that requires.**

The world's solution to our condition of sin grows out of self-idolatry: "Just educate people about right and wrong, and then exhort them to do the right thing." God's solution, however, grows out of surrender to and trust in Him: "Be crucified with Jesus." That is, bring death to the flesh, for without that all human efforts ultimately serve only our sinful nature. Let the merciless powers of the world wear down people's pride until they're ready to confess their powerlessness, give up and die to their own efforts, and cry out at last for a Savior.

Biblical faith proclaims that God created us human beings and pronounced us "very good" (Gen. 1:31). But we have invited a terminal disease that must be dealt with before that goodness can be released to serve God's purposes instead of our own.

Often, this truth is revealed most clearly not in religious folks, but in those surrendered most deeply to the world--perhaps because they experience its evil most graphically (see Luke 16:8). In a fascinating interview about the proverbial "con artist," for example, a professional magician talked about what it takes to "con" another person:[21]

> Regardless of the scale or nature of a con, it has the same basic law: **The only person who can be conned is somebody who wants to take advantage of another person.** In all of these situations you're made to think that you're the smarter person. But, regardless of the scam, the bottom line is that people are greedy and think they know more than other people. It's human nature, and that's why con games work.

With bold insight, the interviewer then asked this professional con man, "Have you ever been conned?"

And with humble insight, the magician answered, "No, but I think it would be extraordinarily dangerous for me to think I could not be. Anybody who thinks he's too smart to be conned is the perfect target."

What a sermon!

Humility is a first-line defense against evil.

The *Heidelberg Catechism* asks, "But are we so perverted that we are altogether unable to do good and prone to do evil?"

The answer is a flat "Yes" (see Rom. 7:18). But the Catechism ends with hope:"...*unless we are born again by the Spirit of God*" (italics mine).[22]

CONGENITAL SIN

Sin--literally, missing the mark God has set for us--is not a temporary illness, but a congenital disease. **Individual acts of sin are merely symptoms of the deeper human condition into which we're all born.** If the kitchen pipe breaks and the floor is flooding, you have to mop the floor --but first, you repair the pipe.

Until we deal with our inborn sin nature, all our efforts to deal with individual acts of wrongdoing ultimately become not only hopeless, but deadly. We either give up, abandon God's will and yield to sin, or we make an idol of "morality" and burn ourselves out fighting it. In the broken pipe model, we either let the water flow and drown us, or we die of exhaustion mopping frantically--instead of calling the Plumber.

In medical language, the wound is not topical, but systemic.

Biology uses the term "parasite" and "host." In some cases, as a tick on a dog, the parasite attatches to the host; healing simply requires taking the parasite off the one spot where it's lodged.

The parasite sin, however, has not simply attatched itself to one spot, but has invaded and suffused the human host, as a virus. As the Apostle put it,

> Sin came into the world through one man (Adam),
> and his sin brought death with it. As a result, death has
> spread to the whole human race because everyone has
> sinned. (Rom. 5:12)

How, then, do you destroy the systemic parasite sin without killing the host human being as well?

The flesh answers, "By constant vigilance, catching individual acts of wrongdoing, punishing the sinner, and exhorting him or her to stop sinning." But this consuming effort is like trying to cure smallpox with an ointment instead of a vaccine.

The biblical faith, in the other hand, answers simply, "It can't be done. The only way for the parasite to die is if the host dies and thereby, gives the parasite nothing more to feed on." On the cross, that is, God announced,

"I'm tired of dealing with symptoms, of forever hassling over nitpicky details of the Law and unending incidents of lawbreaking. It's time for sin itself to be put to death."

STARVING THE PARASITE

Death of the host starves the parasite. It's a radical solution, yet the only one that works for us hopelessly self-centered human creatures. But here's the catch: once both parasite and host are dead, how do you bring the organism back to life?

Only by trusting the God of resurrection power to re-vitalize you with His Holy Spirit.

"We have died to sin," as the Apostle put it. "By our baptism, then, we were buried with (Christ) and shared his death, in order that, just as Christ as raised from death by the glorious power of the Father, so also we might live a new life" (Rom. 6:1,4).

The rub for outsiders comes when some Christians, in an effort to hide their sinful nature, portray this spiritual re-birth as a once-and-for-all transformation. **Yet it's clear--at least to outsiders--that Christians remain altogether capable of sinful acts even after surrendering to Jesus and being born again.** Otherwise, all born-again Christians would be perfect human beings. Their marriages, families, and churches would be perfectly loving fellowships with no strife!

The essential distinction lies here: We are *born* again, not "matured" or "adulted" again. This work of God is a new beginning, not a final conclusion. Newborns are fragile and need much care. At times, that is, the pipes may burst again in our imperfect house, but now it belongs to the Plumber, who lives right here with us. In fact, our sin-nature persists as long as we live in this broken, sin-infected world. Indeed, we must learn to grow into deeper submission to Jesus daily in order to receive more of His power to overcome it.

To be born again, that is, secures your *salvation*. After surrendering your life to Jesus, you're one of His family, assured of life now and eternal with the Father. In this world, meanwhile, you then begin the process of your *sanctification*, of being set apart for God's purposes.

The born-again believer, therefore, can't cop-out by saying, "I can't help the wrong I do, because it's just the sin in me that makes me do it."

Granted we're not accountable for our powerlessness in the face of sin; that's our human state. But if Jesus has come and offered Himself as power to save us, we *are* accountable to confess our powerlessness, surrender to Him, and seek His Spirit to change us.

We can't save ourselves. But we can cry out to the Savior.

Yes, we must "keep on working with fear and trembling to complete your salvation," as the Apostle urges--but precisely "because God is always at work in you to make you willing and able to obey his own purpose"(Phil. 2:12b-13).

Nor can we excuse our faults by saying, "But it's just human nature to be selfish like that." Yes, it's human nature to sin. But God's nature has been made available to us at the cross, where we must dare go in order to be born again of His Spirit.

The Good News in Christ, therefore, is not for those who fancy they have no sin; but neither is it for those who would remain hamstrung by guilt. Liberal-universalists, that is, hold that human nature is good, so sin is nothing to worry about. Conservative-legalists, on the other hand, often imply that since human nature is sinful, sin is all we should worry about.

Both of these views generate a hefty readership for the "guilt-free" Self-worship manuals which line bookstore shelves today: the former, by encouraging people to deny their wrongdoing; the latter, by lashing people so harshly with it that their bruised spirits seek relief elsewhere.

WE'RE NOT OK

The former is illustrated by the title of the old classic, *I'm OK, You're OK*, which seeks to reconcile inner voices of a coercive "Parent" and rebellious "Child" into a rational "Adult." Any "not OK" feelings, the author declares, arise out of hurtful Parent-Child interactions of your past.

That is, the more your rational Adult takes charge and mediates those old conflicts, putting them in manageable perspective, the more your innate human goodness emerges as an "I'm OK" feeling. Parental coercion and childish reactions are thereby the ultimate theater of human wrongdoing, the effects of which are remedied by our rational minds and correct decisions.

Certainly, parental wounding impacts a child profoundly, and as we shall see in a later chapter, Jesus can heal such wounds. But even these most powerful human relationships are not the source of human brokenness. Parents themselves are broken by forces beyond their own childhood--as indeed, the first parents Adam and Eve fell to sin.

At its deepest level, therefore, human brokenness is not about what we do, even to each other, but about who we are. All negative experiences--from plane crashes to emotional problems--do not stem from misapplying our otherwise innately good and ultimately powerful human will. Rather, they reflect a world in broken relationship with its Creator.

The old Pelagian heresy declares that the human self can be ultimately trusted, because we are naturally good. It thereby supplants God--and beckons an epidemic of Self-idolatry.

Christian psychologist Paul Vitz points, for example, to the book, *Your Erroneous Zones*, in which author Wayne Dyer declares that the self is worthy "because you say it is," and advises the reader with headings such as "Taking charge of yourself" and "Useless emotions like guilt."

As Vitz summarizes this popular view:

> Once the self can take charge, you get all the fulfillment you want... The problem, according to Dyer, is that "You must please Jehovah, or Jesus, or someone external to yourself." Throughout the book, the emphasis is on total, blind obedience to your wonderful self. Of course this self is never defined, and the central problem—the tendency of the self to create illusion and to exploit others—is never addressed.[23]

Vitz notes a "final, extreme example" in "est" (Erhard Seminars Training) which proclaims bluntly, "You are the Supreme Being."[24]

Certainly, this belief in the goodness of your own self is well-suited to those who don't want to bother with the needs of others. "Contemporary upper middle class Americans," as Vitz concludes, "have been only too happy to find a rationale capable of justifying their extremely self-centered consumer-oriented world view."

The biblical faith, on the other hand, understands that our human nature is not good, but this condition has been overcome by Jesus on the cross. "I'm not OK and you're not OK--but that's OK," as another has offered. As I thereby crucify my pride and cry out to Jesus to bear my sinful nature, I'm forgiven. Furthermore, I'm freed from beating myself in a corner to make proper amends where necessary, and go on serving God--in all my brokenness and in all God's power.

Neither denying my sin, nor proclaiming it endlessly, heralds the victory Jesus died to give us. As John declared,

> If we say that we have no sin, we deceive ourselves, and there is no truth in us. But if we confess our sins to God, he will keep his promise and do what is right; he will forgive our sins and purify us from all our wrongdoing. (1 John 1:8,9)

Unless we start humbly at the cross, we can't proceed in the direction of God's created purpose for us, because the standard directional marks on our spiritual compass will be mis-marked according to our self-serving goals. That's why the harder we try simply on our own human strength and wisdom to be good, the further we must miss the mark--and why the Law and its striving after righteousness had to be superseded by Jesus.

If we start from the position, "I am by nature good," and ask for directions to God's Kingdom, we can only hear, as in the old joke the farmer tells the lost city slicker, "You can't get there from here."

Indeed, our natural human pride ensures that the more certain you are of your own goodness, the more you doubt that of others. Thus Jesus excoriated the Pharisees as those "who were sure of their own goodness and despised everybody else" (Luke 18:9).

To the extent that we see ourselves as good and powerful, therefore, we don't encounter the God who defines ultimate goodness and power, simply because we fancy we don't need to. We don't see the Kingdom of God because we want only to see our own kingdom.

We want to go to heaven without dying.

TO TRY OR TO DIE

As John Sandford, founder of Elijah House Ministries, has noted, **God's invitation to relationship through Jesus is therefore first a call not to try, but rather, to die.** "Whoever tries to gain his own life will lose it," Jesus proclaimed; "but whoever loses his life for my sake will gain it" (Matt. 10:39). Until that spiritual/emotional death in letting go of our own control, we can never fully trust God's grace and resurrection power.

Most of us balk at so radical and terrifying a call, until some situation threatens life as we cherish it, and brings us face-up against the powers of death--perhaps a substance addiction, divorce, or some other deep loss or fear. This disruption surfaces at last the option to take a chance on Jesus, who came "to set free those who were slaves all their lives because of their fear of death" (Heb. 2:15).

It's as if you were standing on the roof of your house as it's being consumed in flames. Below you, Jesus stands with arms open, but it's terrifying to leap. When at last the flames begin licking at your feet--when it becomes more frightening to stay where you are than to take a chance on God--you leap.

And you're born again.

It's not about obedience. It's about trust.

Thus, author/radio personality Garrison Keillor, himself raised in the evangelical Plymouth Brethren denomination, "marvels" at the "anguish" in the guitar-playing of his teenage son, who has enjoyed all the comforts of a caring Dad and affluent society:

> INTERVIEWER: What do you think the anguish means?
>
> KEILLOR: Maybe it means that the Gospel is true. Maybe it means that getting enough allowance and being reasonably accomplished at what you do and having a nice dad are not, in the end, enough. There is another reality, and it is not the present one.
>
> I: But doesn't the reality of the Gospel make us feel good instead of feeling the blues?
>
> K: I don't know that we're promised a continual diet of feeling good. If I wanted to feel good more often, I'd move to California.
>
> I: You said that there is another reality.... What is it?
>
> K: It is that you must lose your life in order to find it. A man told me a story. He was tilling manure into a field in the spring, using a tractor and a disc plow. It was a long field. The tractor was moving at five miles an hour and the man was bored. It was a warm day and the man wished he could be anything other than a farmer. He was tired of working for his dad.
>
> Out of sheer boredom, he dozed off and started to fall backwards off the tractor seat. He woke up falling

and, because the tractor was an old model with a throttle lever that was notched into place, the tractor just kept moving. The man fell in between the tractor and the discs and, as he hit the ground, he grabbed onto the tow bar. He hauled himself up as far as he could, but he couldn't pull himself all the way up. He just hung onto the tow bar with both hands as the steel discs were moving behind him. His body was literally being dragged through the dirt and the manure. He held on as tightly as he could because, if he lost his grip, he would have been cut in two by the moving discs.

He was just about to lose his grip. He didn't even have enough strength to cry out or to weep--he just kept hanging on. The tractor kept on moving, ever so slowly, until it came to the end of the field, traveled up an incline, and into the woods.

Finally, it hit a tree and stopped, although the wheels kept spinning. It took him ten minutes before he could stand on his two feet, climb up to the seat, and turn the key off.

That man lost his life and got it back again. He stayed in farming after that.

I would think that after an experience like that you would have the feeling of absolute freedom and liberty. All the weight would be gone. You would feel the sort of liberty that you read about in the Epistles when a person has died and been reborn. He, I think, had discovered the meaning of life.

I: What a powerful image of losing your life and finding it.
K: Life is not for the timid.[25]

HOLY PLACENTA

Certainly, to "come to the end of your rope" and "hit bottom" like that young farmer, is humbling--even humiliating. That such a fall might mark the path to maturity and destiny seems patently foolish to the non-believer, who has not been born again, and therefore, as Jesus noted, cannot recognize the Kingdom of God at work. "The message of the cross is foolishness to those who are perishing," as the Apostle noted, "but to us who are being saved it is the power of God" (1 Corinth. 1:18 NIV).

Indeed, as Keillor suggests, **the crunch of life-threatening experiences does not create a new reality, but rather, reveals another, deeper reality, previously hidden by our pride:** in our natural selves, we're being dragged through dirt and manure by our self-centered desire—and powerless to stop it.

Evangelicals testify that those who encounter that truth most graphically and surrender to Jesus in the midst of it become His most powerful witnesses.

Granted, it's a pain unto death.

But for those who want to see the Kingdom of God, it's a birth unto new life.

Even as birth itself brings forth blood, we are ready now to see how the blood of Jesus provides the interface—the holy placenta, as it were—between the definitive "born again" Evangelical experience and the sacrament of communion.

TAKEAWAY

Jesus said we must be "born again"--not "matured again." It's not a completion of your life, but rather, a new beginning, a sure foundation which launches the humble process of learning and growing. We're born the first time physically. In order to be born once more, into spiritual life, we must first die to our self-centered human nature, even as Jesus went to the cross in order to receive the resurrected body. Often God uses the awful brokenness in this world to orchestrate this death to the natural self. This process stirs deep pain and shame, but it's the only way to allow God's life to take over your own.

Do you want to grow into the new life God has planned for you? When has your deepest pain and shame broken your seed-shell of pride? What was it like to be open and vulnerable like that?

The Sacramental Witness:

Meeting Jesus in the Sacrament

5

Nothing but the Blood:

Getting Ready for Communion

"Drink it, all of you," he said; "this is my blood, which seals God's covenant, my blood poured out for many for the forgiveness of sins." (Matt. 26:27,28)

Indeed, according to the law, almost everything is purified by blood, and sins are forgiven only if blood is poured out. (Heb. 9:22)

Shortly after beginning my first pastorate, I was working in my church study while an Evangelical church that rented our sanctuary was holding evening worship. Though busy, when singing arose, I found myself leaning toward the sanctuary and wishing I could join in. One tune in particular caught my ear, and when the service was over, I went in and asked a parishoner for the title.

"That's 'Nothing but the Blood,'" he said, opening his song-book and pointing to the words:

What can wash away my sin?/Nothing but the blood of Jesus.

What can make me whole again?/Nothing but the blood of Jesus.

I drew back at once, as if triggered by some primal reflex. "Uh, well, thank you," I muttered, excusing myself graciously, but quickly. As I closed my office door behind me firmly and settled back into my desk chair, unsettling thoughts and feelings tumbled within me.

Why all this talk about "blood"? I wondered in dismay. *It's all so gory and sensationalistic, if not just plain primitive.* Rationally, I knew that Jesus talked about "the new covenant in my blood" at the Last Supper, but I had comfortably assumed this was just symbolic language. For our communion service, therefore, I had eliminated any talk of "blood," and freely substituted "wine" wherever possible—though even then worrying about offending teetotalers.

The tune, however, stayed with me, and I decided at last to adapt the words to suit our more sanitary tastes. The next Sunday, we sang, "What can wash away my sin? Nothing but the Love of Jesus" at worship. Even as we sang, however, I found myself uneasy with such direct and familiar talk of "Jesus."

BLOOD AND LOVE

Today, I realize that in sanitizing that old Evangelical hymn to accommodate our narrow comfort zone, I was acting out of both pride and ignorance. To sing about Jesus' love instead of His blood denies the power of God in the cross—indeed, the very love which his shed blood demonstrated. "Power without love is demonic." as another has said; "love without power is sentimentality."

Thus, the upending message of the Cross: Love requires sacrifice. Any dad knows this. "Never trust a dad without spit-up on his pajamas" was my motto as a first-year dad.

In fact, the notion that blood must be shed in order for broken relationship with God to be restored, is so basic to the biblical faith that God declares and enforces it at the very outset of human life in Genesis:

> After some time Cain brought some of his harvest
> and gave it as an offering to the Lord. Then Abel brought
> the first lamb born to one of his sheep, killed it, and gave
> the best parts of it as an offering. The Lord was pleased
> with Abel and his offering, but he rejected Cain and his
> offering. Cain became furious, and he scowled in anger.
> Then the Lord said to Cain, "Why are you angry? Why that
> scowl on your face? If you had done the right thing, you

would be smiling; but because you have done evil, sin is crouching at your door. It wants to rule you, but you must overcome it." (Genesis 4:3-7)

At one level, this story says that God requires more than just our surplus, that to give God no more than what we can readily replace is in fact no sacrifice at all. Cain could always get more seed from his harvest to sow again later—but Abel's sheep was the first-born, and therefore, more costly to lose.

Yet the story also teaches that God does indeed require blood in sacrifice, even though our pride makes us balk at the notion. So anxious to prove his own work as superior, Cain was unwilling to see that God was asking him for something else.

God was not judging the merits of meat over farm produce; clearly, both are important to life. Indeed, if either is more important, it's grain, since we can live as vegetarians without meat, but would not survive as well without grain.

The story, however, is not about sustaining bodies, but about sustaining relationship with God; not about what we require of God, but what God requires of us. It says that **God wants our whole being, and therefore requires as a sacrifice something essential to life itself-- namely, blood**.

When no blood has been shed in sacrifice, we're withholding part of our life from God. We're then vulnerable to ungodly forces, like the sin poised at Cain's door, and can't fulfill our divine destiny. Our sin-nature thereby remains untamed and at large, poised dangerously to pounce on our distrust of God and cause us to fall.

GIFT OF MYSELF

This understanding was made graphically clear to me as a pastor by a father whose teenaged son had been critically injured in an auto accident. I didn't know the young man or his family, but when we met at the hospital, I offered them my full pastoral service. Graciously, I told them I'd be happy to visit with them and their son as often as they might like, and that both I and others in the church would be praying for them all.

"We appreciate your offer," the father shot back, "but we don't want you to visit us, and whether you pray or not is your own business. If you really want to help us, what we need is blood. My boy will be having a lot of transfusions. He needs O-positive, and the doctors say their supply is low."

Startled at the man's sharpness—struggling to understand his upset and not to appear defensive--I hastened to assure him that it was fine if they didn't want me to visit. And if they needed blood, our church would indeed come to donate in his son's name.

Still, I left the hospital feeling rejected and not a little indignant. I had presented my very best, hard-earned pastoral offerings, proven effective through years of ministry. But the father did not want my counsel or my prayers. He wanted my blood.

I decided that the father had rejected my offering of pastoral care only because the terrible stress of his circumstance had kept him from recognizing its value. Keeping my word, I did ask our congregation to donate blood in his son's name. But I, instead, would offer only my prayers—much as Cain had offered his farm produce.

A few days later, while in the area, I stopped in the hospital cafeteria for lunch after a pastoral visit and, lost in my newspaper at the table, I felt a quick tap on my shoulder. I looked up as the father passed; nodding, he waved and disappeared out the door.

Disarmed by this unexpected gesture of grace, I realized then what I already knew in my heart: that I needed to release my wounded pride and judgment toward the father. As I did so in prayer, I saw at last that, **important though my prayers were, to stand with him in his struggle I would have to give him something of myself—in fact, my blood, as he'd asked.**

Two days later, after exhausting the last of my excuses, I yielded and went to the blood bank. As I rolled up my sleeve, a strange rush of strength filled me, and continued even as the blood poured out of me. Afterwards, as I walked down the hospital corridor toward the parking lot, tears of repentance filled my eyes, and I sensed that my simple act of surrender might in some way increase the effectiveness of my prayers.

A week later, a thank-you card from the blood bank noted that my blood type is O-positive; it therefore went directly to the young man's body.

Satan is a fallen angel, who can quote Scripture (see Matt. 4:1-11). The act which most frustrates God's purposes is not one which reflects no knowledge of God, but rather, which seizes upon God's word for selfish ends. Such was the evil in my presuming only to pray, as I wanted, instead of give blood, as the father asked and the young man needed.

Cain demonstrated this when he killed his brother out of pride and jealousy--as if to say,

"You say that blood sacrifice sets things right, God? OK, listen: What needs to be set right is not my relationship with you, but my relationship with myself. It's not that you have been offended and I must pay, but that I have been offended, and someone else must pay. If it's blood you want, then blood you'll get: my brother's!"

BLOOD SACRIFICE

The Story says that, when we do not offer our own blood sacrifice to worship the God of Creation, we end up offering our brother's blood as a sacrifice to worship the god of Self. That is, **as we avoid facing our own sins, we ultimately sin against others in order to save face.** God focuses precisely on this perversion of blood sacrifice in responding to Cain's murdering Abel: "Why have you done this terrible thing? Your brother's blood is crying out to me from the ground, like a voice calling for revenge" (Genesis 4:10).

What, then, does it mean to offer your own blood sacrifice?

In the earliest biblical understanding, it meant to kill an animal in place of yourself. As God instructed Aaron during the Exodus out of slavery in Egypt,

...(The priest) shall kill the goat for the sin offering for the people, bring its blood into the Most Holy Place, and sprinkle it on the lid and then in front of the Covenant Box, as he did with the bull's blood.... With his finger he must sprinkle some of the blood on the altar seven times. In this way he is to purify it from the sins of the people of Israel and make it holy. (Leviticus 16:15,19)

Blood is specified because it bears life:

The life of every living thing is in the blood, and that is why the Lord has commanded that all the blood be poured out on the altar to take away people's sins. Blood, which is life, **takes away sins. (Lev. 17:11)**

To say, therefore, that blood is required for the forgiveness of sins, is to say that life must be given up in order to re-establish true

relationship with God. "You must all be born again," as Jesus put it (John 3:7). You have to die first--lose your blood, as it were--before you can be born a second time.

Here, the interaction of the symbolic and the actual becomes critical. Certainly, God doesn't demand that we kill ourselves in order to atone for our sins, else no one would be left to serve Him, since we're all sinners. "Do you think I enjoy seeing an evil man die?" asks the Sovereign Lord. "No, I would rather see him repent and live" (Ezekiel 18:23). Rather, God wants to redeem sinful lives and recycle us to serve His purposes. And so God graciously provided for animal sacrifice, to substitute for our own human lives.

SET APART

To "sacrifice" means literally, to *sacri*-fy, to make *sacr*ed or holy--that is, to set something apart from the world's purposes and dedicate it instead to serving God's purposes--to "distinguish between what belongs to God and what is for general use" (Lev. 10:10). God wants to move us from serving our own self-centered/worldly "general use" to serving specifically His Kingdom purposes--that is, to "sacrify" us, to make us holy, and thereby, serviceable to Him.

In fact, we don't have the inner strength or moral willpower to overcome our selfish purposes and choose God's instead. To compensate fully for our sinful nature would therefore require our own death. What amazing grace: that while only the blood-letting of death can purify our sin-contaminated human nature for our created purpose, God has graciously provided an alternative--even as the goat for Abraham when Isaac was on the altar (see Genesis 22).

In Jesus, God has offered us a life-saving way to overcome our helpless situation besides suicide. The appropriate response at the communion table today, as in the ancient sacrament, is therefore not, "Get on with the ritual so I can pretend how righteous I am!" but rather, "Whew! Thank you, Father God! I want so desperately to get on with real life as you've called me, but my human nature just won't let me stop sinning. I was trapped in a dead end: either stop sinning or die. But in Jesus you provided a third option, a way out of this deadly trap! I can surrender to you, and you will empower me by your Spirit to walk in your calling."

The offering therefore becomes "sacri-fied," or literally, "made holy" to serve God's purposes as you cast your sins upon the lamb, and humbly accept cleansing and forgiveness as it's killed instead of you. In this sense, the "sacri-fice" becomes a "sacra-ment," according to the ancient Church father Augustine's classic definition, "An outward and visible sign of an inward and spiritual grace."

Animal sacrifice serves well for specific acts of sin. Recall, however, that the biblical faith defines sin not as any particular act, but rather, an inborn condition of the human species. Furthermore, you can jump into a pit on your own, but it can be deep enough that you need help getting out. **Our desperate condition of sin is sustained by our proud choice to refuse God's outstretched hand in Jesus.**

RESTORING HUMAN NATURE

God sent Jesus not because we commit various acts against His will. There are plenty enough lambs and bulls on earth already whose sacrifice could atone for that. Jesus came not to patch up particular wrongs, but to restore human nature itself to God's original intention--not simply to reform us, but to re-birth us.

As John the Baptist proclaimed at the coming of Jesus, "The axe is ready to cut down the trees at the roots" (Matt. 3:10). When pointing Jesus out to others, John declares, using the singular, "There is the Lamb of God, who takes away the *sin* of the world" (John 1:29, italics mine).

Focusing exclusively on individual acts of sin is like mopping up individual rooms after the water main has burst; it accomplishes little until the main itself is repaired. Until our central and deepest brokenness is confronted and overcome, all our industrious mopping serves only to divert us from that essential, primary task. Working/sacrificing busily makes us look good, but only allows the terminal wound to fester.

Those who ask, "But why isn't it enough just to make up for each wrong act at a time?" simply haven't yet dared face the awful helplessness of their own sinful condition. They'll see the "axe" as a threat instead of a promise. **You're not ready to know the Savior until you know your need to be saved.**

Hence, the awful wisdom in Cain's sentence, that as sin "wants to rule over you, you must overcome it." In effect, God was telling Cain, "As your

Creator, I know quite well that you can't overcome your own sin. But your cheap offering demonstrates that you think you can. Go ahead and try. But when at last your endless sacrifices exhaust you enough to know you can't do it, come ready for me to change you at the core--with blood."

Life is in the blood.

In the New Testament, the Pharisees mocked God's gracious and loving provision in the sacrament. **They offered animal sacrifice not in order to face their sin, but instead of facing it.** They failed thereby to uphold the vital balance between the symbolic and the actual, substituting the outward sign altogether for the inward grace.

Today, we do this ourselves when we simply "go through the motions" of communion, without first facing our helpless condition of sin and its deadly consequences both in and through us. We do the religious thing instead of the real thing, namely, being honest with ourselves and God. "Everyone should examine himself first," as Paul declared, "and then eat the bread and drink from the cup" (1Corinth. 11:28). Otherwise, we feel better because we've apparently done right, not because we've been made right by God.

CREATURES OF SACRIFICE

On a deeper level, however, biblical faith understands that we human beings are creatures of sacrifice. That is, when we sin, or separate ourselves from God-Who-is-Life, somewhere in our God-created hearts we know it. And we know that restoring proper relationship with God, as with another person we've sinned against, requires payment or restitution.

We might say, for example, that when you hurt me, you take a part of my personhood away and add it to your own; to restore harmony in our relationship, you must yield that part back to me—as by humbly admitting your wrongdoing and asking my forgiveness.

Similarly, my own sin of pride against the young man's father in the hospital required that I "pay" blood to restore relationship. Simply to have confessed my sin without going to the blood bank, would not have accomplished that reconciliation. Hence, the other form of truncated sacrament: when the inward grace lacks the outward sign.

A man I once pastored had a father who disciplined him as a boy with nothing but a disapproving glare. Although he was never spanked or otherwise physically "punished," the man never felt freed from the emotional burden of his wrongdoing. By not affording the boy an opportunity to make amends, the father had turned temporary guilt into an abiding shame. Later, as an adult, the man lived in fear and self-recrimination, endlessly trying to please others, as his un-please-able father, in hopes of someday having paid off his sin-debt.

Likely, the father had only wanted to teach his boy right from wrong. But without providing an outward sign of the inward grace of reconciliation, he left his son in despair. **Indeed, the greatest damage to the human spirit is done not by false accusation, which often you can refute with evidence, but by true accusation without opportunity for restoration**.

The biblical question, therefore, is not *whether* we will sacrifice for our sin, but *what* shall we sacrifice. Even if we try to deny our sin, like Cain, we'll sacrifice our brother's blood, as it were, in order to hide it. If, on the other hand, we face our sin and try to serve out Cain's sentence and overcome it alone, we'll sacrifice our emotional resources in a futile, frustrating effort to redeem ourselves.

BURNT OFFERING

Too often, we substitute our modern sacrifice of time, energy, and money--as to the church, another worthy service, or even to our loved ones--expecting that will pay off our sin and make us feel OK at last. But instead, we just become resentful when our efforts don't earn us respect, but just burn us out--a true "burnt offering"!

A classic example is the spouse, parent, or child of an alcoholic who plays the role of "righteous sufferer"--but actually needs the other to keep drinking, in order to decoy attention from his/her own sin. Such a "co-alcoholic," as Alcoholics Anonymous terms the role, typically sees him or herself as "the healthy one," and the drinker as "the one with the problem"—much as the Pharisees looked down on the prostitutes, and used the sins of others to cover their own.

The co-alcoholic tries to play God and rescue the drinker through endless sacrifices of time, energy, and money. In reality, however, such attempts to "save the drinker" only save co-alcoholics from facing their own insecurities, getting healed, and moving on with their lives without the alcoholic foil. Furthermore, **they save the alcoholic not from danger,**

but from facing the real consequences of drinking, and thereby enable the addict to avoid genuine recovery.

Again, the sacrament is short-circuited. The "outward sign" of doing things to save the alcoholic only fosters the addictive process in both parties, because it lacks the inward grace of trusting God to do what you can't. "Let go, and let God," as AA puts it.

The Snake, meanwhile, knows the access code to your sinful heart: "I'm OK, thanks. I don't need a Savior."

The price for believing your own power and goodness save you is an abiding fear that your weakness and sin will be revealed, and you'll be cast into outer darkness.

When you realize at last that you can't deny your sin, but neither can you redeem it with your own sacrifices, your natural human "flesh" offers only two apparent choices: either to live a secret life in fear of being exposed, or to offer your own blood in suicidal sacrifice.

This is no mere theological concept. Every suicide I've encountered in my ministry felt overwhelmed by shame. Thus the Apostle Paul, after confessing, "even though the desire to do good is in me, I am not able to do it," lamented, "What an unhappy man I am! Who will save me from this body that is taking me to death? (Romans 7:18,24)"

TAKE A CHANCE ON JESUS

But there's another way. Like Paul, you can take a chance on Jesus, and trust God:

> Thanks be to God, who does this through our Lord Jesus Christ!... There is no condemnation now for those who live in union with Christ Jesus. (Romans 7:25, 8:1)

Certainly, ingesting the body and blood of Jesus at the sacrament embodies graphically "union with Christ Jesus." **The food substance becomes assimilated into your body to provide strength to live; similarly, Jesus becomes assimilated into your life.**

As God stayed Abraham's hand over Isaac, so God has intervened in our behalf through Jesus--who has shed his blood once and for all to die in our place, to cover our need for life-blood to be poured out. Because Jesus has covered your sin, you don't have to trudge through life resentfully sacrificing your resources to pay it off. You can make amends where appropriate, receive His grace and the resources of His Spirit, and get on with His plan for you.

Under the Law, we sacrifice to God. In Jesus, however, God has upended the protocols of religion and sacrificed Himself to us. Jesus is not a sacrifice to God, in order to fulfill some legal requirement, but the Father's laying Himself down for us. This reality undergirds the connection between the sacrament and social justice ministry. "God gives Himself to us so we may give ourselves to others," as United Church of Christ pastor Rev. John Martin has put it.

We can come to the sacrament humbly to confess and cast our sin upon Jesus, to receive Father God's liberating mercy and empowering grace. What's more, we can respond at the table with proper appreciation by offering our lives anew--and leave equipped to do God's work in this world.

And so the Apostle exhorts the believers:

> So then, my brothers, because of God's great mercy
> to us I appeal to you: offer yourselves as *a living sacrifice*
> *to God, dedicated to His service* and pleasing to Him. This
> is the true worship that you should offer. (Romans 12:1,2,
> italics mine)

Neither the ancient blood of lambs and bulls, nor the modern sacrifices of time, energy, and money, can save us from our condition of sin. "You do not want sacrifices," as the Psalmist proclaims,

> or I would offer them; you are not pleased with burnt
> offerings. My sacrifice is a humble spirit, O God; you will
> not reject a humble and repentant heart. (Ps. 51:16,17)

From this perspective, when Cain withholds blood sacrifice, he is withholding himself from God, refusing to let God shape him for his created purposes. Authentic Christian sacrifice, that is, takes place at the cross, where our proud selves must be brought to die. There, the life-blood of the natural human self--our pride--must be poured out in humble surrender, and the blood of God's self--that of Jesus--must be transfused to circulate within and among us.

Hence, the sacrament.

What, then, can take away my sin? Not my brother's blood, which just compounds my wrongdoing. Not my own blood and sweat, for that just leads to resentful burn-out as I try to save myself.

Nothing, in fact, can take away my sin.
Nothing can make me whole again.
Nothing, that is, but the blood of Jesus.

TAKEAWAY

I'm drawn by the catchy tune of the old hymn "Nothing but the Blood," and yet repulsed by the words. Why all this gory talk about blood? A pastoral hospital call to a young man in need of blood transfusions opens me to entertain God's answer. The connection between blood/death and born again/life: why we must sacrifice our flesh in order to be purified for God's purposes. You can't cling to Father God if your arms are busy clinging to something else.

Are you clinging to something in your life that you need to surrender to God so He can free you to His purposes?

6

A Protestant Confession:

Power in the Sacrament

He sat down to eat with them, took the bread, and said the blessing; then he broke the bread and gave it to them. Then their eyes were opened and they recognized him. (Luke 24:30,31)

Do this in memory of me. (Luke 22:19)

As a Protestant, I have a confession to make. In fact, I've already confessed it to a Catholic priest.

For over fifteen years, I sneaked into the Catholic mass, taking the elements while knowing full well that Catholic doctrine allows only family members to share in the family meal. A guest in someone's home should abide by the family rules, and I did not. For that, I'm genuinely sorry.

My deeper and abiding sorrow, however, is not for what I did among Catholics, but rather, for what I did *not* do among my fellow Protestants--namely, experience power and joy in the sacrament. In fact, if God hadn't intervened dramatically, I might still be searching elsewhere.

During those fifteen years, I went to mass only occasionally, except for two years when I taught at a Catholic boys' high school and went regularly. Some years later, I was ordained by the United Church of Christ, whose roots lay in the historic German Reform and Congregational Churches.

At my first pastorate, I was surprised to discover that communion was celebrated only quarterly. The U.C.C. was then beginning merger conversations with another denomination, the Disciples of Christ, whose tradition includes weekly communion. How often to offer the sacrament threatened to become a major stumbling block to uniting. The discussions, however, never seemed to reach beyond simply affirming that each congregation was free to do as they pleased. A rich opportunity for education and renewal was thereby miscast as an issue of tolerance and inclusiveness--and lost.

QUARTERLY SEX?

Those who defended our own congregation's quarterly communion generally believed, as one founder of the church put it, "If you do it more often, it's just not special any more." To that, a fellow pastor later scoffed to me, "Quarterly? Would they say the same about making love?"

I encouraged the church to re-consider our policy, and devoted a month to preaching and teaching on the subject. Afterwards, I was pleased when the congregation voted to increase communion celebrations to monthly. Meanwhile, I continued to visit local Catholic masses, as I felt the need more often.

And then, beset by a major crisis in my life, I decided to attend 7 a.m. mass daily at the parish nearest my house, and found myself substantially strengthened for each day. During that time, one of our church leaders mentioned at a Church Council meeting that he would like an opportunity to take communion during the week. I said I'd be happy to oblige, and we began a trial 45-minute communion worship service on Wednesday nights, which drew five or six persons.

And then, strangely, as I entered the local Catholic church one morning for my usual mass, I discovered a funeral mass in progress. This hadn't happened in all the years before, so I decided to skip it. The next day, I had an early business meeting, so decided instead to attend a noon mass at another parish which I had visited before.

As I walked up the front steps, I noticed someone trying unsuccessfully to open the door. "It's locked," he said, puzzled. As several others arrived, we checked the side doors, but to no avail. One man said he'd heard they were remodeling the sanctuary. Confused, I turned and left with the others.

Undaunted, however, I decided simply to wait a few days and return to my "home" 7 a.m. mass.

When I arrived there again several days later, however, another funeral mass was in progress. Turning in dismay to walk back to my car, I puzzled over this recent turn of events. **Being essentially closed out of the mass three times in a row, struck me as more than simply unusual. I wondered: Could God be trying to tell me something?** I decided to forego mass for the next week or two and pray about it.

Two weeks later, I had no further sense of what was happening, but my personal crisis had become more stressful and I missed the uplift from mass. Then one morning as I rolled over to hit my alarm clock "Snooze" button, it occurred to me that I should try at least once more. *Lord,* I prayed, *if for some reason you don't want me going to mass as I've been doing, show me today. Give me some sign, please, so I can see your will more clearly.* Waiting, but sensing nothing, I shrugged, dressed and drove to the Catholic church.

There, the usual mass was being celebrated, and with a sigh of relief I stepped into a pew and knelt down. Later, at the priest's invitation, I joined perhaps a hundred and fifty others in the line to the altar and when I reached the priest, held out my hands for the host. Turning as usual with the wafer in my hands, I took several steps away back towards the pew.

"Excuse me!" a voice rang out suddenly from behind me.

Thinking nothing of it, I continued walking.

"Excuse me!" Louder, the voice sounded again, aiming clearly in my direction and resounding in the high chamber ceiling.

I turned to look, and to my shock, the priest was walking toward me.

Silence fell over the huge, cathedral sanctuary as the dozens of others in line stopped and turned to look at me.

"Excuse me," the priest repeated matter-of-factly, "but you have to take that up front."

"Uh...pardon me?" I blurted out, confused. Struggling, I managed a nervous smile.

"Are you a visitor?" the priest asked.

I nodded, embarrassed.

"Are you a Catholic?"

"Actually, well...no, I'm not."

The priest reached out his hand. "I'm afraid I'll have to ask you to return the Host to me," he said courteously. "But I'd like very much to meet with you after the mass. Would you please wait for me so we can talk then?"

"Uh...well, sure," I stammered, handing him the Host.

The priest smiled genially, then turned and went back to his position.

UPENDING SIGN

Quickly, I retreated to a rear pew and sat down nervously. Heart pounding, I leaned back hard, hoping to blend into the pew wood.

I couldn't believe it. *What in the world was going on?* At least we'd already done the "Passing of the Peace," so I wouldn't have to look anyone else in the eye.

At the last phrase of the benediction, I turned and fled from the sanctuary, bee-lining for my car. When I rounded the corner, I checked my rear-view mirror and glimpsed the priest out front, turning as if looking for someone. And then, at last, I was gone.

A familiar breakfast cafe was not far away, and I decided to go there to settle myself. Uneasily, I drew up to a counter stool. **As I reached for a menu, all at once it struck me:** *My prayer before getting out of bed!*

Sure, I'd asked God for a sign. But I figured maybe just a Scripture would come to mind during the mass, or maybe a responsive reading might sort of "jump out at me" with a message.

Lord, did you have to be so graphic?

It seemed clear that I'd received a sign, though certainly not any I expected. What could all this possibly mean? Shaking my head in dismay, I realized that, at least, I had to go back to the priest and apologize for disturbing the mass.

Gobbling down my eggs and toast, I left and drove back to the church. There, I went directly to the rectory office, and after a moment, the priest came out, smiling hospitably.

"I'm so sorry for the confusion this morning," he offered graciously, drawing me into his office.

"Actually, I'm the one who owes you an apology," I confessed as we sat down. Then, with a deep breath, I poured it all out. "I must tell you that I'm a Protestant minister in town, and I've been taking mass here for some time. I knew quite well that I was acting against your doctrine, and I must ask you to forgive me. I won't do it again."

Taken aback, the priest drew up—and then smiled again. "I certainly didn't know all that; all I know is I prayed that you'd come back so we could talk."

"I'm sure that's partly why I'm sitting here right now," I said. "**I can only tell you that something happens to me at a Catholic mass that doesn't happen when I take communion at my Protestant church.** I don't know what it is, but there's more power here somehow, and I've been drawn to it."

We talked further, and before I left we prayed together that I would see more clearly what God was trying to teach me in this strange experience.

Over the next few weeks, I began to see my attraction to the sacrament of communion as an essential part of my Christian journey.

In fact, as Luke's "Road to Emmaus" story at this chapter's opening portrays, the sacrament of breaking bread offers a major opportunity to "recognize" Jesus. Protestants outside the sacramental tradition haven't often accepted this, and therefore, haven't often experienced it. Ironically, though this opportunity to encounter Jesus is clearly affirmed in Scripture, biblical literalists can be the least likely to accept it, because they are often the most anxious to dissociate themselves from anything "Roman."

CHURCH HISTORY

The price for such pride and prejudice is a truncated relationship with Jesus. As one Baptist pastor declared,

> (C)hurch history did not begin with John Smyth in 1602 nor even with the 16th-century Protestant Reformation. Increasingly aware of the New Testament's suggestion that the normative service for the Lord's Day is a service of Word and Table, I regret Baptist unfaithfulness to Scripture in this area.
>
> If I believe that there are values in the simplicity of our style, I am also "turned on" by the ritual of my Roman Catholic and Anglican friends when I visit their services.[26]

Not only Evangelicals, but also Oldine Protestants are often just as fearful of orthodoxy and ritual, as an apparent threat to individualism. Award-winning author Madeleine L'Engle speaks warmly of the "true Christian community" in her Connecticut farm village Congregational church, then notes,[27]

> But I also discovered that as a storyteller I cannot live without symbol and sacrament, and any symbol was forbidden (in that church) because it smacked of--terrible word--Popery! When the minister said, "Let us pray," we bowed our heads every so slightly, because to do more would have been to capitulate to Rome.

Today, L'Engle notes, "Things have changed, and for the better":

> There is now a plain wooden cross in the church, which would have been impossible then, and there is a beautiful new Catholic church, and each spring the people of the village put on a musical comedy, the proceeds of which go to both churches. **We are, at least, in dialogue, understanding that neither church is perfect, but that we have much to share."**

That is, whenever we balk at encountering Jesus at the communion table--whether as Evangelicals, Pentecostals, or Oldliners--we're simply manifesting our common human pride. It's the old Original Sin of believing our way is better than God's, and we can therefore handle our lives just fine by ourselves.

Sixteenth century reformer John Calvin put it more bluntly: "Whoever abstains voluntarily from the practice of the sacraments, thinking that he does not need them, scorns Christ, rejects his grace, and snuffs out his Holy Spirit."[28]

In fact, whether we allow it or not, I believe the human heart longs for sacramental expression, that is, an occasion to recognize in a community setting certain life events as set apart for God's special purposes.

NEED FOR RITUAL

A clergy friend once told me that when their family's pet parakeet died, his four-year-old daughter was distraught. As the little girl held the dead bird in her hands, the father sensed her sadness and confusion, and tried to comfort her. Eventually, he told his daughter to take the bird out in the back yard and find a good place to bury it as he went for a shovel. At that point, a girlfriend of his daughter stopped by, and the two children walked out back.

My friend paused to watch the two little girls gently carrying the dead bird. The two found a suitably shady spot, and laid the bird on the ground. For several moments they stood quietly, looking down at it with sad and puzzled expressions. And then, to his astonishment and wonder, on no apparent cue, the two girls began to move in a circle around the bird, as if dancing.

This need for ritual—for participatory out-of-the-ordinary drama in order to integrate larger reality--is common among adults as well. Once, a middle-aged professional man called to ask if I would perform a memorial service for his deceased aunt, who "had been loved by all the family." As we discussed arrangements, the man noted that his aunt had died over a year earlier. Startled, I asked why the family had waited so long to hold a service?

"I guess we all just thought it wouldn't be necessary," he replied, chagrined. "But lately, we've all been realizing there's a lot of loose ends over losing Aunt Edith, like something's unfinished or incomplete, and a service of some kind might pull things together for us."

In such humbling moments, we experience God's pressing in to give us His perspective. We realize that our own individual response alone is simply not sufficient to the larger importance of the event, that indeed, a greater-than-human dimension must be acknowledged and engaged. To embrace the full significance of a life-shaping event, to set it aside for God's purposes—indeed, to sanct-ify or make it holy--we need to offer it up to God together.

We need a sacrament.

The daily bread must become the eternal Body of Christ, even as our flesh-and-blood bodies must image the God-who-is-Spirit.

PROTESTANT REVELATION

Too often, we Protestants don't acknowledge this primal need for sacrament, which nevertheless remains as a longing in our human spirits, in spite of our proud attempts to deny it.

The Rev. Terry Fullam, formerly of St. Paul's Episcopal Church in Darien, Connecticut, tells of his Baptist upbringing and being drawn as a college freshman to a Roman Catholic church in Boston, aptly named St. Clement's Eucharistic Shrine. In the ancient Greek New Testament language, *eucharist* means "thanksgiving," and came to mean the sacrament of communion. As Fullam declared,[29]

> I knew all the Protestant reasons, all the things where I disagreed with the Catholics, but there was something about that church that drew me in there.

When later invited to serve as organist at an Episcopal church, Fullam "had never attended an Episcopal service anywhere." Yet because of his experience at St. Clement's, he accepted--and was humbled and amazed much as myself:

> And the Eucharist!...I discovered the Eucharist. I couldn't get enough of it. I looked around--I was like a person who had been without something in his diet--... and found a church that had a daily Eucharist. And for years I went almost every day of the week--up at seven o'clock and drive into Providence....That opened a whole new world to me.

Similarly, former Oldline United Church of Christ pastor and charismatic Elijah House Ministries founder John Sandford recalls when he found himself "ministering among Catholic people a lot," and he first began going to a mass:

> To my surprise--as a Protestant I had never been to a Catholic mass before...I found everything in me saying, "I'm home, I'm home." And I found a love for the Catholic mass I couldn't understand."[30]

In a fascinating essay titled, "Undocumented Protestants," Catholic William Cleary tells of attending a Presbyterian church for its "freedom" and "congeniality," and continuing to attend Catholic mass on Saturday and Sunday nights. He likens the ecumenical issue to the struggle of international refugees, and declares, "It is time for Protestants to start thinking of themselves as Catholics in exile":

> Historically, the homeland of all Protestants is, after all, the Catholic Church. Protestant theolgogian George Lindbeck...compared Protestants to the liberation fighters in voluntary exile from their homeland--to which they hoped to return, some day, bringing more freedom.
>
> But the freedom forces have forgotten that the reason for their existence is to return to their homeland,

a liberated homeland. Instead, they have tried to re-establish their native country abroad, alienated from the depths and continuities of culture and tradition from which they sprang."[31]

Perhaps, I had become so closed off to the power in the sacrament because I had cut myself off from our common Catholic roots as Christians. A sad historical confirmation of that diagnosis lies in a commentary on the Heidelberg Catechism which notes the reformer Zwingli's conviction that in the Eucharist, the bread and wine

> are no more than symbols....The holy Supper is above all a commemoration of the death of the Savior, a ceremony "in memoriam," as it were; Christ is present in the memory of those who participate in this act.[32]

At once, I realized that I had been reared to share this skewed perspective, which empties the sacrament of any power beyond the natural human power of the participants. No wonder I had experienced no transcendent, transforming power in communion!

MORE THAN SYMBOLS

At the same time, I learned that Martin Luther himself had rejected Zwingli's view. His Catechism therefore declares,

> The sacrament of the Lord's Supper is not a symbol, more or less impressive, one that could be dispensed with if necessary...No, **it is a matter of relationship which Christ himself has established. Whenever the holy Communion is celebrated, Christ is present**. The bread and wine of the Lord's Supper become the elements which attest the reality of his work for us and our participation in its benefits.[33]

That was exciting! If the Risen Christ is really present during communion, my job as pastor/celebrant was not simply to remind my congregation what Jesus had done 2000 years ago, but rather, to proclaim that He is among us even now as we share the elements, and welcome Him to act among us.

"W.I.J.D.?" should grace every communion altar.

I began to understand the key difference between Zwingli and Luther when a friend told me about a time when he was working on the East Coast and his wife was working in the Midwest. During that year of geographic separation, they visited each other monthly. Between visits, he said, "we lived on memories, recalling the times we'd shared together--and that was a real comfort." As each next visit approached, however, "we became excited about sharing where we are now and doing new things together."

The difference between remembering a person in the past and actually being with that person in the present--especially someone you love--is dramatic and real. Similarly, the biblical stories of Jesus are a genuine comfort to Christians. But to look forward to communion with excitement--as my friend looked forward to being with his wife again--you must believe that Jesus will actually be there at the table with you, alive and active, even in your behalf.

REMEMBER WITH ACTION

When Jesus breaks the bread and commands his followers, "Do this in memory of me," He's not telling them--nor us--merely to think about what He did in the past. He means what my mother meant when she told me, "Remember your grandmother on her birthday": not simply to stir up a mental image of Grandma, but to write her a letter, buy her a gift, give her a phone call--to interact with her in the present.

Christians are not called simply to live off memories of God. The historical accounts in the Bible prepare us to encounter the Living, Resurrected Christ today. Scripture helps us to know what to expect when Jesus is among us, and in that sense, at last to recognize him with us— even as the disciples on the Road to Emmaus. **Communion is not a time to reminisce about a god named "I Was," but rather, to welcome and celebrate the God named "I Am"** (see John 8:58).[34]

Luther's Heidelberg Catechism refutes Catholic doctrine that the elements become the actual body and blood of Jesus. But this and other detailed theological arguments strike me as fatuous. I sincerely doubt that Jesus worries whether you believe in "consubstantiation" (Jesus is present as we celebrate) or "transsubstantiation" (Jesus becomes the elements)--as long as you come to the Table humbly to welcome the Risen Christ to do His transforming work in and through you. Both Catholics and Protestants, I believe could accommodate that act of faith.

Protestants who surrender their pride to God's larger purposes, are therefore inevitably drawn to the Eucharist.

Significantly, the 1984 World Council of Churches' Faith and Order Commission released a far-reaching document titled, *Baptism, Eucharist, and Ministry*, calling for weekly communion at the principal Sabbath worship. United Methodist pastor and former Catholic priest James Gaughan[35] speculated that among all directives in this "historic" document, the latter "will probably meet with the most consternation or, worse, neglect." Pointing to "the renewal of liturgical understanding and practice" as "the most ecumenical task of the day," he laments that in the case for weekly communion, "for the rank and file, no argument seems persuasive enough":

> To many, it does not seem to matter that the weekly celebration of Christ's resurrection was the universal tradition before the Reformation; nor that Calvin insisted to the end of his life that the full service of the Word include the sacrament as well as Scripture and the sermon; nor that he, like Luther, believed that the Eucharist should be celebrated each Sunday as the culmination of the weekly service; nor that he complained bitterly when the magistrates in Geneva forbade weekly communion.

Focusing closer to home, Gaughan declared,

> Similarly, it doesn't seem to do much good to remind United Methodists that **their original movement was as eucharistic as it was evangelistic**. They don't seem to hear when they are told that the Wesleys received the sacrament at least weekly, and certainly far more often than was the custom in the established church of the time. John Wesley's suggestion (of weekly communion) to the founding conference of the American Methodist Church falls on as deaf ears today as it did 200 years ago.

WORD AND SACRAMENT

Historically, the balance of word and sacrament was often upset not by divine will, but temporal circumstances. The American custom of quarterly communion in Oldline churches, for example, began in some cases with the "circuit rider" preachers, when the frontier lacked enough ordained clergy to celebrate the sacrament more often. In Europe, Swiss reformers simply felt the Catholic Church had so neglected the word that they eschewed the sacraments altogether in favor of Bible-reading and preaching.

Citing theologian Robert MacAfee Brown's *The Spirit of Protestantism*, Gaughan underscores "a basic Protestant conviction that word and sacrament belong together" and concludes, **"The sacraments are not afterthoughts that must be validated by everything else; they validate everything else."**

Significantly, Gaughan finds the call to restore sacramental worship echoed most strongly among Protestants committed to social justice. Affirming "the intimate connection between liturgical worship and social action," he declares that "both meditation on Scripture and participation in the sacraments are complimentary ways of sharing in the mystery of God's self-giving in Christ, providing the knowledge and strength to live a life in the service of others."

He therefore concludes, regarding the WCC document, that "The reforms which *Baptism, Eucharist, and Ministry* calls forth are neither high church nor low church. They are simply biblical, historical, and ecumenical theology applied to the sacraments."

The story of Broadway Methodist Church in South Bend, Indiana, offers a case in point. Located in a declining section of town with a growing ethnic population, the church decided not to close as many of its original, all-white membership fled to the suburbs. A new pastor revitalized the church through programs of visiting the sick and urban ministry--while increasing the frequency of communion.

As Duke Divinity School professors Stanley Hauerwas and William Willimon explain,[36]

> Through (the new pastor's) preaching, by taking the Eucharist to many members in nursing homes and to those too ill to come to church, and in countless other ways, he had helped people see how the Eucharist made caring for one another intelligible. Some undoubtedly put up with the pastor's "high church views" because they loved and respected him; but they were also learning that this type of pastoral care was determined

by the Eucharist.

Eventually, the worship committee suggested weekly communion. When the board moved to vote on the proposal, they were startled when the pastor declared that they should not vote on it:

The pastor seemed to have lost all political sense. A matter for which he had worked for years was coming to a vote, which he would win, and he would not let it happen.

He explained that though it is the tradition of the church that the Eucharist be celebrated every Sunday, the congregation no more had the right to decide how often the Eucharist would be celebrated than to decide whether it would say the Lord's Prayer. Both were obligations it was invited to obey or, rather, **they were privileges in which the church ought to rejoice.**

The pastor suggested that meetings be called for any members who disliked weekly communion, that "if many felt strongly that such a move would make it impossible for them to continue to worship there, then," he said, the church might have to wait a little longer." Not to wait, he suggested, "would belie the very unity of the Eucharist."

None came to the meeting to protest, so the weekly sacrament was instituted.

Later, sacrament informed social justice ministry when unemployment hit the neighborhood hard and the worship committee--significantly, not an outreach or social justice committee--suggested that "since the church had learned the significance of sharing the eucharistic meal together, perhaps it could share a meal with the neighborhood. Such a meal would not be the same as the Eucharist, but at least it would express the kind of community that meal has made possible."

The congregation then proposed to invite the neighborhood to lunch after every Sunday worship. As the authors conclude, **"The presence that comes in the meal sustained the church's ability to be present in the neighborhood, a symbol that all was not lost."**

PENTECOSTAL SACRAMENT

Communion also fosters the "pentecostal" workings of Holy Spirit. This became graphically clear to me one Sunday when I visited St. Luke's Episcopal Church near Seattle, formerly pastored by the late Dennis Bennett, founder of the charismatic Episcopal movement. As the worship band played uplifting worship music, the robed priest stood behind the altar where the bread and wine were prepared. Welcoming the Risen Lord to the feast, the priest blessed the elements and the people. The entire Body then rose to welcome Jesus in praise and thanksgiving.

For perhaps fifteen minutes the worship continued joyously. Then suddenly, to everyone's surprise, a young woman burst into the sanctuary from the back door, raced down the center aisle to the front and threw her arms around the priest's neck, bouncing and whispering excitedly into his ear. After a moment, he motioned the congregation to silence and offered her the microphone.

"Oh, thank you, Jesus!" she cried out breathlessly. "Haleluia! I've been deaf in my left ear for almost 15 years from an accident and this morning as we were worshipping, I thought I could hear with it. I ran across the street to the gas station phone to see if I wasn't just imagining things, and when I put the phone up to my ear, I heard the dial tone perfectly!"

A cheer of praise erupted from the congregation as she hugged the priest—who turned immediately afterwards to lift the cup and proceed with the sacrament.

YES! I thought. *This is how it must have been in the early Church!*

This experience of bodily healing at the communion table opened a whole new dimension to my expectation. I had always understood that the blood of Jesus cleanses us of sinful acts. My prayers before and during the sacrament, therefore, had focused on confessing and asking the Father's forgiveness for my wrongdoing—as David asked God to "search my heart" in Psalm 139:23,24. **But with my new, Evangelical understanding of sin, I saw that Jesus came to the table not only to forgive me my wrongdoings, but also to heal the world's range of brokenness in me.**

"There is the Lamb of God, who takes away the sin of the world!" as John cries out on seeing Jesus first come toward him (John 1:29). Here, John is not simply referring to the plural "sins" or individual acts. He's including the far larger broken or fallen state of this world—including sickness, war, hunger, and the entire host of worldly suffering, injustice, and destruction which comprises the root meaning of "sin," that is, to "miss the mark" of God's intention.

That's exciting. It means I can go to communion not only to find God's forgiveness for my ungodly behavior, but also His healing for my physical problems and power to effect His larger healing of society.

Realizing this today, I can only shake my head in dismay for my ignorance all these years. Who knows what Jesus might have accomplished in and through me had I allowed him this fuller rein at the sacrament? Today, I choose rather to dwell on what he might do now as I allow him such latitude during communion, and how I can proclaim this reality to so many Christians who still don't see it.

SKIMPY THEOLOGY

In my own congregation, the process of moving from quarterly to monthly communion made me regret my skimpy diet of sacramental theology in seminary. In fact, I became convinced that our Protestant fear of "too often" celebrating the Eucharist is rooted in pride. "If it isn't meaningful to me," we seem to say, "then strike it out." But what if it isn't meaningful simply because we haven't allowed God to show us its meaning?

Eventually, during one communion Sunday worship, I prayed quietly, "Jesus, I'm glad you're here. Forgive me and the rest of us for not recognizing and welcoming you here in the sacrament. I release you from my fear and pride, and ask you to do now whatever you want to do here as we celebrate your sacrifice for us."

Through several months of such praying, people began to tell me, as one 38-year-old schoolteacher, that "something special" was happening on communion Sundays. "I feel so uplifted," another declared. Whereas before, fewer people actually came to worship on communion Sundays--"It makes the service too long," as one had complained--now more were coming.

Then a widow in her 60's called me one day and asked, "Could we maybe have a few minutes during worship just before communion, you know, to prepare ourselves?"

Haleluia! I exclaimed in my heart. Accordingly, I inserted a "Time of Preparation" into worship just prior to the sacrament. "Everyone should examine himself first," as Paul noted, "and then eat the bread and drink from the cup" (1 Corinth. 11:28). Occasionally, I would lead the congregation in prayers of confession. Otherwise, I would offer a moment of silence for personal examination.

Everyone appreciated this. "That time beforehand makes the whole thing come alive somehow," as one put it.

Eventually, the mid-week evening communion service folded for lack of participation. Disappointed at first, I came to sense that **God's agenda was rather to bring the power of the sacrament into the whole body on Sunday morning, and not to center it in any smaller, potentially elite group.** Eventually, at a deacon's meeting, one woman spoke up hesitantly and asked if--since we had no altar rail--people who wanted might somehow be able to kneel to receive the elements?

TO KNEEL OR NOT

Prior to my teaching series on the sacrament, this same suggestion had been met with indignation. Gingerly, I offered that indeed, King David wrote a Psalm inviting worshippers "Come, let us bow down and worship him; let us kneel before the Lord our Maker" (Ps. 95:6). "After all," I joked, "David wasn't a Catholic!"

I held my breath--and to my pleasant surprise, all the other deacons agreed that we might now provide an opportunity to kneel for those who wanted to.

One then suggested we use our wedding kneeler. Another noted that the previous year's Maundy Thursday service, instead of serving the elements in the pews, we had invited people to come forward individually; since that service was not far ahead; perhaps we could experiment then?

That Maundy Thursday evening, I stood behind the wedding kneeler with the elements and assisting head deacon. I invited anyone who wanted, to come forward and kneel, and perhaps half the congregation did. "It wasn't a forced, uncomfortable thing," as one remarked. "Everyone who came really wanted to kneel."

Insofar as the typical Protestant service centers about the sermon, the Catholic mass centers about the Eucharist. I knew God had truly begun overcoming our pride—and was taking aim at my own!--when at a following diaconate meeting, one deacon suggested gently, "Could we maybe have a shorter sermon on Communion Sunday?"

A *National Catholic Reporter* editorial jarringly titled, "In Praise of

Bad Sermons," makes the point. Reviewing the spectrum of Protestant preachers from Evangelical conservatives to Oldline liberals, the writer concluded,

> But while there are differences (among Protestant preachers), they are essentially the same. They are performers. Their success depends on their ability to dominate the service with their techniques and their personalities. A Catholic priest's assignment is different. In the liturgy, his job is to pay tribute through the rite, to lead the congregation into a spiritual experience. While the sermon can and should be used for teaching, it would be in poor taste for the priest's preaching to upstage the Eucharist.[37]

Certainly, God can and often does speak through a preacher. But we Protestants could experience so much more of His presence and power in worship if we allowed God to move in the sacrament as well.

As Luke's story notes, the Risen Lord who encountered the two disciples on the road to Emmaus did indeed speak to them. In fact, he gave them much teaching. But it was not until "He broke the bread" that "their eyes were opened and they recognized him." The teaching prepared them, but the breaking of the bread led them to see that Jesus was indeed there in their midst. This real-life encounter with the Risen Christ motivated them to get up "at once" to run and share the Good News with the others that "He is risen, indeed!"

Biblically, therefore, the sacrament of communion may be seen as a preface to evangelism.

A PREACHER YIELDS

After the Maundy Thursday service, many came to me to say "how meaningful" the evening had been. Yet even as I smiled and affirmed everyone's joy, I found myself quietly disappointed.

I know when I've preached well, but that night I was utterly flat. Somehow I just couldn't get pumped up about my message, and I gave myself a resounding "F" for performance.

When later all the sanctuary windows had been closed and the pews empty, I was about to shut the door behind me and leave with that emotional hole in my gut. Instead, however, I paused, and decided to sit down for a minute in a front row pew to relax and center myself.

As I leaned back and took a deep breath, a quiet stillness settled over me--and I knew: the Risen Christ had been present and acting during communion that night, as always. My job then--as whenever I served the Eucharist--was not to preach mightily, but simply to be the faithful doorman who announces the entrance of the Master, then steps back to open the door. **During Sunday worship, my task is "to lead the congregation into a spiritual experience"--sometimes by preaching, but also by presiding humbly and expectantly over the sacrament.**

Rising, I went to the kneeler and fell down. I asked God to forgive me my pride and presumption, and released all my compulsion to "be in charge" of worship, all my responsibility to "make things happen," and my compulsion to perform as a preacher.

Soon, a deep sense of relief washed over me.

I believe that today Protestant clergy and congregations alike could receive more from God during worship by stepping back and allowing the Risen Christ to come and do His transforming work among us. Nowhere is this vision more alive with promise than in the sacrament of communion. I thank God for my Catholic brothers and sisters who have witnessed that promise to me.

The Catholic Church affirms seven sacraments and not just communion alone. During the Reformation, Luther limited Protestants to the two in which Jesus himself participated, namely, baptism and communion. It's beyond the scope of this book to examine all these, but precisely its focus to highlight the one in which Jesus promises to manifest Himself. I therefore pray that we Protestants might be so humble, so expectant, and thus, so hospitable to the Resurrected Lord, that we might experience the fullness of Christ's presence and power "wherever the holy Communion is celebrated."

TAKEAWAY

I experience surprising power in a Catholic mass, as many other Protestants have testified, and ask God to bring that same power to my church's communion service. When I teach to my Oldline congregation that Jesus is present at the sacrament, they want to celebrate it more often.

Have you allowed Jesus to be present when you take communion? Have you let him there not only forgive your sinful acts, but overcome the world's sin in you, from physical to emotional problems? If not, give Him a chance.

The Pentecostal Witness:

Meeting Jesus in the Baptism of the Holy Spirit

7

Faith Encounters
of the Third Kind:

God's Larger Reality

"The wind blows wherever it wishes; you hear the
sound it makes, but you do not know where it comes
from or where it is going. It is like that with everyone who
is born of the Spirit."
"How can this be?" asked Nicodemus.
Jesus answered, "You are a great teacher in Israel,
and you don't know this?" (John 3:8-10)

Shortly into my second year of pastoring, I closed a committee
meeting with a simple prayer that God would guide each one of us in the
week to come--and was startled by one member's response. As others
began chatting and filing out of the room, a lady in her late 60's who had
given untold time and energy to the church lingered behind, troubled.

"Gordon," she murmured, her eyes distant with sadness and frustration
as she touched my arm, "you know when you prayed that God would guide
us during the week...?" Her voice broke, then fell to a whisper as she shook
her head slowly. "You know...I don't think I've ever felt God close enough to
me to really do anything like that. Not in all my years at this church--or in
any other churches before."

She knit her brow, puzzled. "Sure, I've worked on committees like tonight, with sewing circles, programs of all kinds, even been in a lot of Bible studies. I've sat in Sunday worship nearly every week of my life for almost seventy years. And yet...I just never really...experienced anything.

"Nothing...," she whispered, her voice trailing off, "...not in all those years."

Startled, I drew back in fear as I listened to this stalwart, silver-haired pillar of the church pour out her lifelong grief for missing the God she claimed but had never met. If she had needed some advice on a personal matter, I could have counseled her well with my seminary skills. But she was not seeking a better relationship with her husband, her children, or any other person.

She wanted a better relationship with God. **She wanted to feel closer to this God whom for over sixty years she had read about, listened to sermons about, talked about, sung hymns about, and even prayed to-- but had never encountered or experienced in any convincing way.**

Yes, we walk by faith and not by sight. But Jesus died so she could know her true Father intimately. I am quite sure, therefore, that He wept as she talked--and likely had been weeping for throughout those years. I cry in my heart as I recall her words today.

At the time, however, I could only tremble. For I was her pastor, her spiritual shepherd, and I had no idea where lay the green pastures for which she hungered. If I'd had enough courage to be honest, I might have said to her, "I know what you mean, because I feel the same way." And then, maybe, we both could have wept sincerely and deeply enough to find Jesus weeping with us. Broken, together, we might have opened our hearts, and heard Him speak to us at last.

ALL-KNOWING PASTOR

Or maybe, I might simply have trusted Jesus' words to his first disciples, "Where two or three come together in my name, I am there with them" (Matt. 18:20). I could then have said to her, "Let's just sit down together and tell Jesus we want to know him better, and let him respond however He wants."

But alas, I was too proud, too intent on maintaining my "all-knowing pastor" image to cover my inadequacies. I was so heavily invested in my rational intelligence that I couldn't believe that the same Jesus who lived and died 2000 years ago might be real, alive, and active today.

And so, clumsily, I assured my distraught parishoner that I knew she was struggling with a tough issue, alright, but her years of service to His Church had not gone unnoticed by God. And then, quickly, I ushered her out to the parking lot.

Today, I see myself in that story much like Nicodemus--though not as patient as he to listen to others of his faith who differed from him. That "great teacher," though he had likely graduated from the most esteemed religious institutions in Israel, simply didn't know what "born of the Spirit" means

Like Nicodemus, I knew after my own seminary training at Harvard that my intellectual gifts and talent for public speaking would carry me far in the "ministerial profession." But Jesus struck the heart of this religious leader's spiritual ignorance by declaring, "I am telling you the truth: we speak of *what we know* and report *what we have seen*" (John 3:11, italics mine).

Sadly, I lacked precisely that confidence in my faith. **I spoke of what I reasoned to be true, of what I read, of what other people were doing. But I could not report anything I myself had seen God do.** The more I sensed my inadequacy, the harder I tried to compensate with more insightful counseling and better-researched sermons. But I knew something essential was missing, both from my ministry and personal life, which neither intelligence nor diligence could provide.

LIKE THE WIND

I tried to forget my parishoner's unsettling concern. And then, several months later, after teaching a fifth-grade vacation Bible school class, I asked for questions.

"How do we know God is for real?" one boy spoke up, continuing as I strained to appear calm and receptive. "I mean, after all, you can't really see God standing there in front of you, like the people in the Bible saw Jesus back then."

Lord, help me! I prayed quietly.

The very old and the very young ask the essential questions. They experience more graphically their own powerlessness in worldly terms, and thereby have less "face" to save in seeking other power.

As I prayed feverishly for an answer to this young boy's searching question, I thought of Jesus and Nicodemus. "The Spirit of God is like the wind," I replied. "You can't see it, but you can see it moving other things. Just like the wind moves branches and leaves, so you can 'see' God moving people whenever they love one another, like Jesus."

But my fifth-graders were quick to point out that you can tell the wind is around even without looking at other things.

"You can feel it on your face," one noted.

"I've actually felt the wind so strong sometimes that I had to lean against it," another declared. "It was pushing me back from where I wanted to go!"

The implications are staggering. If, as Jesus told Nicodemus, God is like the wind, can you feel God in your face? Can you really feel God pushing you so firmly that even when you lean in another direction, determined instead to do it your own way, you can still feel God pushing you back?

In the Beginning, the Spirit of God moved intentionally over the chaotic waters. **Could that same Spirit still be blowing, pushing, moving in our own lives even now, creating new life and God's order out of the emptiness and chaos in our lives?**

Unsettling questions like these must have driven Nicodemus to pay his secret nighttime visit to Jesus--a "heretic" with whom he dared not be seen by his fellow, well-situated Pharisees. For he confesses right away to Jesus, "Rabbi, we know that you are a teacher sent by God. No one could perform the miracles you are doing unless God were with him" (John 3:2).

Surprisingly, Jesus doesn't rush to welcome this Pharisee with open arms and exclaim, "Yes! At last you've seen the truth!" Instead, Jesus responds as if Nicodemus has not yet gone the full route with his faith.

"Seeing a trace of God, even seeing God at work in the world, is not enough," Jesus seems to be telling him. "Yes, you can see the leaves tumbling and rationally infer that the wind is around. But can you feel the wind in your face? Can you feel the wind pushing your very body in a new direction? You have seen God at work through me, but can you feel God at work in you, even re-creating you?"

That is, "Have you been born of the Spirit?"

SCIENCE FICTION

As Jesus represents to Nicodemus a power beyond natural human abilities, their encounter might be understood via the science fiction convention which spawned the popular old movie, *Close Encounters of the Third Kind*. In sci fi lore, that is, an encounter of the First Kind with extra-terrestrial powers means that a mere trace has been detected.

For Christians, an encounter of the First Kind with God might occur when you notice on American currency the words, "In God We Trust." Or, maybe you hear someone sneeze and another says, "God bless you," or you see the new President place his hand on a Bible at the inauguration and conclude, "So help me, God."

An encounter of the Second Kind means seeing the effects of something clearly from beyond the natural realm. Nicodemus had such an experience when he met people Jesus had clearly healed. Today, this might happen when you actually know a credible individual who was healed either physically or emotionally through prayer, and you can see the difference in that person.

Like Nicodemus, if you've had that close an encounter with God, you're more than curious. Your natural worldview has been challenged. Your comfort in a world controlled by human power has been upended. It's scary, but compelling. **To your God-created human spirit, it's like being lost in the wilderness for years, and suddenly you catch the smell of a campfire in the air.**

Nicodemus is hooked. Against all reasonable standards of his respectable religion, he sneaks over to encounter Jesus for himself.

Why does Nicodemus risk his reputation in order to see Jesus? Because he's a creature of God and therefore bears the essential spirit-nature of his Creator. "God is Spirit," as Jesus noted, "and only by the power of His Spirit can people worship him as he really is" (John 4:24).

Nicodemus therefore hungers to experience the reality of God's *super*-natural presence and action. He's developed his natural intelligence and social/religious power, but that hasn't satisfied his deepest need. He's seen God work in other people's lives, and he's decided at last, "I want God to work like that in my life, too."

He wants a faith encounter of the Third Kind—not just a cultural reference, or even a credible story of someone else's experience, but indeed, his own face-to-face engagement with God.

And so he goes to meet Jesus for himself.

I believe Nicodemus is a paradigm for many Christians today, who secretly long for a real enough experience of God to carry them through life's struggles into their divine destiny.

CULTS AND YOUTH

Youth are often the first to respond to this inner call--again, because they are not so invested in the world's power. Significantly, therefore, over eighty percent of young cult members "come from non-religious or nominally religious homes," according to one survey:[38] "Very few report ever having been active in church, though 90 percent report that their parents were members of a church."

That is, "One of the things the new religions do is supply religion for people who never had it before--except as something other people talk about."

Again, one professor surveyed noted that students at his college who are attracted to "aberrational groups" are moved by a genuine need:

(They) sense a lack of the experiential in their own faith and church life. Such a subjective experience is very important to them. They also miss a sense of drama and vitality about their Christian faith. We lost about two dozen students about ten years ago to the Church of the Living Word, headed by the late Apostle John Robert Stevens. He made things happen. He was exciting and dynamic. Students who came mostly from Baptist, Methodist, and Presbyterian churches saw their churches as well-intentioned, but not excited about their faith. In Steven's church, every service was different. When the Apostle laid his hands on people, the excitement was real.

The Enemy of God is virtually by definition seductive. As another has noted, "At its worst, Evil promises to satisfy a legitimate need in an illegitimate way."

In my own youth during the 1960's, I recall being deeply moved by Beatle George Harrison's popular recording, "My Sweet Lord." When he sang, "I really want to know you, Lord," I knew very well what he meant, because I wanted that myself. By no coincidence, the song moved readily from interludes of "Haleluia" to "Hare Krishna." Indeed, it tapped **a young generation's longing for authentic spiritual encounter--at least, something more real than we had experienced in our sober, well-modulated churches growing up.**

HUNGRY TOO LONG

Surely, that's why the *Close Encounters* film was so popular, and why it birthed a whole new genre of psychic horror films laced with demons: because we in our Western rational mind-set have gone spiritually hungry too long. We've had no encounter at all with God, and so we turn desperately to a celluloid fantasy--like trying to fill an empty stomach with cotton candy.

Yes, we've gone to church, attended youth group, served on committees, built buildings, given money, sung hymns, gone to Bible studies. But too often, we have not encountered palpably the God who animates His Church—and indeed, our very lives.

All human beings long for encounter with their Creator-God, whether they've been to church or not. As in Nicodemus, somewhere in our hearts— respectably muffled but increasingly difficult to restrain--a voice cries out, "I really want to know and experience this God everyone talks about."

Secular psychologist Abraham Maslow portrays how organized religions often ignore this need:

> Most people lose or forget the subjectively religious experience, and redefine Religion as a set of habits, behaviors, dogmas, forms, which at the extreme becomes entirely legalistic and bureaucratic, conventional, empty, and in the truest meaning of the word, anti-religious.
>
> The mystic experience, the illumination, the great awakening, along with the charismatic seer who started the whole thing, are forgotten, lost, or transformed into their opposites. **Organized Religion, the churches, finally may become the major enemies of the religious experience and the religious experiencer.**[39]

Thus, Jesus lashed out at the religious leaders who read the Bible day and night but could not recognize Him standing right in front of them:

> You study the Scriptures, because you think that in

them you will find eternal life. And these very Scriptures talk about me! Yet you are not willing to come to me in order to have life. (John 5:39,40)

Similarly, the Apostle Paul warns his young apprentice Timothy to avoid those who in the coming "last days" will "hold to the outward form of our religion, but reject its real power" (2 Tim. 3:5).

Liberal-universalists would readily identify such a "religious" caricature with conservative fundamentalists. Yet to focus, as Maslow, not on the presence of dogmatism, but the absence of authentic spiritual experience, is to recognize the ideologues of "liberal religion" as bedfellows with the legalists of "conservative religion."

The overriding fear of "emotionalism" and "excess" among both liberal Oldliners and conservative Evangelicals, though valid at times, often simply covers a fear of trusting and surrendering to a power greater than yourself. "No one ever talks about the excesses of reserve, of fear, of suspicion, and pride," as Pentecostal Foursquare pastor Jack Hayford laments. "Much reserve, so-called 'biblical balance,' really is...a horrible imbalance toward an intellectualized spirituality."[40]

THE SHALLOW END

Similarly, Evangelical author Dallas Willard asserts, **"I often say to those concerned about 'going off the deep end,' 'Have you ever considered what happens to those who go off the shallow end?'** Church after church has gone off the shallow end. They're frightened of the spiritual depths."[41]

Significantly missing from "liberal theisms," Maslow notes, are the "experiences of surrender, reverence, devotion, self-dedication, humility and oblation, awe, and the feeling of smallness." The result is

a rather bleak, boring, unexciting, unemotional, cool philosophy of life which fails to do what the traditional religions have tried to do when they were at their best: to inspire, to awe, to comfort, to fulfill, to guide in value choices, and to discriminate between higher and lower, better and worse, not to mention provide Dionysiac experiences, wildness, rejoicing, impulsiveness.

Any religion, liberal or orthodox, theistic or nontheistic, must be not only intellectually credible and morally worthy of respect, but it must also be emotionally satisfying (and I include here the transcendent emotions as well).[42]

Hence, Maslow explains the decline of the traditional, Oldline churches:

No wonder that the liberal religions and semi-religious groups exert so little influence even though their members are the most intelligent and most capable sections of the population. It must be so just as long as **they base themselves upon a lopsided picture of human nature which omits most of what human beings value, enjoy, and cherish in themselves,** in fact, which they live for, and which they refuse to be done out of.[43]

INTEGRATED SPIRITUALITY

Significantly, Maslow does not urge experience as a substitute for either rationality, morality, or social conscience. Rather, he espouses "a pervasively holistic attitude," in which spiritual experience is "integrated with the abstract and the verbal." He therefore affirms the essential relationship "between experientialism and social reform":

Shortsighted people make them opposites, mutually exclusive. Of course, historically this has often happened and does today. But it need not happen. It is a mistake, an atomistic error, an example of the dichotomizing and pathologizing that goes along with immaturity.

The empirical fact is that...our best experiencers are also our most compassionate, our great improvers and reformers of society, our most effective fighters against injustice, inequality, slavery, cruelty, exploitation (and also our best fighters for excellence, effectiveness, competence). And it also becomes clearer and clearer that the best "helpers" are the most fully human persons.[44]

Indeed, as C.S. Lewis noted, "If you read history you will find out that the Christians who did the most for the present world were precisely those who thought most of the next."[45]

Maslow therefore calls for "an integration of self-improvement and social zeal." That is, the best way to become a better "helper" is first to become a better person. But one necessary route to becoming a better person is via helping other people: "So one must and can do both simultaneously."[46]

Maslow's effort to integrate spirituality and psychology invites churches to cry out for God's healing power, precisely in order to promote peace and social justice more effectively. Thus the Apostle Paul proclaims "The God from whom all help comes," who "helps us in all our troubles, so that we are able to help others who have all kinds of troubles, using the same help that we ourselves have received from God" (2 Corinth. 1:4).

What kind of encounter with God do you want in your own life and in your church? Do you feel comfortable with a mention of God here and there, once in awhile? Or, if you're a born-again Believer, is it enough for you to give rational assent to what the Bible says, so that you can lead other people to make that same thoughtful commitment to "follow Jesus?"

Or, indeed, are you like Nicodemus--good, religious, intelligent, and accomplished Nicodemus--longing to sneak away some night and meet Jesus face to face yourself? Do you want to say, like Jesus' first disciples, "We speak of what we know and tell of what we have seen"?

May God bless the Nicodemus in us all. For his is "the way with everyone born of the Spirit."

TAKEAWAY

A stalwart old churchwoman confesses her longing to experience God's presence and power—even as the Pharisee Nicodemus sought Jesus. A prominent secular psychologist witnesses to that need. Because spiritual power supersedes our natural human power, we fear and even deny it—which leads us to deny not only the reality of God, but the cry of our hearts for spiritual connection.

Have you listened to the Nicodemus in yourself? When have you wanted most to meet Jesus for yourself, to see God act more powerfully, even supernaturally, in your own life? Describe encounters you've had with God of the first, second, and third kind.

8

Who Is Holy Spirit?

Meeting the Active Presence of God Today

> While Apollos was in Corinth, Paul traveled through the interior of the province and arrived in Ephesus. There he found some disciples and asked them, "Did you receive the Holy Spirit when you became believers?"
>
> "We have not even heard that there is a Holy Spirit," they answered. (Acts 19:1,2)

Like these ancient followers of Jesus in Ephesus, I had "not even heard that there is a Holy Spirit" by the time I had finished seminary and begun pastoring. Sure, I'd heard about this third Person of the Trinity, at least as the King James "Holy Ghost" as we sang in the traditional *Doxology* and *Gloria Patri*. If pressed, I might even have allowed that there was a Holy Spirit back in biblical times.

Not until I visited a charismatic Presbyterian worship one evening in 1979, however, did I know in my very body that the Holy Spirit is alive and well, continuing even today to work powerfully both in and among us.

SEARCHING FOR STRENGTH

Troubled if not overwhelmed by problems at church and in my home life, I'd made the hour's drive to the Friday evening "Gifts of the Holy Spirit" event, desperate for some release. I'd been reading books about the healing work of Holy Spirit, and was searching for strength both to push through and to learn from this painful season.

During the teaching, I took many notes, and as the minister pronounced a benediction and invited people to come forward for prayer, I stepped matter-of-factly out into the aisle to go home.

"Excuse me, but we've been sitting at the back of the sanctuary watching you, and sense you're distressed."

Startled, I turned to see a middle-aged lady and man standing in front of me.

"We'd like to pray for you, if that's OK."

"Uh, well...," I began, uncertain. "I mean, of course...yes, I guess...that would be fine."

Who are these people? I wondered. *And how did they know I was so stressed out?*

"I really don't know what to pray for," the woman confessed sincerely, "but if it's alright with you, I'd just like to ask the Holy Spirit to come and do whatever He wants."

Standing there on the way to my car, I shifted uncomfortably. "Well, I..." Involuntarily, my eyes turned from her to the man as he stepped away from her side and behind me, facing my back with the woman in front of me. I thought he might be leaving, but he simply remained standing at my back. *What's he doing?* I thought.

Before I could gather myself to ask, the woman lifted her arm and lightly rested her fingertips on my forehead. "Lord Jesus," she began, "we don't know what's causing this man such distress, but we ask you, Holy Spirit, to come now and in the name of Jesus, we ask you to minister to his need."

Suddenly I felt myself falling backward into the man's arms. Utterly relaxed, even rubbery, I dropped, and the man lowered me gently to the floor on my back. From there on the carpet, I looked up as the man and woman smiled kindly and left.

Too much at peace to be puzzled, I lay there amazed, looking at the ceiling. A moment later, the pastor came by and leaned over. "Well," he offered with a reassuring smile, "you certainly got more than you bargained for, didn't you?" And then he, too, turned and left.

I was aware that I could get up if I wanted. But as a sense of refreshment washed over me, I chose to lie there awhile longer and soak in it. After some time, I got up, and was surprised to see maybe half a dozen other people lying on the carpet and various others standing or seated while praying together. As I gathered myself, the woman and man came back, and hugged me. "We'll be praying for you," he said, and they moved to pray for someone else nearby.

Later, on the long freeway drive home, I reflected on the evening's events. No, the woman had not exerted any pressure on my forehead. I was not pushed; I fell.

But how? I wondered. Indeed, *Why*? Nor was I knocked out. What I had experienced was not a de-sensitizing blackout, like a concussion, but rather, the opposite: a heightened sensitivity, unblocked by all my worries.

I remembered the woman had simply asked Holy Spirit to come. As it struck me that Holy Spirit is the third Person of the Trinity, a new and strange question stirred within me: not how or why, but Who? **Who, indeed, is this Person of the Trinity who apparently touched my very body and caused me to fall unto rest and refreshment?**

HOLY SPIRIT'S PERSONALITY

Could this Holy Spirit--like any other "person," even as Father God and Jesus--have a personality?

It was easy for me to recognize that Jesus is a person, and to discern His personality by reading about Him in the Bible. Could I possibly do the same for Holy Spirit?

In a chapter titled, "What Is a Who?" authors C. Brandon Rimmer and Bill Brown declare that Holy Spirit is not "simply a spirit or an attitude of holiness." Indeed,

> We believe that the Spirit is a person because the Scripture gives Him the characteristics of a person. In Ephesians 4:30 He can be grieved. In Genesis 6:3 He strives. In Matthew 3:16 He takes on bodily form. In Matthew 4:1 He leads. In John 3:5 He gives birth. In Acts 10:19 He speaks. In Romans 8:16 He bears witness. In I

Corinthians 12 He gives gifts.[47]

Seeing Holy Spirit as a Person radically jarred my customary view, and I began searching for some way to grasp this new truth. Unfortunately, the English language offers no way to indicate personhood without gender, and whether the Spirit is a he or a she seems pointless to me. But now, referring to a manifestation of God as "it" was no longer appropriate.

Nevertheless, I realized I could begin calling the Third Person of the Trinity simply "Holy Spirit" and not "the Holy Spirit." We add "the" in front of a person's title, but not before their name in order to indicate relationship instead of mere function.

When I preach, for example, people may refer to me as "the Reverend." When they come up after church to talk to me personally, however, they don't greet me with, "Good morning, the Reverend," but simply "Good morning, Reverend." Again, while Jesus is in fact the Messiah, or the Christ, that's a title, not a name. Talking to Him in a personal relationship, we call Him Jesus, not "the Jesus." Nor, when we cry out to God as our Father, do we call, "Help me, The Father," but simply, "Help me, Father."

In that sense, "*the* Holy Spirit" can be used to indicate uniqueness, that is, to distinguish the Holy Spirit of God from other spirits. But **in personal communication, simply talking to or about "Holy Spirit," like "Jesus" or "God," can jar us from our arms-length, function-oriented mentality into the personal relationship we long for—and indeed, already have.**

Certainly, in order to know this personality, we need to understand Holy Spirit's role in God's efforts through history to save us from our sin-nature for His purposes.

CONTINUING WITNESS

At a particular time and place 2000 years ago, the ultimate purpose and power of God was revealed in the flesh-and-blood man Jesus of Nazareth. After Jesus died and was resurrected, another Presence, another Person, was needed to bear continuing witness to God's will and power at other times and in other places.

And so Jesus emphasized to his followers,

> But I am telling you the truth: it is better for you that
> I go away, because if I do not go, the Helper will not come
> to you. But if I do go away, then I will send him to help

you. (John 16:7)

Holy Spirit's major role is to help each new generation to know what God has done in Jesus, and empower us in what God is calling us to do now in Jesus' Body, the Church:

> The Helper will come--the Spirit, who reveals the truth about God and who comes from the Father. I will send him to you from the Father, and he will speak about me....
>
> I am telling you the truth: whoever believes in me will do what I do--yes, (that person) will do even greater things, because I am going to the Father.... I will ask the Father, and he will give you another Helper, who will stay with you forever. He is the Spirit, who reveals the truth about God. (John 15:26; 14:12,16,17)

The disciples to whom Jesus was speaking, that is, would all be dead years later. The ongoing, here-and-now witness to God's saving power in Jesus would therefore be Holy Spirit:

> All that the Father has is mine; that is why I said that the Spirit will take what I give him and tell it to you. (John 16:15)

Furthermore, this telling Word of God is portrayed from the outset as poised expectantly and "hovering" over pre-creation (Gen. 1:2). **Holy Spirit therefore does not simply express an idea, but in fact, accomplishes a new reality as the extension in this world of the Father's will—even as God said, "Let there be light" and "there was light"** (Gen. 1:3 RSV).

LIFE-CHANGING REALITY

In speaking about Jesus, therefore, Holy Spirit speaks life-changing reality into God's people. As the Apostle declared, "We brought the Good News to you, not with words only, but also with power and the Holy Spirit" (1 Thess. 1:5).

In this present age, since the death and resurrection of Jesus, the workings of God are therefore accomplished among believers through Holy Spirit. Thus, James directly linked spirit and actions: "(A)s the body without the Spirit is dead, also faith without actions is dead" (James 2:26).

The Body of Christ requires God's Holy Spirit to animate it.

Without the third Person of the Trinity, therefore, we are for all *practical* purposes lifeless. A church that does not invite and welcome Holy Spirit to animate it, is *practically* dead. It cannot be a "Christ"-ian church, because it does not have the resurrection power to do what Jesus does.

With Holy Spirit, on the other hand, we experience ultimate vitality and power. "If the Spirit of God, who raised Jesus from death, lives in you," as Paul declared, "then he who raised Christ from death will also give life to your mortal bodies by the presence of his Spirit in you" (Romans 8:11).

These are no small claims to make about this Holy Spirit, whom so many of us Christians, like our early forebears in Ephesus, don't even know exists beyond "First Encounter" hearsay. The third Person of the Trinity is a full-fledged Presence of the Living God--indeed, *the* active Presence of God in this present age. **Our sense of identity and effectiveness as God's people today therefore hinges upon knowing and allowing Holy Spirit to work in and through our lives.**

To recap: to know Jesus as he was, therefore, and appropriate what he accomplished for us 2000 years ago, you begin by facing your own sin, with a desire to repent and be forgiven. You go to the cross and die to yourself, confessing your sinful nature, and beg Jesus to save you from its effects. Being thereby born again is the Spirit's work of salvation.

SAVED AND SANCTIFIED

To know the Risen Christ as he is today--to do what he wants to do in and through us even now--you must want not only to be saved from the consequences of your sin, but also to be sanctified, that is, set apart and empowered for your unique calling. You need to face where you have wounded God and others by turning away from Him. You need not only to ask His forgiveness, but also His healing for wounds others have caused you.

Holy Spirit bridges the gap between receiving God's forgiveness and forgiving others. Thus, Jesus "breathed on (the disciples) and said, 'Receive the Holy Spirit. If you forgive people's sins, they are forgiven...'" (John 20:22,23).

Since the Spirit witnesses to the ongoing purpose and power of God in Jesus the Son, to know Jesus without knowing Holy Spirit is ultimately to know only the Jesus of the past, and not the living, active Christ today. In worship, for example, you can sing songs *about* Jesus, but not *to* Him; you can read what Jesus did, but not experience fully what He's doing now-- even in your own life. Thus, WWJD.

John the Baptist portrayed the relationship between the second and third Persons of the Trinity when he proclaimed, "I baptize you with water to show that you have repented, but the one who will come after me will baptize you with the Holy Spirit and fire" (Matt. 3:11).

Water cleanses; fire not only purifies, but empowers as well. As the second Person of the Trinity, Jesus blazed the path to God, so we can face our sin honestly, repent, and recognize God as our true Father (see John 14:6).

But a cleansed vessel can't accomplish much until it's filled. That's what vessels are made for. In Holy Spirit, God poured out upon us the firepower to do His godly works in this world—indeed, to bring the Kingdom of God on earth even as it is in heaven.

That is, "The Holy Spirit is present in conversion to introduce the unbeliever to Jesus Christ as savior," but also to exercise a "subsequent empowering ministry for the believers."[48] This in-filling of God's Spirit is therefore "required, not for salvation, but for truly victorious Christian living."[49]

If Jesus the son is God coming among us, the Spirit is God bringing Himself into us. Hence, Paul's benediction to the church in Ephesus:

> For this reason I kneel before the Father, from whom
> His whole family in heaven and on earth derives its name.
> I pray that out of his glorious riches He may strengthen
> you with power through His Spirit in your inner being, so
> that Christ may dwell in your hearts through faith. (Ephes.
> 3:14-17 NIV)

The most common progression in the Christian journey, therefore, is first to come humbly to Jesus at the cross, confessing your sins. That empties you of self-centered natural human power. Then, you ask to be filled with Holy Spirit's super-natural power to be healed and equipped, in order to serve a broken world. Thus, Holy Spirit empowers social justice ministry.

WARNING

For those who would know Holy Spirit, but have not dared to face the reality of your sinful human nature, a warning is in order.

The God who sent Jesus is revealed in history. We must therefore take seriously the historical fact that Jesus came before the outpouring of God's Spirit. The gospels come before the book of Acts. That is, in order to receive and manifest the full power of the Spirit in your life, you must first go humbly to the cross to receive cleansing for your sin. **You must be born again in order to grow into spiritual maturity on its authentic foundation.**

Certainly, no one of us is perfect so long as we remain in this broken world. But it would seem that, even as God longs for us to receive and exercise His Spirit's power, He requires the water-baptism cleansing of the second Person of the Trinity before giving that power.

Even as new wine bursts old wineskins, pure water is contaminated by dirty vessels (see Luke 5:37). The self-centered, un-regenerated human being thereby would too easily seize God's power for selfish purposes, which--like the proverbial sorcerer's apprentice run amok—could ultimately prove misleading if not patently destructive. Thus, "God is kind because he is trying to lead you to repent" (Rom. 2:4).

Occasionally, I have seen Holy Spirit's supernatural workings manifest through persons who have not yet confessed their need for Jesus to save them from their sinful condition, and thereby, have not yet been born again. God knows each one of us and thereby, how best to draw each of us to the cross for regeneration. Seeing the Spirit's supernatural work is an electrifying experience, not easily dismissed or forgotten. Perhaps the Spirit works to a degree in an un-regenerated person as a "taster" or enticement to seek God's fullness of life by later surrendering to Jesus.

Nevertheless, I advise caution when someone not yet born again seeks to exercise Holy Spirit's supernatural giftings—not because it's immoral or wrong, but because it's dangerous. **In our natural state, that is, we're simply unable to discern spiritual reality accurately.**

Those who have ventured into the spirit realm with any humility, soon encounter in addition to Holy Spirit other, evil spirits which manifest genuine but destructive powers that do not serve God. We have a spiritual Enemy, clearly portrayed in the Bible. In spite of our attempts to water it down for more sanitary sensibilities, the Lord's Prayer in the original language begs to "deliver us" not simply "from evil," but indeed, "from the Evil One."

An essential "gift" provided by the Holy Spirit is therefore "the ability to distinguish between spirits" (1 Corinth. 12:10). Those who strut into the spiritual realm thinking they can identify accurately and control the powers they encounter, are courting great danger. To fancy that we can manipulate spiritual powers to get what we want for ourselves—as in most New Age practices--is a seductive and ultimately destructive deception.

The biblical faith therefore warns believers explicitly not to engage in occult spiritual practices, such as astrology (Isa. 44:24-26; 47:12-15), seances (Deut. 18:11), fortunetelling (Deut. 18:10; Acts 16:16-18), and the like. Number One of the Ten Commandments, in fact, is "You shall worship no gods before me"--that is, surrender to no other spiritual powers.

Most churches today have abdicated the supernatural dimension of faith to the "dark side." Our popular culture, therefore, has tagged the word "supernatural" with negative connotations--as at Halloween.

EVIL AS COUNTERFEIT

Indeed, a casual observer might note that the supernatural workings of Holy Spirit resemble occult practices. A "prophet," for example, might be seen as "channeling Jesus." But that's like saying, "Wool looks like orlon-polyester"; it confuses the counterfeit with the original.

The Bible portrays Evil as a fallen angel--not wholly independent of good, but rather, a fallen, and thereby deceptive imitation of good. In encountering spiritual powers, therefore, anyone who has not surrendered to Jesus can only respond out of natural human self-centeredness as a reference point, and eventually be deceived.

Even as it's thereby dangerous trying to know the third Person of the Trinity without knowing the second, it's impossible know the Son without knowing the Spirit. Indeed Holy Spirit alone empowers us to recognize Jesus as Lord, and thereby, enables us to be born again. "No one can confess 'Jesus is Lord' unless...guided by the Holy Spirit," as Paul declared (1 Corinth. 12:13).

Holy Spirit, in fact, is the Primary Evangelist, who communicates to sin-blinded human beings the Good News of what God has done in Jesus. A gifted human being, such as Billy Graham, may at best be called *an* evangelist, that is, one who ministers the gift of evangelism given by The Evangelist—namely, Holy Spirit. In fact, it would seem that today God's strategy is less often to lift up singular personalities as in the past—thereby spreading His witness more foundationally by His Spirit moving broadly among the Church fellowship.

Becoming born again is therefore a work of the Spirit. As Jesus declared, "A person is born physically of human parents, but...spiritually of the Spirit. Do not be surprised when I tell you that you must all be born again" (John 3:6,7).

In bringing us thereby into new life, Holy Spirit

> makes you God's children, and by the Spirit's power
> we cry out to God, "Father! My Father!" God's Spirit joins
> himself to our spirits to declare that we are God's children.
> (Rom. 8:15,16)

The new birth, or "born again" experience itself is mediated by the Third Person of the Trinity, who ushers us from the death of self at the cross into the renewed life of serving God in the world. Without Holy Spirit's leading, therefore, both personal healing and social justice ministries can easily mask the activist's own sin-nature and eventually miss God's mark.

HISTORICAL CONFLICT

Indeed, in my early ministry at an Oldline church, I lumped all other churches together as a monolithic "conservative Church." Years later when I ventured out in my faith, I was startled to discover the deep historical conflict between Evangelicals and Pentecostals.

With sincere openness, I set out to experience the supernatural workings of Holy Spirit, described in the Bible as common to Jesus' ministry and that of the early Church. I was surprised to find that the Evangelical tutors who had led me to be born again and taught me God's Word in the Scriptures nevertheless rejected those workings for today. "The supernatural miracles only happened in the Apostolic Age," as one told me. "They don't need to happen any more, because we have the written Word."

I was astounded to discover that both conservative Evangelicals and liberal Oldliners share an altogether similar disregard for Holy Spirit's present-day supernatural workings.

In avoiding the third Person of the Trinity--whether by trivializing

the supernatural or banishing it to the past, we presume ourselves to define God and limit His power. The terrible price for such pride is that we remain spiritual infants, vulnerable to a host of spiritual deceptions and unable to appropriate Holy Spirit's power to recognize and fulfill your divine calling in this world.

In fact, the third Person not only brings us new birth and identity as God's children, but also proceeds to rear us into godly maturity. "But we Christians have no veil over our faces," as Paul put it; "we can be mirrors that brightly reflect the glory of the Lord. And as the Spirit of the Lord works within us, we become more and more like Him" (2 Corinth. 3:18 TLB).

Since the second and third Persons of the Trinity are so closely interrelated, I believe that Holy Spirit's power becomes available to the believer when you first surrender to Jesus. Yet the workings of the Spirit may remain dormant in you until you affirm and release God to use them.

If all we seek is God's forgiveness for our sinful acts through Jesus, God will give us that. But I believe God wants to give us more, to overcome our very sin nature so we can build His Kingdom on earth as it is in heaven. **Human kingdoms can be built with human power; God's Kingdom can be built only with God's power—which in this present age is mediated by Holy Spirit.**

Holy Spirit therefore brings into our personal lives today the Father's workings 2000 years ago through the Son. That is, the Spirit enables us not simply to believe that Jesus rose from the dead, or even that He lives now somewhere out there in the spiritual realm, but indeed, that He lives even now, in me—as in His Body, the Church.

The third Person of the Trinity defines and manifests God's power today. Those who humbly welcome Him can unite to celebrate that power as He leads--regardless of church affiliation.

As Quaker theologian Robert Rensing has declared,[50]

> We need to follow the promptings of the Spirit to the real but inexpressible experience that transcends logic, explanations, and models. It is that experience that leads to true universality!

INTELLECTUALIZED RELIGION

Biblical faith understands that not all spiritual power is good and serves the God revealed in Jesus. We must check all human experience against biblical standards. But Rensing reflects an appropriate concern as well for many other Oldliners, Sacramentalists, and Evangelicals alike in fearing that today "Quakerism is in danger of being an 'intellectualized religion'":

> If we are truly to remain the Religious Society of Friends, our focus must remain on the experience in worship of the Presence of the Spirit. Denial of that Presence would change us into a "Political Society of Friends."

Declaring that Christianity as practiced today is too often "a religion that essentially lives in the past, trying to project onto today in some meaningful fashion what happened 2000 years ago," he laments that we are prone simply "to discuss that 2000-year-old information":

> Thus, it is small wonder that today many persons who have not been exposed to an experience of the Spirit, do not, in view of the present world situation, find much relevance in Christian religious thought as having at least some practical answers to contemporary questions.

Many fear that to engage such spiritual experience is to deny the practical needs of the world. To these, Rensing argues rather, that

> It is the immediate and personal experience of the Spirit that can unite the world and transform us into channels for the healing energies our world needs so badly right now. And, to be very mundane, **it is that experience that the legions of people, young and old, who are turned off by the perceived hypocrisy of organized religion and seek a substitute experience in drugs or material possessions, are hungering for.**

Jesus is far less glitter and hype than many religious TV showmen would have us believe. But He's far more power than the conservative legalists or liberal universalists among us would allow.

God's ministry to unite humanity is therefore presided over today by Holy Spirit. How, then, do we become hospitable to that ministry? As we shall now see, the Third Person of the Trinity asks only for an open heart.

TAKEAWAY

Being born again prepares you as a vessel for God's Spirit. When Paul visited the ancient church in Ephesus, members had not even heard of Holy Spirit. 2000 years later, even as a seminary-trained pastor, I found myself similarly unacquainted with the Third Person of the Trinity--the very Presence of God in this present age. As James declared, the Body without the Spirit is dead. Have you heard that there is a Holy Spirit? Have you allowed Holy Spirit to act freely in your life today, even as in the Scriptures? What work of the Spirit does your church need most, and how might you and your congregation facilitate that?

9

Healing Emotional Wounds:

Seeing the Past as Jesus Sees It

> I ask God from the wealth of his glory to give you
> power through his Spirit to be strong in your inner selves.
> (Ephes. 3:16)

What began as an ordinary pastoral counseling appointment literally upended my lifelong belief system.

Beth (not her real name), college-educated and in her mid-20's, had been dating a man for some time and found herself emotionally blocked whenever they drew close physically. At the outset of our appointment, she asked only that I not pray for her. "I'm just not comfortable with that sort of thing," she explained.

"That's OK," I said. "We don't need to pray."

Indeed, my seminary counseling class and further reading had equipped me in standard psychology techniques, and I felt confident as we began that I could help Beth without either praying or otherwise mentioning God. As we talked, in fact, I sensed clearly that some childhood wound was making her afraid of men; I loaned her Hugh Missildine's sturdy secular classic, *Your Inner Child of the Past*,[51] which she found "very helpful."

Midway into our third weekly session, I asked if she had ever experienced any particular trauma as a girl--maybe some hurtful or fearful encounter with a man?

"No!" she insisted quickly, her voice shaking.

"You seem a little nervous about that," I noted, and waited as she shifted uneasily in her chair.

"Well, nothing really all that bad happened," she declared, straining to relax. I said nothing, and in the silence, she took a deep breath and sighed loudly.

"Actually," she began hesitantly, "when I was eleven, my girlfriend's father tried to assault me." Gathering herself, she sat upright and folded her hands conclusively. "But that's all in the past."

"Really?" I asked. "Your nervousness makes me wonder if what happened is still affecting you now."

Beth hesitated. "Well, it was pretty upsetting," she allowed finally.

"Can you tell me what happened?"

"Well, I was there in the living room at their house, waiting for my friend--she'd been late getting home from school--when he suddenly walked in, exposed himself and came toward me. I was terrified. I mean, I didn't know what to do. But I was just so scared I turned and ran out of the house, slammed the door, and ran home."

"Did you tell your parents what happened?"

"Oh, no! I mean, not at first. Then a few weeks later (Mr. X) was arrested for assaulting his daughter, my girlfriend. My folks heard about it, and since they knew I'd been over at her house a lot, they asked me if I knew anything about him. Finally, I broke down and told them everything."

"What did they do?"

"It was awful. Mother got all hysterical, just screaming and angry. Dad was furious. He said if Mr. X wasn't in jail, he'd take his gun and go shoot him."

FEAR OF FEELINGS

"How did that make you feel?"

"What do you mean?"

"I mean, did your mother's and father's reaction make you feel better, or did you need something else from them to help you with your upset?"

Beth fidgeted. "Oh, it was OK. I mean, I've pretty much dealt with it by now. My folks are who they are, you know? You just have to accept people after awhile."

"I'm not asking who your parents are. I'm asking who you are. How did you feel when your mother was hysterical and your father furious like that?"

"Oh, I don't think there's really much more to say about it," Beth snapped, gripping her hands together tightly.

I tried another direction. "How did you feel toward Mr. X after he tried to assault you?"

"Oh, I don't know," Beth mumbled, her hands now shaking. "I've pretty much taken care of the whole thing by now...."

Clearly, she had only repressed the memory, the feelings from which were now subconsciously dictating her responses to men. I wondered: *How could we surface those feelings fully enough to release her from their grip?*

"I sense you still have some deep feelings toward Mr. X inside you that want to come out," I offered.

"Oh, no...," she said, dropping her eyes. After a moment's hesitation, she looked up. "Well,...maybe."

"Did you feel angry at Mr. X?"

"Well," she declared, leaning forward in determination, "he was clearly a sick man, don't you think?" Her eyes narrowed. "I mean, he was obviously mentally ill to do that kind of thing!"

"You sound angry," I noted.

"Well, I certainly didn't like what he did, if that's what you mean!"

"What I mean is, are you angry at him?"

Quickly, Beth withdrew to the back of the couch. I guessed that she had not been given permission as a girl to be angry, so she now felt guilty as a woman for feeling anger--even toward a rapist/child molester. "I don't understand what you're getting at. What good would it do now, fifteen years later, to get angry at Mr. X? The whole thing is done with, over, in the past, isn't it?"

"Is it?" I asked rhetorically.

"What do you mean?"

BOTTLED-UP ANGER

"I'm not asking you to be angry. I'm asking you to be honest, and tell me what's already in you. I sense you still have a lot of bottled-up anger in you toward Mr. X, and it's controlling your responses to men."

"I don't know...maybe I do," she said, shaking. "I think I'm going to cry," she added defiantly, and tears began to form in her eyes.

Her tears seemed more a defense than a release, and I decided to push ahead. "I think you're really mad at Mr. X, but you're afraid to say so because you were taught as a girl it's wrong to get angry." Recalling my psychotherapy training, I pushed further. "In fact, if you want, you can tell Mr. X right now, at last, how angry you are at him."

"How do you mean?" she shot back, her defiance unable to cover a trace of hopefulness in her face.

"Just a minute," I said, and dashed across the hall to the church lost-and-found, grabbed an old sweatshirt and returned.

"Here," I said, handing it to her. "Go ahead and wring this sweatshirt as tightly as you can. As you do, go ahead and pretend Mr. X is right here now, sitting in that chair across from you. Tell him what you think of him."

Uncertain, then with determination, Beth seized the sweatshirt. "Mr. X," she said matter-of-factly, "I'm angry at you for what you did to me."

"Yes," I urged, "tell him how angry you are at him."

"Mr. X," she said, slowly wringing the sweatshirt, and then with growing intensity, "I'm angry at you!" She gripped the sweatshirt fiercely--then stopped, afraid.

"Go ahead. Don't stop. Tell Mr. X what you feel!"

She took a deep breath, then began wringing again, tighter this time. "I want to wring your neck, Mr. X!" she cried. "I hate you! I hate you!" Suddenly, she paused and turned to me. "Is it alright if I curse?"

I could hardly conceal my delight. The therapeutic scene was working great! "Sure, it's OK," I replied excitedly. "Go ahead!"

With a flash of prudence, I sat up. "Uh..., in just a minute!" Quickly, I leapt up and dashed around the church, closing the windows.

When I rushed back, Beth was wringing the sweatshirt furiously. "Mr. X, you (expletive)!" she cried out. "You destroyed me! You ruined me when I was just a helpless little girl! You dirty, filthy old man! You (expletive)!" She leaned back in rage, then looked at me. "I want to scream. Is that OK?"

"Go ahead!" I urged. "Tell Mr. X!" This was going textbook-great, I smiled. Once she gets all this rage out at last, she'll be a new person!

"I HATE YOU! I HATE YOU!" Beth screamed. Eyes blazing fury, suddenly she sat bolt upright, threw the sweatshirt aside, and seized a pillow off the couch. "I want to kill you! I've got a knife in my hand!" Panting, she lifted her fist as if grasping a dagger, ready to plunge it into the pillow.

Yes, of course! I thought, smiling with self-satisfaction. *This is the way to finish off Mr. X from her memory once and for all!*

OK TO KILL?

"Is it OK if I kill him?" she asked suddenly, interrupting my delight.

"Wh-what?"

"Is it OK if I kill Mr. X?" she repeated angrily, her hand and imaginary dagger poised and shaking above the cushion.

A dark uneasiness swallowed my enthusiasm. Sure, I realized, that would be fine and effective according so some secular therapies. But should a Christian kill someone, even if only in their imagination? Could I as her pastor tell her to kill someone? Nervously, I prayed under my breath: *God, help me!*

Confused, I balked. And then, I remembered a technique from my seminary counseling class. "Uh..., do what you feel you need to do," I said quickly, holding my breath.

In that terrifying moment, I realized I had lost control of the healing process. **What I didn't realize was that the Kingdom of God had invaded my ministry.** All my secularized training pointed in one direction: Get her to "kill" Mr. X in her imagination, and she's healed. But even though my seminary training allowed that response, and thus associated it with God's blessing, in my heart I knew that killing, even in fantasy, could not be God's will.

Here, I knew, lay a major turning point in my faith and ministry. The secular therapy with which I'd felt so confident, had led me to a dead end, a point beyond which my Christian principles would not permit me to go. Yet, where did the Christian path to healing lead from that point?

Uneasily, I held my breath as Beth lifted her dagger-fist and paused for the thrust. Then suddenly, she opened her hand, "dropped" her "knife" and fell sobbing into the pillow. "I can't do it!" she burst out, tears flowing-- real, defenseless tears this time. "I can't kill him!"

Whew! I sighed in relief--but was drawn up immediately as Beth lifted her head crying and pleaded, "What am I going to do now?"

Oh, Lord! I cried out silently. *What have I done? What* are *we going to do now?* Indeed, how could Beth resolve these deep and frightening emotions that had surfaced at last?

Panicking, I looked at Beth, her face streaked with tears. "Well," I managed finally, "I...I know you asked me not to pray, but frankly, I...really don't know anything else to do. Would you really mind that much if I said a prayer right now?"

"Well, I guess not," Beth sniffled. "Anything at all is OK at this point."

"Well, then, let's...pray," I said, and bowed my head, uncertain. If ever I needed a good, flowing prayer, now was the time. But instead, words spilled mechanically out of my mouth. "Lord Jesus," I heard myself saying, "we don't know what to do here. Heal Beth from this terrible wound in her past. Show us what to do. Lead us, please."

Sitting there in awful silence, I recalled a book I'd read in which the author told of inviting Jesus into a painful memory and being released from its fears.[52] At the time, I'd scoffed at so much "Jesus talk" as the sort of foolishness I'd come to expect from uneducated people.

But there lay my patient, cut open on the operating table--and I had no other idea how to get the disease out and sew her up again. It was worth a try.

"Beth," I began slowly, "I...want to try something a little different, if it's OK with you--sort of a prayer, that's helped out some other people who've tried it."

Wiping her eyes, Beth shrugged her shoulders. "Whatever," she sighed. "I'll try anything right now."

"OK, then, this time let's close your eyes, and I want you to see if you can picture the scene years ago when Mr. X came toward you. Can you do that?"

"Sure," she said, closing her eyes--and to my pleasant surprise, adding, "I can see us both right now in that living room."

INVITE JESUS

"Alright, now I want you just to invite Jesus to come into that scene. Ask him to come into the living room with you and Mr. X. Can you do that?"

I hesitated. Maybe all this was just too bizarre. What if...

"OK," Beth interrupted matter-of-factly. "Jesus, will you please come into the room with Mr. X and me?"

I paused cautiously. "Is...is He there?"

"Yes, he's there. I can see Him standing beside me."

Amazed, I drew up in fear. *How could that be? What was going on?* Curious, I leaned forward. "Wh-what's Jesus doing?" I asked.

"Jesus bends down and picks me up in his arms and rushes me out the front door, and he locks the door behind us," Beth reported.

I hesitated, astonished. Was Beth again trying to run away from the whole episode? Just running out of the scene didn't sound like "good therapy" as I'd studied it. Still, my "good therapy" had left us in the lurch. *OK, Lord,* I prayed, *I give up to you. Keep leading us.*

"And...what happens then?" I invited.

"Jesus puts his arms around me," Beth noted, smiling now with her eyes still closed. "'You're alright, Beth,' he says. 'You're alright. I still love you. You're alright.'"

Puzzled, nevertheless I recalled Beth's shame over the incident. Surely, she did need reassurance that she was still an acceptable human being after the ugly thing some sick old man had done to her. Beth's parents had done nothing to reassure her, but had simply reacted in their own fear and anger. It occurred to me that some unfinished business remained with the parents.

As my mind reeled, Beth sat peacefully on the couch, clearly comforted. Encouraged, I waited a moment, then spoke up. "I wonder if you'd like to go home with Jesus to see your mom and dad. Can you let Jesus walk you home?"

"Yes," she replied immediately—and soon added, "Jesus and I are walking down the street together, hand in hand."

At that point, I decided that it might be good for me to get involved myself in the scene, so I pictured in my mind a girl walking down a street, hand-in-hand with Jesus on her right. In my imagination, I saw leafy trees along the sidewalk, and among several houses ahead on the left I saw one painted white with a white picket fence around it. That seemed imaginative enough to me, and I returned to Beth. "Where's Jesus now?"

"He's walking on my right," she said.

That's a coincidence, I thought. *Same as my picture.* "Which house is yours?"

"Over on the left--the white one with the white picket fence around it," Beth replied.

Abruptly, I sat up. *Amazing! How can that be?* I wondered. **Something real and powerful was definitely going on here. And so far, at least, it seemed altogether good.** Shaking my head incredulously, I pushed ahead. "When you get to your house, can you let Jesus walk in with you?"

"OK. We're there, and inside now."

And in my mind's eye, I saw that indeed, they were! "Where's your mother?" I asked.

"She's out in the kitchen."

"Can you...maybe let Jesus take you out to the kitchen to her?"

"We're there," Beth declared, to my amazement. "She's surprised to see Jesus there with me. 'What's going on?' she asks. 'What's the matter? Is something wrong?' Mother is beginning to get all nervous and upset. I tell her what Mr. X did--all of it. (pause)

"She's wringing her hands. Now she's crying hysterically, just like she did when...but wait. Now Jesus is walking over to her. He puts His arms around her and all of it seems to pour out of her into Him, like a dark cloud or something. But nothing happens to Jesus. It just disappears into Him.

I STILL LOVE HER

"Now he's talking to Mother. 'Beth is alright,' He says. 'I still love her, and I want you to love her, too.' Mother stops crying. She's calm now. She looks down at me. She's smiling. She bends over and hugs me. 'I love you, Beth,' she says."

Beth relaxed as tension drained out of her. "Oh, Mother!" she sighed, smiling broadly.

For a few moments, I simply let Beth receive at last the love God had wanted to give through her mother.

"Where is your father?" I asked eventually.

"He's coming in the front door right now from work. He's surprised to see Jesus there with Mother and me. He comes over. 'What's happening here?' he asks. I turn and tell him everything that happened, everything that Mr. X did." She hesitated, shifting uneasily.

"What's your father doing?"

"Daddy's angry, then he begins to get furious. He's shouting that he's going to get his gun. Then Jesus is there, putting His arms around Daddy.

'Don't worry,' Jesus tells him. 'She's alright. I love her, and I want you to love her, too.'

"All of Daddy's anger just seems to pass out of him, like a dark cloud, and into Jesus, where it disappears, like with Mom. Then Daddy turns to me. He bends down and gives me a big hug. 'Oh, Beth—are you alright? I love you, Beth!' he says. Oh, I love you too, Daddy!"

For several moments, Beth sat beaming, clearly receiving at last the reassurance and love God had wanted to give through her parents, but was now giving sovereignly Himself. Quietly, joyfully, Beth continued. "Now Jesus has His arms around all three of us and we're standing there, looking happily at each other."

Beth rested in her joy, then opened her eyes, smiling and amazed. "What in the world is all this that's happening?" she exclaimed brightly.

"Well," I said, sighing deeply and shaking my head, "I'm not really sure. But it seems like Jesus is healing you from those painful old memories." As I spoke, I remembered that in the book I'd read, the person experienced full release only after forgiving the perpetrator.

"In fact, I wonder if...maybe, he wants to do a little more. Could we go back to the prayer again, just for a minute?"

Glowing, Beth paused--then nodded. "OK."

We bowed our heads.

"I think...Jesus may want to go back and see Mr. X again," I began, uncertain. *Would it be too much to ask Beth to go back with Him? Or could Jesus just do it for her by Himself?* I decided to proceed slowly. "Is there anything you'd like Jesus to tell Mr. X?"

A pause, then, "Yes. Tell him that what he did was very wrong, that it hurts little girls very much and he should never do it again."

"OK. Anything else?"

I FORGIVE YOU

Another pause. "Yes," Beth declared finally. **"Tell Mr. X that I forgive him."**

Yes! I thought, sensing clearly now the direction and green light. "Would you go with Jesus back to see Mr. X?"

"Yes, I'll go," Beth replied, with uneasy determination. Soon, she reported that she was walking hand-in-hand with Jesus, back down the street to the X's house. "I'm standing on the doorstep, and now I'm knocking.

"Mr. X opens the door," Beth continued. "Jesus says, 'We want to come in and talk with you.' But Mr. X says, 'No. I just want Beth to come in alone. You stay outside!' But Jesus says, 'Beth will only come in if I come with her.' Mr. X says, 'Well, OK, you can both come in.'

"We both walk into the living room and look at Mr. X standing there. 'Well, what do you want?' he asks. (pause) "I came back to tell you that what you did was wrong!" Beth declared, sitting up with determination. "You made me feel afraid and ashamed. Don't you ever do that again, not to me or any other girl, ever!"

Trembling, Beth sat upright now, vindicated.

"Then...Jesus walks over to Mr. X and puts an arm around him. He looks Jesus in the eyes... and begins to cry. He's crying and crying. 'I'm sorry,' he says, 'I didn't want to hurt her.' Jesus hugs him and all Jesus' power is going into Mr. X and it's filling him up. 'You don't have to hurt little girls any more,' Jesus tells him, 'I can make you a real man now and you can love a real woman from now on.'

"Then Jesus says, 'I forgive you, Mr. X.'

"Then, Mr. X looks at me. All of a sudden, I'm getting taller and taller... until I'm tall enough to look at him in the eye."

The air was bright, electric. *What's happening now?* I wondered, recalling the scene from *Alice in Wonderland* where Alice shoots up in height. **Was the present-day sense in which Beth still carried the old wound, being brought forth at last into adult resolution?**

"I...I," Beth was saying--balking, trying, balking again. And then it poured out. "I forgive you, Mr. X," she burst out. "Yes, I forgive you!"

And indeed, she did. With a deep sigh, a brightness broke forth at last onto her face and her voice sang out, "Jesus is putting his arms around us both and he hugs us. We hug each other. Then Jesus takes my hand and leads me to the door. Mr. X calls out, 'Goodbye!' and I turn in the doorway..."

GOODBYE TO FEAR

Her eyes still closed, Beth paused, smiled, then sighed again. "Goodbye, Mr. X!" she called out with gusto. "Goodbye!"

Relieved, I took a deep breath. "Goodbye, Mr. X!" I echoed. "And thank you, Jesus, thank you!"

Beth's eyes burst open. "I feel free!" she cried out. "I'm free at last! It's really done and out of me!" Exultant, she leapt up and stretched. Then suddenly, she dropped to her knees. "Can I say a prayer?" she asked, turning to me.

What a day of glorious surprises! This was the woman who weeks ago had insisted I not pray with her! "Of course," I smiled, "as long as I can get down on my knees and pray, too!"

I knelt on the carpet with Beth.

"Jesus, thank you for leading me here," she prayed. "Thank you for taking that awful fear out of me. Thank you for setting me free!"

"Thank you, Jesus," I echoed. "And let this be just the beginning of new life for Beth."

"I want to sing!" Beth exclaimed suddenly, leaping up. "Can we sing some hymns?"

"Sure," I said, rising to pull a hymnal off the shelf. Seizing it, together we turned to #1 and sang forth,

> Holy, holy, holy! Lord God Almighty!
> Early in the morning, our song shall rise to thee;
> Holy, holy, holy! Merciful and mighty!
> God in three persons, blessed Trinity!

"Merciful and mighty," indeed! And "three persons": the loving and powerful Father who heard her cries, the Risen Son sent to stand beside her in the truth of her wounding and the grace of His healing, and Holy Spirit giving her power to be real in her pain and forgiving in her strength. (see John 1:17)

In that day, in my very office, Holy Spirit came in the Living, Resurrected Christ and dramatically changed a life before my eyes. **My comfortable, controlled naturalistic worldview was shattered—thankfully, beyond restoration.**

Months passed before I dared share this story. Yet during that time, others came to me seeking healing for traumatic memories, and in each case, inviting Jesus into the troubling scene led to His remarkable resolution and freedom.

INTO ALL TRUTH

Thus, even today, Holy Spirit witnesses to the ongoing power of God in our time, bringing us "into all truth" (John 16:13).

In fact, as Jesus declared in our prayer, Beth was "all right" after her encounter with Mr. X, but her shame and fear had convinced her she was shameful and dirty.

In fact, her parents did love her, even after the event, but their anger kept them from expressing it.

In fact, Mr. X did not want to molest a little girl, but his own deep sense of inadequacy as a man drove him into treachery.

In fact, Beth did not want to kill him, and even wanted to forgive him, but her fear and anger kept her from seeing him accurately, in his brokenness.

"You shall know the truth," as Jesus declared, "and the truth will set you free" (John 8:32).

Certainly, these truths do not excuse Mr. X from attempting to molest--or Beth from attempting to kill. But if the sum of our response to evil is simply, "Kill the wrong-doer," we never move beyond Old Covenant justice toward New Covenant grace and truth in order to protect against further wrong-doing.

Inviting Jesus into the scene, therefore, beckons the saving presence and power of God, who sets you free to walk in the truth without fear. "Where the Spirit of the Lord is present, there is freedom," (2 Cor. 3:17) as Paul declared. Holy Spirit witnesses to Jesus as the One who enforces the freedom of truth when our fear and anger would bind us in the illusion of control.

Beth's initial desire to kill Mr. X, that is, was itself a false cover-up for her profound sense of powerlessness, which became unnecessary once she invited Jesus into the painful scene. Indeed, her true and deepest desire was to maintain her own integrity by confronting Mr. X openly with his wrongdoing and its effect upon her. But as long as she believed no power greater than that in Mr. X was available to her, she dared not do so.

In the presence of Jesus, however, she experienced what John proclaimed, "But you belong to God, my children...(and) the Spirit who is in you is more powerful than the spirit in those who belong to the world" (1 John 4:4).

Through the eyes of her own genuine powerlessness, Beth could see only two possible outcomes from the event in her past: either Mr. X destroys her--and she bear that destruction in her truncated relationships with men--or she destroys him, as with the dagger.

"Fantasize the very worst," as a *Redbook* magazine article instructs women to deal with anger toward men:

> Indulge yourself with a little harmless violence. Mentally beat up the person who makes you angry; then kill him off as imaginatively as you can and completely destroy the body. (Make sure you get rid of every trace of the corpse, lest you be nagged by guilt.) In fantasy, I pummeled someone I was fond of, but angry with, until he was magically reduced to the size of a tennis ball. Then I threw him into my typewriter and typed him into a thousand tiny pieces, which I sprinkled over New York's Central Park. By the time he had melted into the earth, I was amused and no longer angry.[53]

NO HARMLESS VIOLENCE

In spite of *Redbook's* glib reassurance, research has demonstrated a high correlation between indulging visual media images of violence and committing violent acts. Watching film violence is no harmless way of releasing violent impulses.

The same logic would conclude that reading pornographic magazines is good for curbing sexual fantasies. "How can Satan drive out Satan?" as Jesus declared (Mark 3:23).

The prayer with Beth demonstrated that **Jesus' power focuses on setting free both antagonist and victim from the world's vicious cycle of destruction and vengeance.** In fact, at the moment Beth forgave Mr. X in my office, I believe he was set free to receive God's forgiveness and his life was genuinely changed. "Receive the Holy Spirit," the Risen Lord said to his disciples. "If you forgive people's sins, they are forgiven; if you do not forgive them, they are not forgiven" (John 20:22).

Certainly, Mr. X retains freewill choice thereafter either to accept that forgiveness and walk in God's healing, or refuse it and continue to let the shame of his inadequacies fuel his perversion. But Beth is not responsible for Mr. X's choices, only her own. **And in her choosing to let Jesus lead her into forgiveness, she has done her part for the Kingdom of God and can release Mr. X--both spiritually and emotionally--to his own part.**

Searching the Scriptures, I have concluded that several basic elements of faith undergird Holy Spirit's ministry to heal past wounds:

1. Jesus is risen, alive, and available even now in Holy Spirit to save those who call upon him:

> Whenever two of you on earth agree about anything you pray for, it will be done for you by my Father in heaven. For where two or three come together in my name, I am there with them. (Matt. 18:20)

2. Jesus was present in every past event, no matter how upsetting:

> Jesus Christ is the same yesterday, today, and forever. (Hebrews 13:8)

> I will be with you always, to the end of the age. (Matt. 28:20)

3. Even now, Jesus wants to enter and apply his saving power to all our past wounds, and awaits our invitation:

> Listen! I stand at the door and knock; if anyone hears my voice and opens the door, I will come into his house and eat with him, and he will eat with me. (Revel. 3:20)

4. As Risen Lord, Jesus is not magic, but manna for the journey. He doesn't change past events, but rather, frees us from our narrow, self-centered, self-sabotaging view of events to see the past with God's eyes. This revelation of truth releases our future for God's Kingdom purposes.

JESUS HEALS A MEMORY[54]

In the "Road to Emmaus" story (Luke 24:13-35) following the crucifixion, for example, two disciples were walking "about seven miles" from Jerusalem to Emmaus with "their faces downcast" (24:17b NIV). Their hopes and expectations for Jesus to save them and their nation Israel had been dashed. This deep wound in their hearts was distorting their present perceptions, and thereby threatened to sabotage God's purposes for their future.

Suddenly, the Resurrected Lord comes alongside them, but they don't recognize Him. They tell their discouraging tale to this apparent stranger, pouting, "We had hoped that (Jesus) would be the one who was going to set Israel free!"

Whereupon Jesus scolds them for their short-sightedness and

explains for them "what was said about himself in all the Scriptures." That is, he shows them this wound of their past through God's eyes. This truth heals their myopia and frees them to participate in His future.

Fortified with God's Kingdom perspective on their past, these formerly downcast mopers exclaim, "Wasn't it like a fire burning in us when he talked to us on the road and explained the Scriptures to us?" Uplifted and energized, they race the seven miles back to Jerusalem and share the good news with the other disciples.

We might ask here, But what about the many times when evil does have its way, as for example, innocent girls like Beth don't escape and are in fact molested?

Such evil events demonstrate tragically that this world is broken unto death by sin. In fact, that's why Jesus came: not to take us out of the world but to bring His Kingdom into it, that is, not to eliminate all pain and suffering from our lives, but to redeem it for His Kingdom purposes.

Jesus did die. When the disciples invited Jesus into the scene of their despondency, He came--but did not give them all lobotomies or brainwash them to forget the awful reality of His death. **Rather, He showed up in the midst of their pain, re-interpreted what had happened from God's view, and that re-vitalized them to press on in the task to which He had called them.**

Thus, Beth leapt up to sing after our prayer. Again, Jesus did not heal her wound by "re-scripting" her past and giving her instead a warm-fuzzy image of the scene with a nice, un-broken Mr. X. Rather, He walked her through the whole scene in all its ugliness, unto his saving purposes. Jesus--resurrected and present to us today in Holy Spirit—comes alongside us to heal our near-sighted vision so we can walk, even run with joy, into God's future.

Several additional Scriptures highlight this inner dimension of God's healing.

In Romans 12:1,2, Paul urges,

> Offer yourselves as a living sacrifice to God.... Do not conform yourselves to the standards of this world, *but let God transform you inwardly by a complete change of your mind.* Then you will be able to know the will of God--what is good and is pleasing to him and is perfect. (italics mine)

We can humble ourselves before God because He wants to heal our emotional wounds and fulfill our divine calling.

Significantly, the prayer for healing proceeds not upon the counselor's skill, but only upon Jesus and His initiative. As always, the things of God can be counterfeited, and wisdom is required here. **The counselor does not suggest any "visualized" outcome and ask the client to affirm or "claim" it.**

Looking back over my prayer with Beth, I realize how at several points I became fearful that Jesus would not do anything, and tried to nudge things along. Since then, I've learned that God, working through Holy Spirit, is well up to the task. He needs me only to testify to Jesus' love and invite the person to welcome Him into the wound. Because God so highly values relationship with us, He gives us freewill either to ask for or to eschew His help.

To suspend your will for any guided human re-programming, as in hypnosis, is therefore suspect because it presumes that Holy Spirit is not up to the task—and thereby dangerous, because such spiritual surrender apart from God invites other spirits besides Holy Spirit (for a complete discussion of this topic, see my chapter "How Demons Enter—and Leave" in *No Small Snakes: A Journey into Spiritual Warfare*). Rather, the person is asked only to recall the actual scene of the painful event, to invite Jesus into it at last, and let Him do what He's been waiting to do since it occurred.

PRAYER COVERING

The counselor simply provides a "prayer covering" at that point, praising God for His power and healing, and praying protection from any spiritual forces which might hinder that.

As for the client, he or she must simply be willing not to "conform...to the standards of this world"--that is, to renounce all claims to vengeance and be open rather to God's will as that's revealed during the prayer (Rom. 12:1,2).

Sometimes, when you have remembered the painful scene and invited Jesus to come into it, you may not sense or see Him there, or you may see Him present, but not doing anything. Most often, this is an invitation by faith to trust Jesus is present and waiting for you out loud to tell the person who hurt you how you feel about that. When you have fulfilled that part of your own responsibility, call on Jesus again and let Him now take his turn, as it were, to speak and/or move.

Again, the Apostle declares,

> I ask God from the wealth of his glory to give you
> *power through his Spirit to be strong in your inner selves,*
> and I pray that Christ will make his home in your hearts
> through faith. I pray that you may have your roots and
> foundation in love, so that you, together with all God's
> people, may have the power to understand how broad
> and long, how high and deep, is Christ's love--although
> it can never be fully known--and so be completely filled
> with the very nature of God. (Ephes. 3:16-19, italics mine)

Holy Spirit heals our emotional wounds, therefore, as we invite Christ into our hearts through faith--in order to root us in the love of God made flesh in Jesus. As we surrender to Jesus and draw from God's love, we receive God's nature--in fact, the very Spirit of God, who empowers us to bring His Kingdom "on earth as it is in heaven."

Beth had no idea how much God loves her or how deeply Jesus could heal her painful memories. Indeed, when she finally forgave Mr. X, she herself was "completely filled with the very nature of God" in a mercy that exceeded her natural abilities. Then, she could forgive, and at last, be set free from the pain and fear in her past.

Indeed, as Jesus declared, "It is like that with everyone born of the Spirit" (John 3:8).

TAKEAWAY

As I become more open to supernatural reality, a woman with deep emotional wounds comes to me for pastoral counseling. Secular psychological techniques lead us to a root memory and surface her repressed anger at last. But the apparent natural resolution via violence violates God's heart. In desperation, I pray and ask Jesus to come. To my astonishment, He does, and proceeds to heal the woman's heart by showing her the wounding event from His perspective.

Do you remember a painful event in your life that wounded you deeply—and still does? Can you to trust the living, Risen Christ to come into that wound and heal it?

10

Cleaning Lady to the Rescue:

Power to Heal Bodies

> There are different kinds of spiritual gifts, but
> the same Spirit gives them. There are different ways of
> serving, but the same Lord is served.... The same Spirit
> gives faith to one person, while to another person he
> gives the power to heal. (1 Cor. 12:4,5,9)

Of all Holy Spirit's gifts, none draws us so universally as His ministry of physical healing. We may not all share the same denomination or even be "into religion." But we all have bodies, and when we become sick or injured, we're definitely into healing.

The above scripture notes that the gifts of the Spirit empower us to serve God. Certainly, a debilitating physical illness or injury can sorely limit or destroy your ministry of service, whether in peacemaking, social justice, or visiting a nursing home.

Although the Gospel accounts are literally filled with stories of Jesus' healing bodies supernaturally, many churches—even those who allow that Jesus did in fact heal 2000 years ago--have denied that Holy Spirit heals today.

For the earliest believers, however, Jesus' healing ministry could not be separated from His identity as Messiah. Even after baptizing Jesus, John the Baptist was not convinced that He was the Christ. When John sent his disciples to ask, **Jesus held up His physical healings as clear proof, even linking them explicitly with a social justice component in ministry to the poor:**

> Go back and tell John what you are hearing and seeing: the blind can see, the lame can walk, those who suffer from dreaded skin diseases are made clean, the deaf hear, the dead are brought back to life and the Good News is preached to the poor. How happy are those who have no doubts about me! (Matt 11:4-6)

Nevertheless, in my early ministry, I was anxious to "bleep over" the healing stories in the Bible. Such supernatural acts revealed the limits of my own natural power, and therefore, made me feel inadequate. To cover my shame, I seized upon popular, negative images of shouting "holy rollers" and people fainting in hysterics. *If that's what "Christian healing" is about*, I reassured myself, *then it's all a fraud*.

SENSATIONALISTS AND SKEPTICS

Certainly, if these sensationalists were the only Christians who had ever witnessed a physical healing through the power of God, the skeptics could get off the hook and go their way snickering. Significantly, however, the biblical accounts are not limited to the Gospels—nor are credible stories of Holy Spirit's healing limited to biblical times.

In fact, the earliest followers of Jesus continued that ministry immediately after Holy Spirit had been poured out on them. At the outset, in Acts 3:1-10, Holy Spirit heals a crippled beggar outside the temple. When Peter and John later proclaim the power of God present in Jesus Christ as the source of that healing, "Many who heard the message believed; and the number of men grew to about five thousand" (Acts 4:4). The very birth of the Christian Church—the first evangelical crusade, as it were--was thereby sparked by an act of physical healing.

We must therefore release the sensationalists long enough to ask the serious question, Did Jesus really heal broken bodies?--and its even more serious counterpart, Does Holy Spirit still heal even now, 2000 years later?

This question was settled dramatically for me as a pastor one Sunday after worship, when a parishoner asked me to visit her mother, who had suffered a heart attack and was in the hospital awaiting a series of pre-operation tests. I had a wedding later that afternoon, and decided to stop by the hospital for a brief visit beforehand.

Walking down the corridor, I noted the relative quiet and inactivity characteristic of a Sunday, when many hospital personnel are off-duty. I checked my watch and realized I had only about fifteen minutes for the visit.

As I entered the room, Jane (not her real name) was standing on one side of the bed where her mother lay, and a middle-aged lady stood on the other side.

"Gordon!" Jane exclaimed amiably. "I'm so glad you're here. I want you to meet my mother, Mrs. Smith, and Sue, a very special friend of the family."

I'd never met either Jane's mother or Sue, and had no idea of their religious orientation. As we greeted each other and chatted, time drew short and the question soon struck me, *Should I offer to pray?*

"Well," I began hesitantly, glancing at my watch and then looking at Mrs. Smith. "It's been nice meeting you and I...wonder if you might like, maybe...to say a prayer together before I leave?"

"Well, OK," she said quickly, with a trace of uneasiness.

NON-THREATENING PRAYER

"Alright," I offered gingerly, still uncertain as I sought to formulate a suitably non-threatening prayer in my mind. "Why don't we all just hold hands together, and we'll go ahead and pray?"

My confidence was buoyed as Jane took one of her mother's hands and Sue took the other. Moving closer, I was about to reach out and join hands with Jane and Sue when suddenly I heard a gentle but distinct knock on the door. Startled, unnerved at being interrupted at such a tentative moment--I turned abruptly. There in the doorway, a short, dark-skinned lady stood wiping her hands on a water-splotched apron, a mop handle beside her.

"Ex-cooz," she stammered, pushing a gray curl from the side of her face. "I am clean lady. Come to clean room."

Exasperated, I drew myself up with polite restraint. "Actually--if you don't mind--we were just going to pray!"

"Oh," said the cleaning lady. Nodding matter-of-factly, she set her mop aside. Thinking she was going away and simply leaving her mop for later, I turned back to our prayer circle. To my astonishment and dismay, however, she promptly stepped up to the bedside between Sue and myself, and quietly bowed her head.

Stunned, I realized at once that I had no choice but to stuff my consternation and proceed with the prayer, holding hands not only with Jane on my left, but also with the cleaning lady on my right. With a controlled sigh, I reached out and took Jane's hand, then reluctantly but resolutely, extended my arm to the cleaning lady. Involuntarily, I winced as her hand--cold and damp from the mop--took mine.

"God who loves us," I began quickly, aware of the time--and then fell strangely silent. In a flash, I saw my ugly fear of "not performing well" and the awful pride that prompted it.

Oh, God! I cried out quietly in my heart. *Forgive me!*

STRANGELY WARM

In that moment, I was aware that the cleaning lady's hand was no longer cold. In fact, it had become strangely warm, even more than normal. Catching myself, I began again.

"God who loves us," I said once more, louder this time as an unusual sense of conviction arose in my voice; "we thank you that you love Mrs. Smith even more than any one of us here, and that your power is greater than anything we can do or imagine ourselves."

I paused, uncertain but determined, as a feeling of freedom and power swept over me. "Lord," I continued, "touch Mrs. Smith's heart right now."

In that moment, prayer thoughts sprang into my mind--words so bold, so outrageous, that it took some effort to restrain them. As I resisted, other thoughts crowded in: *What in the world will everyone here think of me if I dared to pray like that? They'll all dismiss me as a crackpot. The word would get around the church and...*

On the other hand, I'd never met Mrs. Smith or Sue before, and might never see them again. Jane and I were close enough that I knew she wouldn't say anything about it if I asked her not to. Actually, I had nothing to lose--and Mrs. Smith might gain a lot. A glance at the clock showed I had little more than a minute.

The warmth in my right hand increased, and I decided to go with it.

"God who loves us," I proclaimed again: "In the name of Jesus, I crush any hardness in Mrs. Smith's heart and in all her arteries, and I ask you, Lord, to flush it all out of her system by the power of your Spirit. And in the name of Jesus, I speak to her heart muscles, the arteries around them, and all the nerves to them, and I say, Be strengthened, be restored, be made whole again, by the power of the God who created you. Let the blood of Jesus flow freely and freshly through all her blood vessels, and let the Spirit of the Living God fill her heart."

Startled by my own boldness, I paused and took a deep breath. *Lord, what have I done?* Quickly, I stole a peek around our circle--and all the others still had their eyes closed and heads bowed. No one was sneaking disgusted looks at each other, sighing impatiently, or ready to bolt. Relieved, I turned back to the prayer.

"Lord, we...uh...thank you for your love and...for all that you're doing even now for Mrs. Smith." I paused as a surprising sense of peacefulness rushed over me. Realizing I had nothing else to say--and that I needed to be leaving for the wedding--I squeezed the hands on either side.

"Amen," I said finally, looking up and dropping hands.

A strange quietness had settled upon us all.

Oh, no! I thought. *You really blew it this time. They all think you're crazy.* "Well," I declared quickly, backing for the door and bowing slightly. "It's been great meeting you all and I...uh, I have to get on to a wedding soon, so I'd better be going. Good to see you again, Jane. Nice to meet you Mrs. Smith, Sue."

Turning to go, I saw the mop and bucket against the door--and stopped. Uncomfortably, I stepped over to the cleaning lady and hesitated.

To my surprise, tears were streaming down her face.

"Um...thank you," I managed, reaching out and shaking her hand.

She nodded, smiling brightly.

Waving clumsily to the others, I turned and left.

Driving to the wedding moments later, I puzzled over what had happened. Should I have given in to the impulse to pray so unusually like that? At any rate, it was done. Now what would happen? Maybe I should call Jane later and apologize for going off on a tangent in my prayer. Still, Mrs. Smith had agreed to pray, and nobody seemed upset afterward. Confused, maybe...

As the church and bridal limousine came into view, I sighed. "Lord, I place all my worries about this in your hands, and trust you to show me if there's anything else for me to do with Jane and her mother."

SURPRISED BUT THRILLED

Several days later, Jane called me at the church.

"Oh, Jane….," I offered tentatively, realizing I hadn't thought about her or her mother since the hospital visit. "Well, uh, hello…"

"I wanted to get back to you on my mother's situation," she said, a strangely uncertain tone in her voice. "And I need to ask you about when you prayed for her."

Oh, no! I thought. *Here it comes!*

"Well, of course...I'm...I'm glad you called," I said, attempting a casual but concerned tone, and shifting to the edge of my chair. "I really didn't...I mean, how's your mother doing?"

"Well, it's all...very strange, actually," she replied, hesitating. "Nobody quite understands it, but after the test, the doctor told Mother that her heart was like a baby's--strong and healthy. They never did the operation."

With a start, I slumped back in my chair. "What?" I exclaimed--and then, catching myself, "What...do you mean?"

"All I know is that Mother's been on heart medication for twenty years," Jane replied, with a mixture of elation and confusion. "But the doctor just took her off all of it and said there's no reason for her to be taking anything. Of course, Mother's really happy, and we're all...well, thrilled. Surprised, for sure. But...really thrilled."

She paused, waiting for my response. But I could only sit there, speechless.

"So...could you maybe just tell me, what happened with that prayer? I mean, we're all wondering--what did you do?"

Fumbling, I thanked her for getting back to me and said I was overwhelmed myself at the news. **"Frankly," I added, "I really can't say I did anything but speak out what I sensed God wanted me to. And now….it seems like God…, well, healed your mother's heart."**

Another pause. "Yeah,…it sure seems like that," Jane allowed. As I sat there stunned and elated, we said good-bye.

As I hung up, a mop and bucket leapt into my mind.

OBSERVATIONS

After years of reflecting on this and other experiences since, I offer several observations about prayer for physical healing.

1. God still heals bodies today through Holy Spirit, even as in the Bible.

Both my Harvard seminary training and the liberal/Oldline church tradition hold that such healing does not occur today, nor did it ever occur in fact as the biblical accounts describe. Rather, such stories are merely symbolic tales, like myths, designed only to communicate ideas and values. To note that Jesus "healed the blind," for example, means only that he helped those with limited intellectual understanding to "see" otherwise difficult concepts.

Liberals and evangelical "dispensationalists" become bedfellows at this point, for the latter also hold that healing does not occur today. Yes, they allow, it happened in the past as the bible records, but healings and similar supernatural phenomena claimed today by Pentecostals are largely rooted in a false spirituality and not truly Christian.

Seeing God heal bodies myself, however, led me to grant increasing authority not only to the healing stories in the Bible, but to its teaching as well. Far from "conservative" fears of entertaining a false spirituality, or "liberal" fears of abandoning social justice ministries, the convincing reality of healing prayer has led me to grant greater authority not only to the Living, Risen Jesus Christ, but to the Scriptures and to His ministry to the poor—who often cannot afford medical treatment.

2. Healing through prayer proceeds upon God's design, and not our own.

Healing prayer is not about mastering a healing technique, but rather, deepening relationship with the living, acting God.

Indeed, Jesus uses many different "methods." On one occasion, healing results from the sick person's faith (Matt. 9:22); on another, from his friends' faith (Matt. 9:2). Sometimes, it requires driving out a demon (Matt. 9:33). Another time, healing is connected to the sins of the sick one (Matt. 9:2).

Often, Jesus says nothing whatsoever about sin (Matt. 8:2-4). Indeed, he declares of one blind man, "His blindness has nothing to do with his sins or his parents' sins. He is blind so that God's power might be seen at work in him" (John 9:3). In some cases, Jesus simply commands healing (Matt. 8:3); in the latter case of blindness, he applies a mixture of mud and spit to the eyes, and in fact, two treatments are required for the complete healing.

GOD ORCHESTRATES

My prayer with Mrs. Smith is a case in point.

The coming of the cleaning lady in that brief moment on a short-staffed Sunday afternoon was extremely unusual. God had apparently orchestrated the "healing procedure" entirely according to the unique demands of that particular situation. Clearly, she was instrumental in opening the door to Holy Spirit—Who used me once I let go of my own authority. I needed only to confess my own prejudice and powerlessness in order to receive and minister Holy Spirit's power.

God wanted to heal Mrs. Smith's heart, and chose that occasion to do it. The words I spoke simply reflected the "procedure" which He showed me in my mind, as it were, before I spoke them.

The flesh, however, is not easily overcome. After Mrs. Smith's heart was healed, I was chafing to run out and pray for other heart patients exactly as I had prayed for her.

Soon afterwards, in fact, an aging parishoner of mine had a stroke and her husband was crushed. Anxious to comfort the husband--and to demonstrate this wonderful healing power that I'd discovered--I rushed to their home, laid hands on the woman's head and right away prayed, as with Mrs. Smith, to crush any obstructions in her arteries. The next day, I called her husband expecting great reports.

"Well," he began hesitantly, "actually, I'd have to say she's worse off now. We had to call an ambulance a few hours after your visit."

Devastated, embarrassed, I apologized profusely for any misjudgments on my part. After hanging up, I fell to my knees and asked God what had gone wrong?

"Did you ask Me how to pray?" I immediately sensed His response.

Convicted, I asked Him to forgive me for my presumption. As I prayed further, I eventually sensed deep lifelong emotional wounds in the lady, and adjusted my prayers accordingly. Over the next few weeks she became slightly more alert and responsive to her family, and shortly thereafter, she died peacefully.

Similarly, Francis MacNutt tells the story of a Christian friend who saw Holy Spirit heal, and promptly ran into a hospital, laying hands on every patient. No one, however, was healed, and when he complained to God, he heard, **"Did you ask me if I wanted to heal that person at this time, or whether you were the person I wanted to use for that?"**

3. The process of healing through prayer cannot be separated from its purpose.

God's ultimate purpose for us is to draw us so close to Him as to reflect the divine image. This is the work of Holy Spirit, who "transforms us into (God's) likeness in an ever greater degree of glory" (2 Corinth. 3:18). The ultimate healing for us human beings is to become one with God. It's not only about affecting bodies. After all, even the people Jesus healed eventually died.

While healing conferences, books, and courses may be helpful, we do not follow the healings; we follow Jesus.

Christians understand that the way for us to unite with God is through Jesus Christ. The purpose of healing prayer, therefore, is to draw us to Jesus, by witnessing to his presence and power. "The Lord himself first announced this salvation," as Hebrews declares,

> and those who heard him proved to us that it is true. At the same time, God added his witness to theirs by performing all kinds of miracles and wonders and by distributing the gifts of the Holy Spirit according to his will (Heb. 2:4)

Certainly, physical healing reflects the wonderful kindness of God. Wonderful as that may be, however, it only hints at the larger, ultimate kindness in drawing us toward God Himself. Healing prayer, therefore, serves God's purposes insofar as it leads us to give up on our human power in order to receive God's power.

Holy Spirit, after all--who witnesses the power and love of God through Jesus unto all generations--was poured out only after the crucifixion. The ultimately healed, resurrected body came only after Jesus offered his physical body as a sacrifice to be broken. The pains of the flesh can be awful indeed, but the Father's "medicine" for healing often requires such willingness to be broken for His sake.

PURPOSE OF HEALING

This doesn't mean that God sends illness to bear as a cross. Nowhere do we read that Jesus laid such a burden upon any sick person. Rather, it means that the ultimate divine purpose for our lives is brought about not by healing our bodies alone, but by bringing us to the cross--where our proud human nature is broken unto death in order to receive God's nature unto life eternal.

4. While sickness may not be the result of any sinful act, a major purpose of God's healing is to bring us into an awareness of our sinful condition.

Our sin-nature separates us from God, and Jesus came to lay himself down and bridge that terrible gap. The primary attitude which re-connects us with God is humble repentance—possible only because Jesus shows us God's extreme compassion and mercy. We need not fear being destroyed as we confess our wrongdoing to Him; in fact, we can hope for new life precisely as we do.

Thus, Paul chided the Romans for regarding themselves as deserving: "(D)o you presume upon the riches of (God's) kindness and forbearance and patience? **Do you not know that God's kindness is meant to lead you to repentance?**" (Rom. 2:4RSV).

Jesus was therefore dismayed when only one of ten lepers he healed returned to give thanks (Luke 17:17). Indeed, he states clearly that God's major purpose and hope in healing us is that we would turn away from our pride:

> How terrible it will be for you, Chorazin! How terrible for you too, Bethsaida! If the miracles which were performed in you had been performed in Tyre and Sidon, the people there would have put on sackloth and sprinkled ashes on themselves, *to show that they had turned from their sins*! (Matt. 11:21, italics mine)

The response which God seeks from us to His healing is not, "Eureka! I've discovered the technique!" or even "At last! This proves I didn't do anything wrong to deserve my illness!" Rather, God hopes we'll be overwhelmed by such mercy, fall on our knees and cry out, "Thank you for healing a sinner like me!" And then, forgiven and overwhelmed by grace, we rise to trust His provision and walk out our divine calling.

King David modeled this humble response when, after his many sins, God nevertheless promised to establish his kingdom eternally on earth. Convicted of his sin, David could have refused God's grace, withdrawn from exercising any godly authority, and lived out his life truncated by shame and self-pity. But instead, he fell on his knees and praised God:

> Sovereign Lord! I am not worthy of what you have already done for me, nor is my family. Yet now you are doing even more, Sovereign Lord; you have made promises about my descendants in the years to come.
>
> What more can I say to you! You know me, your servant. It was your will and purpose to do this; you have done all these great things in order to instruct me. How great you are, Sovereign Lord! There is none like you; we have always known that you alone are God. (1 Sam. 7:18-22)

When God gives you His gift of healing, don't give it back. Receive it. It cost Him a lot. Let it remind you of who God is—and who you are as His beloved child. Respond by letting Him use your healed body for His larger purposes.

5. Healing prayer is not magic, to achieve our desires, but rather, an effort to draw closer to God and let Him achieve His desires.

Healing power is not intrinsic to some special words, but only to the God who inspires what the words merely reflect. Nor is healing power intrinsic to any visual images.

The early healing prayer movement often focused its efforts on formulating a visual image of health in your mind to replace that of the person's illness. To pray for a crippled child, for example, you had to picture in your mind that child with altogether healthy legs, running and playing sports with other children. Thus, you demonstrate your faith in the child's healing, and God is obliged to follow through on your vision.

DANGER

Such an approach, however, dangerously effaces God's personality and purpose from the healing process. Indeed, it shifts the burden of healing to your own human faculties, allowing you to conclude that the person prayed for was healed not because God is gracious, but rather, "because I held the positive image in my mind." Worse, it's your fault if the person is not healed.

Certainly, the Bible records many instances in which people had images of God's intention in their minds. For example, Peter "sees" the various "unclean" foods arrayed above him before the "unclean" Gentile Cornelius comes to ask his prayer (see Acts 10). But again, the purpose of this image is to draw Peter closer to God through repentance, because it leads him to realize that he has proudly regarded himself as better in God's sight than any Gentile.

A vision given by God, such as Peter's, is not the same as a humanly-contrived mental picture. **Rather than conjure our image of how we want the sick person to be, we must first surrender ourselves and the sick person to God, and seek God's vision or plan**. If no vision comes thereupon, we must faithfully resist the impulse to manufacture one of our own. Even if a vision does come, we cannot assume outright that it has come from God and speak it immediately.

Rather, a simple check on whether a vision is from you or from God, is to pray with several others and wait to see if they receive a similar image or sense of confirmation. This complies with the biblical injunction that whenever some would offer anything as a "message from God," then "others are to judge what they say" 1 Corinth. 14:29).

Insofar as healing through prayer is a work of the Spirit, it's a function of the Body of Christ, not of individual believers. We must therefore trust God's healing design will be revealed in several persons as confirmation. In this present age, when God's messages to us must be filtered through our broken human nature, we "see through a glass darkly" (1 Corinth. 13:12) at best. That humble confession is our best safeguard against rash and potentially harmful miscues—like my hasty prayer for the aging lady with a stroke.

While a vision from God can help focus your prayer, certainly you don't always need a supernatural leading to pray for healing. Physical brokenness is a natural part of this fallen world, and the Father honors a direct request. A heart for a suffering sister or brother—not religious expertise--is your license to pray.

Indeed, the "success" of our prayers for physical healing cannot be judged by our human expectations. Often, I pray and people are not healed. In those times, I'm left with many questions, and often, great frustration. **Yet the God who allows painful, even deadly brokenness in this world yet remains the only One who can save us from its eternal effects.**

Meanwhile, I will continue seeking Holy Spirit's ministry to heal broken bodies. For indeed, it is Holy Spirit "who reveals the truth about God" (John 14:17. Whether or not our prayer leads to the physical healing we seek, therefore, I trust that in the very exercise of praying together, both of us will be drawn closer to God--and in that ultimate sense, healed.

TAKEAWAY

I stop by the hospital to visit a parishoner's mother whose arteries have hardened. Before leaving, I offer to pray for her, but am interrupted by the hospital cleaning lady, who to my surprise joins in the prayer—which emboldens me to pray for a supernatural healing. Later, I find the patient's arteries were healed.

Have you ever sought Holy Spirit to heal yours or someone else's body? If so, what did you learn from that experience? If not, who could you pray for right now?

The Social Justice Witness:

Meeting Jesus in the Poor and Oppressed

11

From Pier to Ocean:

Adventuring into the World with Jesus

> Jesus got into a boat, and his disciples went with
> him. Suddenly, a fierce storm hit the lake, and the boat
> was in danger of sinking. (Matthew 8:23-24a)

Some years ago, I visited the Los Angeles Museum of Science and Industry. There, I was fascinated to see on display a gigantic, 30-ton steel propeller taken from the *Queen Mary* ocean liner when it was bought by the nearby city of Long Beach.

The son of a Navy officer, I grew up captivated by ships. In the 1950's, before passenger jets, I enjoyed great boyhood adventures sailing with my family on ocean liners round-trip from New York to Pakistan, one of Dad's duty stations. When years later I began pastoring in Los Angeles, the chance beckoned actually to board the fabled *Queen* and I embarked on a pilgrimage to Long Beach harbor, where she had been retired as a floating hotel.

Driving excitedly onto the wharf, I was not disappointed. Majestic and massive—sleek black hull with white trim, crowned with giant red and black smokestacks—she stood glistening in the evening floodlights. Reverently, I approached the gangplank stairway, and could hardly believe it; my boyhood dream was about to come true! Moments later, I stepped out at last onto the graceful bow and gazed over the railing at the magnificent ocean beyond.

As I glanced down, however, my fantasy was rudely shattered.

Forty feet below me, permanent cement and steel walkways locked the *Queen* to shore. In the middle of one gangplank an elevator protruded, and in another, an escalator. The water lay well below the regular, sea-bound waterline, and giant breakwater boulders in a neat row penned-in the mighty ship from the sea--which lay hardly a hundred yards away.

TAMED AND EMPTIED

The mighty *Queen*—having braved sea and storm on the wild oceans of the world--was now hopelessly trapped and bolted to shore by a cluster of pipes and walkways! That great and powerful vessel had been tamed, diminished, and emptied of her power.

Like a punctured tire, I sighed.

The spirit was gone.

Today, the *Queen Mary* riveted to the pier serves as a prophetic image, an apt warning for the Church. In fact, the early Church often compared itself to a ship; hence, the church architectural term "nave" for the front vestibule, derived from the same root as "navy."

Granted, the *Queen Mary* will last longer, look prettier, and have fewer problems fixed to shore. She may well make more money for her owners. But is an ocean liner really an ocean liner when it sits in a puddle?

Indeed, Is a church really The Church of Jesus Christ when it languishes safely moored at home, unmoved by the great and powerful currents in the world beyond its doors?

Once, the disciples--who included several skilled fishermen--sailed with Jesus in a boat, and a storm threatened to capsize their craft while Jesus was sleeping. Their faith drowning in fear, they shouted to awaken Jesus, "Don't you care that we're about to die?" (Mark 4:38).

We can imagine their panicky thoughts: *Why didn't we stay safely back at shore? If we weren't going somewhere with Jesus, this never would've happened to us. And there he is, sleeping --ready to let us all go down with the ship!*

When Jesus awakes, he rebukes the storm and the lake calms. But then, he rebukes the disciples as well for their own unseemly tempest: "Why are you frightened? Do you still have no faith?" (Mark 4:40).

The Story is clear: When you sail with Jesus, you don't stay safely tied up to shore. Rather, you're under orders and given power over death itself to go out where the winds and storms buffet, out into the real world where powers threaten to overwhelm you. Thus, **biblical faith redefines safety--indeed, peace itself--not as the absence of threat, but the presence of Jesus.**

With Jesus in your boat, you're not at the mercy of the world's power. You can sail into the world with authority to affect the very waves and powers that threaten to overwhelm you—and others.

NOT A TRUE PICTURE

Hundreds of years ago, the Pope commissioned an artist to paint the Church living and working in the world. [55] After laboring for months, the artist proudly unveiled his masterpiece before the Magisterium.

The painting showed a wild sea, with ships sinking amid angry white-capped waves and scattered swimmers struggling in the stormy current. The center of the canvas featured a calm and peaceful area where the sun shone on smooth water. There, a ship stood quietly; sitting in it were the Pope and his cardinals.

The Pontiff frowned in dismay. "Your artistry is excellent," he told the painter. "But this is not a true picture of the Church of Jesus Christ."

The Church is not an untroubled island in the midst of a troubled sea, but a vessel amid that sea. As the cross itself demonstrates, the Body of Christ is in the middle of the world's turmoil, itself affected, always going through ups and downs, as if on waves. The Church is forever struggling amid that turmoil, as it tries to bring the Kingdom of God on earth as it is in heaven—not to avoid the waves, but rather, to restore their Creator's order to them, as even Jesus commanded them to be still.

The ancient pagan Greeks among whom the early apostles ministered wrote classic dramas in which the hero often found himself cornered by powers of evil and destruction. At that point, the stage crew behind the scenes would lower a basket onstage, like a cherry picker machine, carrying a character dressed as a familiar god. As from "on high," this god-character would draw the hero into his basket and whisk him up and away from danger. Hence, the Latin term *deus ex machina*, literally, "god from a machine"—used unto today to suggest a cheap exit from conflict.

NO CHEAP EXIT

On the cross, however, God demonstrated clearly that He's no pagan deus ex machina. In response to our cry, He comes not to take us out of this broken world, but to put Himself squarely into it. That is, **the Father's mission in Jesus is not to whisk us out of danger, but rather, to stand with us decisively in the midst of it.**

The Good News is not that we're spared all pain and suffering, but that we're not abandoned to it. Rather, we're met in our darkest hour with the very Presence of God, who in Jesus has promised, "I will be with you always, to the end of the age" (Matthew 28:20; see also Joshua 1:9).

What, indeed, will people see when they board His ship, the Church? Will they see an unmoving, powerless vessel whose propeller Holy Spirit has been "safely" removed and displayed as a museum curiosity? Will they see an isolated people bolted to the world's power structures, living quite comfortably all by themselves—a people who have built a neat, protective breakwater of self-preserving excuses around themselves just outside vast oceans of human conflict and suffering?

Will they see a people comfortably ensconced just across the freeway from unemployment, violence, and despair; around the corner from neglected seniors; down the street from lost and angry youth; a news report away from global hunger?

Will people investigating our faith see a museum church, with Christ safely and securely nailed to the cross, where he can't interfere with the programs and desires of the congregation? Will they find the Spirit of God-- who literally fired the first Christians to speak new languages, cross worldly boundaries, and forge new community--now properly tranquilized by rigid worship forms, performance standards, and self-serving programs?

Will they find the God who led His faithful community out of slavery through a desert wilderness now comfortably locked to shore, wed to Pharaoh and the self-sufficient ones who've "got it made"? Will they meet people who once followed faithfully after security in Jesus now securely assimilated into the world?

Or indeed, will those who visit the Church of Jesus Christ find **a people who know there's no shore, no permanent ground in this world to which we can tie ourselves for security?** Will they find a craft with its propeller connected to the Power source and stirring with His Spirit, eager to head out into the unknown after God's purposes—undeterred by the threatening waves of the world?

Will they find a people pooling their talents and gifts toward new visions, ready to go places they've never dared, and to reach out in ways they never thought possible?

Our God calls us into uncharted and uncertain seas to restore His Kingdom to this world. The Good News in Jesus is not that we're lifted out of this world, but rather, sent into it and all its brokenness with resurrection power to redeem and reshape it in God's image.

It's time to leave the comfortable pier. The Captain is ready to set out into the oceans.

Are you?

TAKEAWAY

I visit the proud old ocean liner *Queen Mary* in permanent dry dock, and am dismayed to see that she's been tamed and stripped of her true identity--no longer an ocean liner, but merely a museum, featuring exhibits of past power and glories but no longer moving out into the world. Hence, the Church without social justice outreach.

As you hear the daily news, what human problem or need grabs your heart and stirs you to make a difference? What if Jesus is out there among the broken people and calling you to come minister to Him there? How might you and your church respond?

12

Of Jogging and Cat Food:

Meeting Jesus Where It Hurts

> Then the King will say to the people on his right,
> "Come, you that are blessed by my Father! Come and
> possess the kingdom which has been prepared for you
> ever since the creation of the world. I was hungry and you
> fed me, thirsty and you gave me a drink; I was a stranger
> and you received me in your homes, naked and you
> clothed me; I was sick and you took care of me, in prison
> and you visited me." The righteous will then answer him,
> "When, Lord, did we ever see you hungry and feed you, or
> thirsty and give you a drink? When did we ever see you
> a stranger and welcome you in our homes, or naked and
> clothe you?" The King will reply, "I tell you, whenever you
> did this for one of the least important of these brothers
> of mine, you did it for me!" (Matt. 25:34-40).

While leafing through a magazine some time ago, I found myself transfixed by a sportswear ad showing a man running.[56] The picture didn't include where he came from or where he was going; he was simply running. And for a strange moment I was with him--not loping through a glossy layout in color-coordinated jogging shoes and warm-up suit, but in the tiny, remote Nigerian village where I had served years before as a Peace

Corps Volunteer.

In a flash, I saw the one-lane bush road outside my cinder-block house, a road that ambled through jungle and scrubland to the nearest town with electricity and running water--a two-hour bike ride away. And I remembered how the adventure of the first few months gave way, through steamy-hot tropical afternoons and candlelit nights, to long daydreams about boyhood sandlot ball games.

PERFECT JOGGING PATH

For some time, I pondered over what, if any, sport I could play at my unlikely outpost. **At last, it occurred to me that right there on that narrow bush road, under ancient layers of naturally crushed terra cotta, lay a perfect jogging path!** Back then in 1965, before the advent of running shoes, I had never jogged anywhere before in my life. But at 6000 miles from the nearest sandlot ball game, I was willing to expand my sporting horizon. And so, later that same afternoon, as the equatorial sun dipped below the palm trees, I laced up my old canvas US Keds and set out running on the road, stretching my arms exultantly.

I had guessed right; its firm but resilient surface was perfect underfoot. Overhead, giant banana leaves seemed to wave me on amid the squawking cheers of myriad birds invisible in the surrounding palm trees.

Just as I was about to hit my stride, I heard the distinct rattle and whirr of oft-repaired local bicycles. In seconds, I was joined on either side by two cassava farmers, pedaling their way back home from the fields after a long day's work in the equatorial sun.

Managing my best American Peace Corps smile, I turned each way and nodded to them without breaking stride. To my surprise, they slowed and did not pass. Holding even with me, they stared.

"You got trouble?" one asked gravely.

"Oh...(puff)...no," I said, holding my pace. Again, I smiled quickly to each side.

"You need help?" the other farmer urged.

"Uh...no...(puff)...thank you," I wheezed. "No help. Everything... (puff)... OK. Thank you...(puff)."

The soft, chipped clay crunched beneath my feet as the two bicycles rattled along beside me. Ahead, a chuckhole the size of a manhole cover loomed; as the bicycles swerved, I leapt it and continued. The two drew back beside me.

"You run," one noted.

"Yes...(puff). I run...(puff)."

"You run...," the other repeated, hesitating. "Where?"

With some discomfort, I shifted my stride. I was out of shape, and had expected the running to get difficult, but carrying on a conversation at the same time was beginning to tax my patience. "Up the road!" I snapped.

"You run up road," the two echoed. Rattling and whirring together, they looked ahead and, seeing only the same road and trees that they and their ancestors had seen for generations, they turned back to me with blank expressions. For a brief second, their mutual bewilderment slowed their pedaling, and I strode ahead. Catching themselves, they pulled even with me again.

"No trouble. You run. Up road." Brow furrowed, the one farmer spoke studiously, as if writing the problem before himself on a mental blackboard, the more clearly to grasp its components.

"WHY you run up road?" the two burst out at once.

It was no use. I did what is forbidden to all joggers. There, beneath the waving banana leaves and cheering birds, I stopped. We all stopped. Panting, sweating in the humid dusk, frustrated at being interrupted on my very first jog, I struggled to remain calm and American Peace Corps friendly.

"You want to know...(puff)...why I am running up the road," I offered, panting, "....right?"

Standing patiently beside their bicycles, they nodded.

"Right," I repeated, stalling as a feeling of being oddly out of place crept over me. Drawing a deep breath, I exhaled matter-of-factly. "OK, I am running to get exercise."

"'Ex-er-cise'?" one echoed, as the other looked up the empty road ahead, his brow knit in confusion. "What is 'ex-er-cise'?"

RUNNING NOWHERE

For a long second, I stood there, mouth open, beginning to sense the scene's absurdity: two thin, overworked, barefoot cassava farmers sitting astride broken-down bicycles that represented a measure of their success;

an over-caloried white man in canvas shoes running nowhere to get something that no one had ever heard of.

Words failed me. Where we stood, farmers had for centuries harvested barely enough calories to continue toiling in the fields. **We were an arm's length apart, but a hopeless cultural gulf yawned between us.**

Lifting my shoulders, I spread my hands, palms upward, and shook my head helplessly. At last, clumsily, I reached out and shook each man's hand. "Thank you...for stopping to check on me," I said, faltering. "You...you are good friends."

And then, wiping my brow quickly, I turned and ran back to my house.

If we meet Jesus at the cross, where our sinful self must be confronted and surrendered unto death, His ministry of social justice for the poor and oppressed introduces Him graphically to us well-fed Americans. Our self-centered human nature forever seeks to justify our own comfort and ignore the plight of others--especially when called to share our bounty.

Even when we begin to recognize their plight--as myself, while jogging in Nigeria--our difference may appear so overwhelming that we simply want to run away from it. Yet biblical faith declares not only that we meet Jesus among those rejected and broken by the world, but that the ultimate reward of eternal life—as Matthew notes above--belongs to those who minister to His needs there.

Significantly, Jesus saves this teaching until the end of his ministry, just before the Last Supper. It thereby focuses on what "the King will say" at end-time judgment--and His ultimate distinction between "the righteous" (Matt. 25:33) and those "under God's curse" (:41), even as a shepherd separates the goats from the sheep. Referring to creation itself, Jesus implies that these "righteous" ones, precisely because of their unknowing generosity, will have overcome the innate pride to which Adam fell.

Indeed, God reserves this ultimate blessing not for those who have taken the sacrament, been born again, or baptized with Holy Spirit-- though certainly each of these reveals Jesus among us. His ultimate goal for us is to follow Him and overcome the sin of the world, that is, to restore the world's brokenness to God's purposes. Clearly, the poor and oppressed reflect how the world misses His mark and thereby, reflect its sinful state.

Ministry to the world's needy--not just in spirit, but with physical/material help—therefore ranks high, if not supreme, on His agenda.

Thus, James defines faithfulness in contrast to those who merely espouse correct belief, without acting on it to serve others:

> My brothers, what good is it for someone to say that he has faith if his actions do not prove it? Can that faith save him? Suppose there are brothers or sisters who need clothes and don't have enough to eat. What good is there in your saying to them, "God bless you! Keep warm and eat well!"--if you don't give them the necessities of life? **So it is with faith: if it is alone and includes no actions, then it is dead.** (James 2:14-17)

IMELDA'S SHOES

A classic example of James' concern was reflected in the brutality of former Philippine dictator Marcos and his free-spending wife Imelda. As one Catholic priest wrote in a newspaper letter to the editor after the despotic Marcos was at last deposed,

> Ferdinand Marcos says he was kept from committing suicide by his Roman Catholic religion. It's too bad the same religion did not keep him from stealing his country blind.
>
> And Imelda is upset over the press reports of her obscene collection of thousands of shoes, expensive gowns and extravagant gifts, which are now being shown to the Filipino people "while they are not being shown the prayer room which would prove how pious we were."
>
> Will some good atheist please help finish this letter while I throw up?[57]

The God of Spirit who became flesh in Jesus is served not merely by piety. As John declares,

> Little children, let us stop just *saying* we love people; let us *really* love them, and *show* it by our *actions*. Then we will know for sure, by our actions, that we are on God's side, and our consciences will be clear, even when we

stand before the Lord. (1 John 3:18,19TLB, italics mine)
That is,

> If someone says he loves God, but hates his brother,
> he is a liar. For he cannot love God, whom he has not seen,
> if he does not love his brother, whom he has seen. The
> command that Christ has given us is this: whoever loves
> God must love his brother also. (1 John 4:20,21)

The very first generation of Christians wrestled with this issue amid a growing "Gnostic" movement, which insisted on separating body and spirit. Gnostics considered the material world as base, lower, with no hope of being redeemed--and therefore, entirely distinct from and insignificant compared to higher glory in the spirit realm. Therefore, they saw no responsibility to affect the temporal order, including society and government, nor compassion towards those who suffered its inequities.

The Gnostics, in fact, were offended by the incarnation, in which the God of all purity and goodness becomes carnal flesh. A Gnostic arrogance, therefore, took shape in their doctrine of Docetism, which held that the divine Christ could not possibly have stooped to take on corruptible flesh and blood. In fact, these of "higher spiritual perception" affirmed that Jesus had no real body, but was actually pure spirit with only a physical appearance, or *dokesis*--the Greek root word of Docetism.

The Gnostics embodied the most graphic spirit of division and separation by splitting spirit from body--which God had sent Jesus to unite, even as Holy Spirit with His Body the Church.

The ancient Gnostics offer a prophetic warning, in preferring to lift their elite gaze above the world's brokenness, even above the crucified Jesus and his enduring presence among the broken of the world. Docetism lurks in Christians unto today when we insist that the only valid revelation of Jesus lies in personal conversion, sacramental participation, or supernatural phenomena—and otherwise ignore the material needs of the poor and oppressed.

WORD AND DEED

The Christian license for social justice ministry, that is, lies in the unity of body and spirit. It's issued by the Spirit-God who has not abandoned the material world, but indeed, has come in the flesh

to save and redeem it for His purposes. Like the Gnostics, we may be pessimistic about the world itself and our sinful human nature. We're forever optimistic, however, about God's determination to struggle with us and overcome that nature and thereby, transform this world on earth as it is in heaven.

As Baptist theologian Gabriel Fackre notes in his book *Word and Deed*,

> The marriage of word and deed is consummated in the birth of Jesus Christ. Here the word is made flesh. The converging lines of action and interpretation meet at the incarnation. The Word of God becomes the Deed of God. It is out of this fusion that the ministry of Jesus comes. And from it proceed the Acts evangelism of the apostles, and the word-in-deed mandates and miracles of today's evangelists.[58]

Here, the Pentecostal witness is also essential. The New Testament letters emphasize this theme that "through faith we might receive the Spirit promised by God" (Gal. 3:14), and thereby, see others with God's eyes, in the fullness of their need. Holy Spirit empowers us to live a "faith that works through love" (Gal. 5:6). Those who by faith receive the Spirit within them can do what God wants done, even—especially--ministry to the poor and oppressed.

Thus, an article "Charismatics Shake Hands with Social Activists" reports on a consultation of Pentecostal/charismatics and Oldline social activists, drawing forty-five Christian leaders from six continents. Participants asked "hard questions of one another, challenging weaknesses or inadequacies in one another's perspective and practice."

Nevertheless, the reporter noted, "the overall impact of the meeting was the sense that both emphases are integral to the spread of the gospel: **the good news must indeed be brought to the poor and powerless and their needs addressed--not by mere human effort, but in the full power of the Holy Spirit**."[59]

Jesus demonstrated that true integration of spirit and flesh manifests in great humility. Thus, He portrays the "righteous" ones who meet the needs of the downtrodden as not even realizing that they've been doing anything special: "When, Lord, did we ever see you hungry and feed you, or thirsty and give you a drink?"

That is, as you surrender yourself to Jesus to be born again, allow Him to baptize you with His Holy Spirit, and receive his empowering body and blood in the sacrament, his nature begins to pre-empt your self-centered human nature. You become not only thankful for what He's given you, but like Him, determined that others might have it, too.

Kindness is a fruit of the Spirit, not humanly conjured (see Gal. 6:22). Compassionate, godly acts thereby become "naturally super-natural"[60] responses when Holy Spirit animates your flesh. In fact, when the Lord calls you forth for the ultimate reward of life everlasting, you can only ask ingenuously, "When, Lord, did I do all that?"

That's eating from the Tree of Life, not the Tree of Knowledge—being empowered by relationship with Jesus, not by religion.[61]

SACRIFICE REQUIRED

Still, no matter how powerfully we've encountered Jesus spiritually, we often balk at the here-and-now sacrifice required to meet him in the poor and oppressed. "But I don't know any poor people," we may protest.

Social justice ministry, however, in its very overarching focus is not primarily about relationship with other individuals, but rather, relationship with Jesus, for it is He whom we serve in that ministry. In fact, **we don't minister to the needy primarily because we care about them, but rather, because Jesus cares about them--and indeed, is them.**

This is why the Evangelical, Sacramental, and Pentecostal witnesses all undergird social justice ministry. Insofar as you allow these three to draw you into heartfelt relationship with Jesus, you'll know Him well enough to recognize Him among the downtrodden and be sustained in His call to uplift them.

Certainly, visiting a suffering community or Third World country and seeing firsthand the pain of poverty and injustice can—and often does—stir your heart to action. But ultimately, we do not serve the poor and oppressed. We serve Jesus. Indeed, serving the downtrodden can often get messy. Human nature inevitably provides excuses for you not to do so, and you'll either quit or shut down your heart and retreat into ideology.

Human nature does not want to face the poor and oppressed, because they reflect the brokenness of the world, even our own world--from local panhandlers to international martyrs—which inspires shame. In this fallen world, therefore, God's vision is often pre-empted by the old factional squabbles which divert attention from that shame—and from Jesus, who would bear it.

On the one hand, conservative legalists seek to eliminate the poor and oppressed altogether, either by denigrating or ignoring them. In fact, poverty is not often pretty, and can stir considerable evil, from crime to domestic abuse to war.

Yet the political Right would often sacrifice grace to truth. As fellow human beings, something of ourselves lives among the downtrodden—even as the crucified Jesus. Compassion, therefore, is in order. "There is no difference at all," the Apostle Paul declared. "Everyone has sinned and is far away from God's saving presence. But by the free gift of God's grace all are put right with him through Christ Jesus, who sets them free" (Rom. 3:22b,23).

On the other hand, liberal universalists often idealize the downtrodden, casting their suffering as righteous heroism. Certainly, the tenacity of many who suffer poverty and oppression can truly be called heroic. Yet the political Left would often sacrifice truth to grace.

Suffering, however, is not intrinsically redemptive. We're not saved by our suffering. We're saved by Jesus' suffering. When we surrender to Jesus in the midst of our pain, our suffering becomes His own—and thereby sanctified, made holy, set apart for His purposes and not merely an obstruction to our own.

No human condition—no matter how unfair or destructive-- overcomes sin; only Jesus' blood does that. Rich or poor, free or oppressed, we're all sinners, and delight the Father when we surrender at last to Him. In fact, because sin is a part of creation itself, poor people are as bound by sin as rich people—but just lack the resources to hide it.

The truth is, Father God does want to eliminate the poor and oppressed. The grace is, He does that not by marginalizing or romanticizing them, but by providing their material needs and setting them free from oppression.

The best way to get rid of poor and oppressed people is to give them resources to get out of poverty and to walk in freedom.

That's where we affluent Christians come in. The question for us is therefore not—to paraphrase Scripture—"Shall they continue in suffering that grace may abound?" (see Rom. 6:1), but rather, "Shall we mobilize our resources and join God's efforts to overcome their suffering?"

Father God wants us to face and confess our need for Him. Yet He is less concerned with our sin, which is a given in this fallen world, than with our readiness to bring it to Him--which allows for our free will and thereby beckons the overcoming relationship He longs for. Most often, however, we surrender to God only when our human resources fail.

That's why the poor and oppressed are close to the Father's heart: not because they're inherently more righteous or even deserving, but because having fewer worldly resources—from food to political clout--makes you recognize more readily your dependence upon Him. In fact, **those who have little of the world's resources reflect the deeper reality that we all have nothing except what God has graciously given us.**

Thus, Jesus blessed "those who know they are spiritually poor," declaring that "the Kingdom of heaven belongs to them" (Matt. 5:4). "Spiritual prosperity," as Mary-Andrews-Dalbey paraphrases, "belongs to those who keenly recognize their inadequacy and unworthiness, and earnestly seek God's mercy to save them."[62]

Jesus is precisely what the Father has graciously given us; in that sense, He thrives among the poor and oppressed. Insofar as you know Jesus as the One who has died for you, you can't be satisfied with your own well-being as long as Jesus is hungry, imprisoned, unclothed, or otherwise in need.

Our human nature, however, often sabotages the spiritual sensitivity which such awareness requires.

Once, a woman came to me with chronic resentment toward her husband. In order to break the vicious cycle of criticism between them, I sensed the Father wanted her to do some special act of kindness for him.

"But he's hurt me so badly," she protested. "I just don't think I have it in me to do something nice for him."

"Ask Jesus to put it in you," I offered. "Even if you can't do it for your husband, do it for Jesus."

A sincere believer, the woman agreed, and decided to cook her husband his favorite meal. "He was so kind and loving at first, I could hardly believe it!" she reported later in excitement—then fell silent. "But things really haven't changed."

Puzzled, I asked if she'd done anything else.

"Well," she declared, eyes narrowing, "later, after the dinner, of course, I told him, 'I want you to know I'm being kind to you only because I'm doing it for Jesus, not for you!'"

The old Adam does not yield easily!

We can do good deeds for Jesus. But He has more room to work His healing when we surrender our control and give freely, without agendas and asking, When did we....? Indeed, **if someone you've helped asks how to repay you, you can reply, "Don't repay me, repay God, by doing something good yourself for somebody else."**

FOREVER CRUCIFIED

The natural self-centered, comfort-driven desires of the flesh must forever be crucified in order to meet Jesus among the poor.

I learned this myself some years ago, when I bought the most lively and playful kitten you could want for yourself—the friendly kind that sleeps at your shoulder and wakes you with a fuzzy paw on your chin.[63]

Soon after bringing the kitten home, I went to buy cat food at the local supermarket. Strolling there along aisles overflowing with cans, boxes, and hefty bags of animal food "with all the high protein your pet needs"—as one ad proclaimed—a strange and unsettling vision lurched into my mind.

Flanked by walls of nutritious dog and cat food, I remembered a little boy named Igwe, then about seven years old, who lived in the thatch hut behind my comparatively upscale cinderblock, tin-roof house in rural Nigeria. Igwe's stomach always bulged unnaturally, like his playmates'—not from overeating, as I had naively assumed, but from malnutrition and not getting, as it were, "all the high protein your fellow human being needs."

There in the supermarket, I watched a father lift his son playfully to a top rack, where the boy seized a bag of dog food and held it to him like a teddy bear. As father, son, and dog food disappeared laughing around the aisle, I remembered the day Igwe came to me with a broad smile to tell me the good news: "My father bought our family a puppy at market today!"

"Hey, that's just great!" I exclaimed.

"Yes," he burst out, eyes dancing, "and Father says we can eat it very soon!"

"What? Oh, no!" I blurted out indignantly--then caught myself as Igwe's smile broke in confusion.

For a painful, embarrassing moment, I stood there, lost in a new and terrifying world. Here was a little boy for whom meat on the family table was an almost unheard-of luxury. And there was a man who had allowed his own customary riches to cut himself off from the suffering of others.

"Oh, uh, well..., I'm... happy for you," I fumbled at last, reaching out awkwardly to pat Igwe on the shoulder. As I now reached out as awkwardly for the box of "100% nutritionally complete cat dinner," I winced at the irony and prayed for forgiveness.

Perhaps—just perhaps—that prayer was answered when later it occurred to me **to keep an account of how much I spent on cat food, and give that same amount to a world hunger fund.** The more I enjoy my friendly, fuzzy cat, the more I hope that this sacrifice is acceptable to God. If not, I confess that I'm not sure I want to hear about it, since I'm not yet fully converted from the religion of Me-ism. I still prefer to do what I like, without worrying how that affects others.

Nevertheless, I know that my own actions here in this land of abundance do indeed affect others. Certainly, I would never kill someone else to keep my cat, much as I enjoy it. And yet, people die of hunger while my none-too-skinny pet eats his fill.

How can we make this essential connection between Christian spirituality and the practical effects of our lifestyle upon others? Can a personal faith address the larger call to social justice?

FASTING AND JUSTICE

The answer was suggested to me at an ice-cream break during our church's spring confirmation class, when I was surprised to see one youngster not eating anything. Curious, I asked him, "Why not?"[64]

"I'm giving up sweets for Lent," he explained, his voice wavering as friends chattered nearby over cones and sundaes.

"Oh...," I murmured, shifting my own cone uncomfortably and easing away as another youngster called to him.

Several minutes later, I was taken aback to see the same boy walking by licking a large ice cream cone.

"I broke my Lent," he confessed sheepishly.

"I'm really curious," I said. "Why did you want to give up sweets in the first place?"

"Well, you know—you give up something for Lent, right?"

"Yes, but why?" I urged.

He hesitated. "I guess I really don't know," he said at last.

No wonder his Lenten fast couldn't hold up against temptation.

As a Protestant who had never actively observed church liturgical seasons, I felt challenged: Is "giving up something for Lent" simply an outmoded, meaningless custom? Is it just an ingrown, personalized piety with no effect beyond the individual? Or can it be redeemed and reaffirmed as a significant Christian witness—even to the poor and oppressed?

The ancient prophet Isaiah answers decisively, in response to those who have been fasting in order to get something they want from God, and not getting it:

> The Lord says to them, "The truth is that at the same time you fast, you pursue your own interests and oppress your workers. You...spread out sackcloth and ashes to lie on. Is that what you call fasting? Do you think I will be pleased with that? The kind of fasting I want is this: Remove the chains of oppression and the yoke of injustice, and let the oppressed go free. Share your food with the hungry and open your homes to the homeless poor. Give clothes to those who have nothing to wear, and do not refuse to help your own relatives. (Isa. 58:3-7)

Christians do not fast as punishment for our wrongdoing, nor, as the pagan Greek Docetists, as an act of self-denial in order to dissociate from the 'evil sensory world of the body.' **The God who created the human body clearly says that it's good and its needs are important—so important, in fact, that He's determined to meet those needs in the poor.** Faithful fasting thereby requires that we sacrifice our "own interests" in order to serve the pressing material needs of others in this world.

Social justice ministry counters the religious temptation to hide from the world's brokenness behind pietistic, other-worldly spirituality.

If you don't believe the material world is important, you won't honor the pressing material needs of the poor. A classic story from the Hasidic tradition of European Judaism makes the point:

> A very pious and very wealthy man wanted to impress (his rabbi) with a description of the austerity to which he subjected himself. "Tell me what you eat every day," the Maggid inquired. — "Oh, almost nothing. Bread and salt." — "That's bad," said the Maggid, "that's

very bad. I order you to eat white bread and cake, and also to drink sweet wine." — "But, Rebbe, why?" cried the astounded Hasid. — "I shall tell you why. You see: if you are content with black bread and water, you will come to the conclusion that the poor can subsist on stones and spring water. If you eat cake, you will give them bread."[65]

Certainly, Christian fasting can affirm giving up something in order to remember what Jesus gave up for us, namely, his very life. Such a fast reminds us of how deeply God loves us, sinful as we are. This must lead us not only to know God loves me, however, but also to discover that God loves others, and thereby would use me to serve their needs.

As a start, you might give to a world hunger fund the money not spent on food while fasting.

HUNGER AND GASOLINE

Meanwhile, the larger political dimension to global hunger must be faced if our fellow human beings are to be fed. To understand better how a hungry person in today's world might feel, think of the average American buying gasoline. Periodic upheavals in the Middle East often affect our oil supply, resulting in higher gas prices.

Certainly, American oil companies share the responsibility for price increases. What angers Americans, however, is that the price of gas at our neighborhood pumps is not totally controlled by our own people, but often by other people in other countries halfway around the globe.

To us, gasoline is not a luxury, but a need, something we can't live without. As former President Bush noted, we're "addicted" to oil; life as we know it depends upon gasoline-powered vehicles. But **what if our dependency on foreign oil parallels Third World dependency upon foreign food?**

Imagine that you're a small nation with few resources. The price of food is dictated by a handful of foreign countries with food surpluses and controlled by their commodities market in New York and Chicago. The price of food goes up or down—and your people are either fed or starved—at the apparent whim of greedy foreigners.

If Americans are to food as Arabs are to oil, it's an awfully good thing that the poorer, starving countries of the world don't have nuclear aircraft carriers, or they'd be headed right now for Los Angeles and New York to clean out our supermarket distribution centers. You can get pretty hungry—and angry--waiting on someone else's charity.

But, you say, certainly those small countries have land of their own. Why don't they just work hard, grow their own food, and feed themselves, like we do?

Part of the answer is simply that you can't farm a desert or jungle. Beyond topography, however, most farmland in hungry nations is already being used—pre-empted in fact, by a very few rich landlords who oppress very hard-working laborers to grow non-nutritious crops for export to America and the world's wealthy. Coffee, tea, sugar, cocoa, rubber, tobacco, and such "luxury produce" are all grown on land that could be used instead to grow beans, vegetables, fruit, and other food to feed malnourished citizens.

Nor let us be misled to scoff, "Well, it's their land to do what they want with it. If they choose to grow sugar instead of beans, that's not America's fault."

SUGAR OR BEANS

A study of the Dominican Republic, for example, revealed that more than two thirds of the island's agricultural produce is exported, with three quarters of that going to the U.S., mostly in sugar. As a *National Catholic Reporter* feature noted[66], the sugar is grown on large estates that take up most of the country's arable land, owned by one per cent of the population. **Clearly, an elite few rich Dominicans—not the people—are choosing to grow sugar instead of beans.**

What's more, this fateful decision was enabled by the American government. U.S. Marines invaded the Dominican Republic in 1965, and shortly thereafter the American corporation Gulf & Western bought controlling interest in over 100,000 acres of Dominican land for sugar production. Among other benefits, Gulf & Western enjoyed a 20-year tax exemption from the government set up after the U.S. invasion.

Sugar plantation workers at that time earned an average of $200 per year.

For some time, hunger has been a way of life in the Dominican Republic. A Columbia University report showed that one out of ten children there died then of malnutrition in their first year; half the survivors were anemic and suffered from chronic malnutrition.

You don't need a personal relationship with any sugar plantation worker to know that's cruel and inhumane.

What does the faith of a "Christian" nation have to say about this? Certainly, in Isaiah God tells us to give food to the hungry people of the world. But before God tells us to give food away, He commands that we "remove the yoke of injustice."

It's not enough for us simply to give food away, necessary though that may be as an emergency stopgap. As Christ's Body, we're called not just to avoid contributing to world hunger, but to act against the powers that keep people hungry. **We're called to attack the fundamental causes of hunger and no longer simply to "pursue our own interests," to end the cruel systems and self-serving institutions which leave people starving upon heaps of sugar**.

We're called to speak out against those who "oppress your workers" with $200-a-year wages—at the very least, to withdraw our support from political regimes that practice such evil, and not to reinforce them.

God is not mocked. To ignore our larger, corporate responsibility for world hunger is to sacrifice the soul of our nation—and to abandon Jesus as He labors even now among the poor and oppressed.

How about a well-researched church campaign to help your political representatives understand world hunger and change national polices that foster it? Also, a congregation could fast for a season from coffee, sugar, tea, tobacco, and other non-nutritious crops, and give money saved from that to a world hunger fund--not to punish themselves out of self-righteous piety, but to better remember how much God has sacrificed for us in Jesus.

During that time, they could meet weekly and explore ways to serve the poor at home and beyond. This would offer God a chance to show your church not only how to avoid contributing to world hunger, but to act positively, even politically, to insure public policy that would end it.

Granted, it would be hard to give up coffee, sugar, and tobacco for us Americans, who are often as addicted to our caffeine, sweet-tooth, and smokes as to our gasoline. The Alcoholics Anonymous 12-Step Program declares that the first Step to overcoming an addiction is to admit that your compulsive behavior is affecting your life, even beyond your ability to control it. This honesty allows the addict to see how his/her addiction affects others. A coffee/sugar fast could thereby bring the Body of Christ to face and confess our dependency upon sweets, and convict us of how that dependency harms others around the world.

In fact, the addictive quality of those non-nutritious crops in question indicates the spiritual source of their attraction, and promises thereby that evil will be engaged in producing them.

Indeed, the power of addictive behavior is indicated by how hard it is to stop. I know that, because when I first began a sugar fast, that craving for a chocolate chip cookie fairly overwhelmed me. Humbled and ashamed, I began to see how that part of me which demanded my cookies and desserts could seize a society filled with others like me, and lead us collectively as a nation to oppress other, weaker nations to serve our addiction.

CUL-DE-SAC THINKING

Social justice issues jar us into God's larger perspective. When we look no further than our own selves for what's good and right, then what's different from me begins to look evil and wrong. To be another race is to be inferior; to be poor is to be lazy. Avoiding this cul-de-sac mentality is a painful, lifelong process that requires crucifying our natural appetites and surrendering regularly to Jesus. It is, in fact, the life process of growing into Christian maturity.

A tiny infant knows nothing beyond its own desires; a major component of childishness is selfishness. A child's greatest desire is to affirm, "You love me!"

Maturity, however, requires seeing the needs of others, and giving thanks for your own talent and treasure as tools for serving others. It means no longer looking to others to give you the love only God can provide (Romans 2:28,29). The adult's greatest desire is to affirm "I love you"—not just with words, but with deeds of compassion and mercy.

"Do you love me?" Jesus asked Peter three times. And each time Peter answered "Yes," Jesus responded, "Feed my sheep" (John 20:15-17).

The essential question remains: Is it bad for me to seek the material security and comfort I want for myself?

I offer this answer: **Material comfort and security are good insofar as they are seen as the undeserved gifts of a graceful, loving God, and evil insofar as they separate us from the needs of others and make us**

unresponsive to their suffering.

God gives generously to us, that is, in order that we might give generously to others. As Paul explained,

> And God is able to make all grace abound in you so that in all things at all times, having all that you need, you will abound in every good work. As it is written: "He has scattered abroad his gifts to the poor; his righteousness endures forever." ... You will be made rich in every way so that you can be generous on every occasion. (2 Corinth. 9:8,9,11 NIV)

Certainly, it's very hard to think of others if, like an animal, you have to expend all your energy for mere survival. But most of us with enough money to buy this book don't need more material security. Rather, we need to learn how to celebrate and thank God for His abundant provision, so He can use our thereby opened hearts to serve others as He has so graciously served us.

Thus the Apostle declares,

> Let us give thanks to the God and Father of our Lord Jesus Christ, the merciful Father, the God from whom all help comes. He helps us in all our troubles, so that we are able to help others who have all kinds of troubles, using the same help that we ourselves have received from God. (2 Corinth. 1:3,4)

I learned this lesson graphically when in seminary I took a part-time job ministering in a nursing home. I'll never forget the awful fear that swept over me when I first walked down those halls: so many frail people with broken bodies, just sitting there and doing absolutely nothing with their lives! Only my large seminary debt held me to that ministry—until in desperation, I cried out, "Lord, you've got to set me free from this fear or I can't endure these people!"

In time, I began to see that the idle nursing home residents were forcing into my consciousness a deep sense of purposelessness that had long haunted my own life. Among so many people apparently so much nearer to death than myself, I began to face as well my deep fear of death. I realized that none of us dictate our own lifespan, that indeed, in this broken, uncertain world we all live near to death, no matter what our age or physical condition. Accident and disease can strike the young as easily as the old.

At first, I panicked: "What in the world can I possibly preach to so helpless a condition?" In that moment of terror, my human nature saw only two options: either quit the nursing home ministry, or shut down my heart when I visit. Eventually, I fell on my knees in despair and cried out, "Lord Jesus, I haven't got anything to give these people and I'm literally scared to death to be around them!"

At that, I bottomed out into a third option, namely, Jesus. He, I realized, is the only help and hope for us all, the only vital response to death, no matter what your age or physical condition. **"Father, I can't do this,"** I **sighed. "You're going to have to give me what I need to do it."**

I believe this humble surrender was the lesson God had sent me to learn at the nursing home—so I could proclaim it not only to the residents there, but wherever I preach.

HIDE FROM HELPLESSNESS

Through prayer and counseling, I found not only courage to endure in the nursing home ministry, but also the strength of faith to rejoice in it. I began to see myself among residents there as simply a fellow human being broken by the powers of the world and drawing hope for each day from Jesus alone.

Whereas previously, I had always left the home feeling overwhelmed and guilty, now I could sense the Father's "Well done" in my heart as His signal to bless and release the residents to Him, and leave. Eventually, the flood of appreciation for my song-leading, preaching, and listening caringly to individuals, allowed Holy Spirit to refresh my own heart, and I began to leave each visit more uplifted than when I had arrived.

Preaching to those nursing home residents gave me a freedom no church could offer. These people on the threshold of death could not be moved by my fancy words or style. They literally had no time for religious games. They wanted the truth. They wanted the love of God. They wanted a safe place to lay down their masks and get ready to meet Jesus. Anything more was fluff, anything less was cruel.

In their powerless state, in fact, they were closer to the natural human condition of powerlessness than the rest of us with youthful energy and material resources to hide it. In that sense, they were

closer to Jesus—and as I dared to draw near to them, they drew me closer to Jesus.

Ministering in a nursing home led me to my own fears of death, which led me to Jesus, who then gave me his heart for the aging and infirm. Similarly, being among the world's poor can lead you to your own fears of deprivation, which can lead you to confess that all you have comes from God, who can then give you His heart—and outstretched arm—for the poor.

Thus, God's heart for the poor and oppressed manifests in acts of compassion. "Compassion" means literally, "com" = together + "passion" = suffer; that is, "suffer with." Thus, **the best way to recognize Jesus among others who suffer is to invite Jesus into your own suffering**. Otherwise, it's too risky; their suffering will exhaust your natural resources and drag you down. Thus, we're tempted to minimize, deny, and shun poverty and oppression.

Your pride has to break in order to meet Jesus among the poor and oppressed. And that, of course, is the Good News: it's a great place to crucify your fantasies of self-sufficiency and control.

That's why the Evangelical witness in humbly letting go of your life and being born again is foundational to social justice ministry.

The classic old fear that "If I give my life to Jesus, He'll call me to the darkest jungle," is thereby revealed as a handy excuse if not demonic deception. To recognize Jesus among the poor and oppressed, you don't have to join them in squalor the rest of your life. You just have to be humble enough to confess your own brokenness unto death and let Jesus reveal Father God's heart for you.

In that process, He'll give you His heart for others as well. You'll know that when your own heart breaks along with His for some particular outreach need—from nursing home to inner city, from broken suburban families to yes, even the darkest jungle. Thus bearing His heart, you can beg Father God with *heart-felt com-passion*, "Give me what I need to help these people—even as you have given so graciously to me."

Social justice ministry therefore begins with confessing your sin of self-centeredness and of not trusting God to run your life. Thus an angel anointed and purified the ancient prophet Isaiah's mouth by touching his lips with burning coal, declaring,

"This has touched your lips and now your guilt is

gone, and *your sins are forgiven.*
    Then I heard the Lord say, "Whom shall I send? Who
will be our messenger?"
    I answered, "I will go! Send me!." (Isaiah 6:5-8, italics
mine)

If you're surrendered to Jesus as your Lifeline, with one hand securely in His and the other reaching out, you can enter into the pit of others' suffering as He calls and witness there to His saving power with both word and deed.

Again, Christians are not limited in social justice ministry to one-on-one encounters, but are called to confront the larger societal conditions which perpetrate the suffering recognized in those encounters. God can use governments and systems for His Kingdom purposes—if we cooperate.

I recall one well-known politician who offered "gladly" to share his own lunch with any hungry child. And then, he voted against a school lunch bill that would have fed a million hungry schoolchildren. **This man had not faced the awful depth of his own neediness and surrendered there to Jesus. Therefore, he could not entertain the depth of others' needs, nor exercise his authority to fulfill them.**

FALSELY DIVIDED

In the churches, meanwhile, the enemy has divided us.

"Conservatives" say you don't need legislation, but only a personal relationship with Jesus. Sharing your lunch and carrying Christmas bags of groceries to the poor is enough. "Liberals" say you don't need relationship with Jesus, but only a universal concern for human need and proper legislation to fulfill it.

Yet the God who became one particular person in one particular time and place in order to save all people in all times and places, can only be frustrated by such fragmented views. Like body and spirit, both personal relationship with Jesus and an outstretched arm to the poor are necessary to God's purposes in this broken, beloved world.

Thus, Russian Orthodox Archbishop Krill of Smolensk, in a call for "the moral and spiritual renewal of humanity," declared,

> One should not accept the distorted situation
> where fundamentalists preach personal morality while

ecumenists are left in charge of social morality. To emphasize one at the expense of the other involves a division of essentially indivisible moral standards, thus distorting Christian life and weakening Christian witness.[67]

The aforementioned consultation of charismatics and social activists concluded with a worship at which an Anglican minister's wife from Singapore told a parable about a village that discovered a child was lost:

Each little group went off on its own to search for the child. Then the father of the lost child said, "We must work together. We must form a line and join hands and conduct a sweep of the fields and forests." The group assembled at the base line, joined hands, and moved out together. They found the child, but too late; the child had died. Over the grieving community was heard the mother's lament, "Why didn't we join hands sooner?"[68]

If, as He said, Jesus is among the afflicted, **we can't presume to "bring Jesus to the poor and oppressed." He's already there.** That's why evangelism among the poor and oppressed often begins primarily not with spiritual conversion, but with material service.

We might ask, "If He's there, why doesn't he call in legions of angels to heal the sick, feed the hungry, visit the prisoners, and uplift the poor? What is he waiting for?"

The question, however, is not "What?" but rather, "*Whom* is he waiting for?"

TAKEAWAY

My jogging in the jungle as a Peace Corps Volunteer baffles local villagers, whose daily struggle for life does not allow for "exercise." We don't bring Jesus to those in prison, in poverty, in hospitals, or otherwise in need. He's already there. We must know Jesus therefore, in order to see Him there and be sustained in social justice ministry. As a loving Father, God does not want His children to suffer poverty and oppression.

At what point does material comfort blind us to the suffering in the world? How has it blinded you? Where amid that suffering does God want to open your eyes, give you His heart, and minister His outstretched arm to the needy?

13

The Mirror of Prejudice:

Overcoming Personal & Corporate Racism

> Whoever fears God and does what is right is acceptable to him, no matter what race he belongs to. (Acts 10:35)

A white minister serving a church of color?

"Nobody was more skeptical than I was myself at the beginning," the pastor from an Oldline Reform denomination told me. "In fact, I probably never would've thought to candidate for the position unless people from the congregation itself hadn't approached me. Frankly, I was scared when they did."

Yet, in the several years since this man answered their call, the congregation has grown steadily in caring fellowship, mission outreach, and spiritual maturity.

How did that happen?

Looking over the church's profile, the man sensed several areas where he might serve its needs significantly. "But no matter what its goals, the congregation was still not white," he said. "Over and again, I kept struggling with the question, What right do I have as a white man to exercise any authority among people of color?

"Without a solid answer to that question, it just seemed presumptuous of me even to consider serving that church. I mean, every one of those people had suffered in some way from white racism--their parents and grandparents, too."

He shrugged his shoulders, both puzzled and amazed. "And yet, something felt strangely right about the whole thing." Honoring the congregation's desire and effort to seek him out, he decided not simply to decline graciously, but instead, spent considerable time in prayer and reflection: "I was really forced back to the absolute basics of my faith and sense of ministry."

Finally, he "got a real answer" to his question:

> I realized that by all natural standards, I had absolutely no right to pastor that congregation-- certainly not because being white makes me in any way superior, but neither because being white there would be some kind of example or statement against racism. I also realized I couldn't take that job just because I'm ordained, or have special talents, need a job, or even because people wanted me there.

WHITE POWER, GOD'S POWER

He sighed, smiling thinly.

> I mean, I could go into most white churches and get by on all the tricks of my good breeding and education-- but these people would see through all that in a second. **They've seen enough of white power; what they haven't seen enough of--and really need--is God's power.** That was scary, knowing that all my usual sense of security and power would have to go out the window.

"In fact," he declared, "I realized that the only right I had to enter that pulpit was because God had called me to it, and the only right I'd have to stay would be as a sinner saved by Jesus, trying to bring Him and His saving power to the people there."

To his credit, this pastor realized that the overriding issue for his ministry was not who he is, but rather, who Jesus is. His job, therefore, was not to apologize for the evil past of his own racial heritage--necessary as it might be for him to recognize that and be prepared to do so. Rather, he was called simply to proclaim to whatever congregation God sent him the Good News of their common spiritual heritage: **that Jesus' life, death, and resurrection has saved us from the sin nature in us all, and His Holy Spirit empowers us to accomplish what God has called us to do together.**

That's spiritual ecumenism.

His decision at last to follow that call harkens yet again that of Paul as he went to preach at Corinth: "Your faith, then, does not rest on human wisdom, but on God's power" (I Corinth. 2:5). And again, "For it is not ourselves that we preach; we preach Jesus Christ as Lord, and ourselves as your servants for Jesus' sake" (2 Corinth. 4:5).

Significantly, this pastor's deliberately Christ-centered approach led him and his church to one of the most productive outreach ministries to the poor in his denominational region.

As "the greatest work of the Lord among us," he points to a church "food pantry" for hungry families, many of whom are recent immigrants who don't qualify for state aid. "The idea just came to me," he said, "and I sort of primed the pump by taking my truck a couple of times to get surplus food for a few needy mothers. Now, it's mostly run by lay people and we serve over a hundred families a week."

A church delegation visited their congressperson and other local government representatives to discuss how to alleviate hunger by political means. The pastor invited denominational officials to visit the food pantry and help with packaging dry goods, bagging produce, and other tasks.

"This ministry has been good for all of us in the church," he declared. "When I see some mother with two hungry children standing in line, I swear it's like I see Jesus right there in front of me."

As an old "sixties radical" accustomed to political models of unity, I was astonished, if not embarrassed by the success of this man's ministry among people of color.

Most denominations that minister social justice gained their perspective through the civil rights movement of the sixties and its focus on injustice against African-Americans. In fact, I first began to notice a division among churches when, as a college student in the early 1960's, I realized that virtually all white Christian opposition to racism was coming from the Oldline Reform churches.

In all the "brotherhood" rallies and civil rights demonstrations I attended, I met no Pentecostals or Evangelicals. This surprised me, since the anti-slavery movement in the 1800s had been generated by Evangelicals, and the Pentecostal movement had been sparked by African American Pastor William Seymour in 1906 at the Azusa Street Revival.

RUSH WEEK RACISM

In the early 1960s, I attended a private university in the Southeast, which at that time refused to admit any but white students. I remember during "rush week" hearing members of a fraternity—which like most campus Greek organizations, was founded in the Confederacy--singing in the quad, "There'll never be a n----r Sigma Nu!" In my junior year, the "sit-ins" began, not far from my university, with black students' deliberately sitting in "white only" areas of restaurants, bus depots, and other public facilities.

As a freshman in 1960, I remember when Alabama Governor George Wallace—later wheelchair-bound but remarkably healed spiritually as a firm supporter of African-American causes--visited our campus to speak out for segregation. That evening in the university auditorium, hundreds of white students listened as Wallace promoted white supremacy and racial separation. After his hour-long speech--punctuated by occasional cheers from the audience--the moderator rose to the microphone and invited questions.

A few scattered white arms went up. But before anyone could speak, suddenly from the balcony above and behind us--almost as an invisible choir from on high--a deep, steady, and yes, compassionate chorus of the civil-rights theme song "We Shall Overcome" broke forth and filled the auditorium.

Startled, the crowd of white faces below turned to look where perhaps a hundred black students from a nearby "Negro" college sat with hands joined, swaying and singing above us. A few catcalls went up, but were overcome by the rising crescendo, "Oh, deep in my heart, I do believe, we shall overcome, someday!"

In that moment, perhaps for the first time, I suspect many of us below did believe--in a way we'd never experienced in church.

Though my own parents had never allowed racial epithets at home, breathing the germs of a racist society had infected my soul. Almost fifteen years later--after two years in Nigeria, three years of teaching junior high school in a California Latino *barrio*, and participating in many civil rights advocacy programs--I faced at last my own racism and begged God to deliver me from it (see my chapter, "Battling Racism," in *Fight like a Man*).

In that process, I came to believe that racism plays upon a primal sense of "not belonging" in every one of us, no matter how popular we may be or esteemed by others.

The biblical faith, that is, understands that this world is not our home, that we are "foreigners and refugees on earth" (Heb. 11:13). Insofar as we do not turn to Father God for our true home, we fear this reality and it's associated shame in feeling outside, apart from, and therefore, unacceptable.

DISPLACED SHAME

Most of us don't want to face that "outsider" part of ourselves, and would avoid it by displacing and projecting it onto others, acting out against them our feelings toward that unacceptable part of ourselves.

For example, once whites agree that blacks are "unacceptable," we promote housing discrimination insofar as we don't want to live with the part of ourselves that seems "different" and alienated, and thereby, beckons rejection. Thus efforts to promote exclusiveness, from college fraternities to country clubs—stem from the same root as racism.

Unlike such exclusive social organizations, Christianity makes no attempt to massage our shame by fabricating an "in-crowd" and reassuring those who belong. The Apostle therefore chides his fellow Jews for insisting that relationship with God depends upon keeping laws such as circumcision, and for seeking acceptance and approval from other persons by keeping up such outward appearances:

> Rather, the real Jew (i.e., man of God) is the person
> who is a Jew on the inside, that is, whose heart has been
> circumcised, and this is the work of God's Spirit, not of the
> written law. Such a person receives his praise from God,
> not from man (Rom. 2:29).

Indeed, the world is alienated from its very Creator by the power of sin. Those who choose to alienate themselves from the God who created them thereby forsake their true identity and will look for it instead in the world—that is, to receive their praise from others and not from God. They'll be defined not by their Creator for His purposes, but by popular expectation—and miss their created destiny.

Those who don't face their intrinsic separateness from this world will be consumed by its shame and fabricate social structures to hide it. Ultimately, they'll displace it onto others whom they deem "outcasts." Biblical faith, meanwhile, understands that we're *all* "foreigners and refugees on earth" (Heb. 11:13), and hail rather, from a "heavenly country" (11:16).

When you recognize, confess, and surrender to Jesus your common human alienation from this present world, you're freed from a desperation to "fit into" it. Instead, you can recognize and pursue the destiny for which God created you—"even before the world was made" (Ephes. 1:4).

We were never meant to fit into this world. That's why Jesus came explicitly to call "not respectable people, but outcasts" (Matt. 9:13). Those who feel altogether connected to the human constructs of society, who feel wholly affirmed, a part of, and belonging within those structures—as in most exclusive organizations--simply **will not seek Jesus, because they fancy they have all they need in other people like themselves.**

Certainly, we do not function fully in God's calling as "Lone Rangers" apart from fellowship. Nevertheless, the Church is not the Body of Believers, but the Body of Christ. It's no coincidence that often the first generation of Christian converts were drawn from among those whom the larger society scorned--even the prostitutes and tax collectors.

Outcasts have nothing more to lose in the world's society, and everything to gain in the fellowship of Christ. In that defining sense, outcasts are the seeds of the Church, the genetic code of the cross.

The Igbo people where I lived in Nigeria, for example, considered multiple births to be a curse, and cast off such unwanted newborns into *ofia njo*, or "bad bush," to die. Igbos also marginalized others among them to the *nsu* slave caste. Missionaries often rescued twin and triplet babies from death and befriended *nsu* youngsters, raising them to become mission teachers and priests. These outcasts knew they were dead without Jesus, which is in fact the reality of life in this world—and the next.

Rejected by society, they had none of the world's esteem to lose, and everything to gain by serving Jesus. Indeed, they did so joyfully as they received their newfound status in the Church as God's beloved and respected children. In fact, when the missionaries and Western culture effectively abolished the old traditional lifestyle, these former outcasts became prime candidates for leadership.

Certainly, great joy abounds in the fellowship of believers—not, as some exclusive club, because we're so much better than others, but simply because our no-good-ness has been covered by Jesus and we can therefore get on with our life's purpose by the power of his good-ness.

The world warns: "You're an outsider until you measure up," and promises, "If you strive to perform well—or if you look good trying--you can cover up your inadequacy and fit in." At least, you can scorn groups of others as "bad" and "out," which will make you appear "good" and "in" by comparison.

The Good News in Jesus, however, is this: **You're an outsider, because God created you to transform the world, not to adapt to it.** As Martin Luther King, Jr., declared, Christians are called to be thermostats, not thermometers.

DUMPING SHAME ON OTHERS

Because sin is intrinsic to our human nature, none of us can overcome it by ourselves. The shame of thus not measuring up to God's call is too much for any human heart to bear. That's why Jesus had to come and bear it for us on the cross. If we don't trust Jesus to bear it, however, we either bear it ourselves and burn out unto suicide, or displace it onto others, so we can appear OK by comparison.

Whatever shame we don't give to Jesus, we dump onto others.

Both the intolerant "religiously correct" and the all-tolerant "politically correct" mentalities feed on this shame of inadequacy and breed racism— the former by attempting to cover sin with religious performance, the latter by denying sin altogether. Thus Christianity divorced from the Living Christ--both on the "Left" and the "Right"--becomes an addictive/ compulsive effort to mask sin, rather than an avenue to face it and let God overcome it.

Jesus came not to foster the appearance of goodness, but to expose and save us from the reality of evil--even the sin of racism (see 1 John 3:8).

Give up, therefore, to Jesus. Cry out to Him your longing for acceptance from other people and the shame you feel from not having it, and leave it at the cross. Seek first your identity in Jesus, not in other persons. As you thereby surrender to Him, you allow Holy Spirit to make you God's child and empower you to transform this world "on earth as it is in heaven."

Our human nature, however, won't give up hoping for the world's approval until its false promise of "belonging" is wrested away from us-- perhaps through some deep loss, or simply by the universal, un-attractive and disempowering process of aging. Only then do we begin to realize that the world cannot offer the acceptance and fellowship we long for, and we're set free at last to go to the Source and receive it from God—even in the Body of Christ.

Thus the Apostle declared,

> So then, my brothers, because of God's great mercy to us, I appeal to you: Offer yourselves as a living sacrifice to God, dedicated to his service and pleasing to him. This is the worship you should offer. *Do not conform yourselves to the standards of this world, but let God transform you inwardly by a complete change of your mind.* Then you will be able to know the will of God--what is good and is pleasing to him and is perfect. (Romans 12:1-2 italics mine)

We do not and cannot fit into this world. When we dare to face unto death this fact of life, we no longer need to project our alienated self onto persons of another race. We can cry out our shame and surrender to Jesus, experience the grace of our Father's love, and let God transform us spiritually into brothers and sisters. We can then join together with believers of all races to restore the Kingdom of God to this world.

THE SAME FATHER

I was once asked to minister at a church in Belfast, Ireland—a city torn by generations of Catholic vs. Protestant hatred and violence. In order to expose me to the culture, my Protestant hosts on the afternoon of the conference drove me to the inner city. There, I saw the hateful graffiti slogans on walls, street curbs painted either blue or red to indicate either a Catholic or Protestant block, and armored police tanks patrolling. Stunned, I was moved to both fear and tears.

At one point, as the host pastor was driving, two black taxi cabs drew menacingly alongside us from both sides. "Those are IRA (Irish Republican Army) agents," my host whispered nervously. "Gordon, if they stop us, you must do all the talking!"

Startled, I sat bolt upright. "What? I mean, …p-pardon me?"

"You have an American accent, and they won't do anything to cause an international incident," the pastor explained quickly.

Preparing hastily to smile broadly and shout my best "Howdy, Y'all!," I held my breath as the cab drivers squeezed alongside, looked us over— then as suddenly, turned and drove away.

Lord! I exhaled, my heart pounding. *I came here to preach about knowing you as Father and how you heal the shame of fatherlessness in men. I feel embarrassed; my ministry seems like a frill, a psychological luxury when people—even fellow Christians!-- are so ready to kill each other like this. What am I doing here? How in the world can this message you've given me for men speak to this awful hatred and violence in Belfast?*

Almost at once, I sensed the answer—in a question: "What do you call men who have the same father?"

At last, I understood. When we do not allow Jesus to do what He came to do, namely, restore relationship with the Father, we don't see ourselves as God's sons and daughters. Therefore, we cannot recognize Christians of other races and ethnic groups as our brothers and sisters (see John 1:12,13, Gal. 4:5-7).

Racism and other cultural division is the outward sign of our inward pride in not letting Jesus restore us as children of Father God. **Social division and hierarchy demonstrate that a people do not know God as their Father. Otherwise, they would regard each other as brothers and sisters.**

"Don't we all have the same father?" as the ancient prophet Malachi declared. "Didn't the same God create us all?" (Mal. 2:10).

For persons of color in America, meanwhile, the painful truth of our cosmic alienation intrudes all too readily. African-Americans, for example, don't need to wait until they get divorced, fired, or aged before they realize how fragile and uncertain human acceptance can be. Everyday encounters with the larger, white society--from seeking a job to buying a house to being arrested for a "DWB" (Driving While Black)[69]--can slam the message home.

Early in my faith journey, therefore, I avoided religiously any church which preached exclusivism. For I knew that ultimately I could not measure up perfectly to any such church's standard, and would be rejected there if I didn't join their act.

The Oldline churches, on the other hand, offered me protection against being judged and rejected. As a starving person eats anything without examining it for germs, I longed so badly to be acceptable that I rushed to embrace their ideology of "tolerance and inclusiveness"--without ever questioning whether it was based securely in the person and work of Jesus.

I therefore quoted often in those days the scripture, "So there is no difference between Jews and Gentiles, between slaves and free men, between men and women…" (Gal. 3:28). Christian liberalism, in fact, has long marched under the banner of this text. Yet somehow in those days we conveniently dropped its final words, namely, "you are all one *in union with Christ Jesus.* (italics mine)" We proclaimed oneness in union with everything from ideologies to political parties. But in all our anti-war demonstrations and civil rights rallies, I never heard anyone proclaim our union "with Christ Jesus."

Being thereby cut off from its Source of life has sapped the Christian social justice movement of vitality—even as happened in my own heart.

UNIVERSAL AND PARTICULAR

That scripture, I now know, is no political manifesto, but rather, God's melding of the universal and the particular--His reconciliation, in fact, of liberal and conservative. That is, only in and through and because of Jesus—who has saved us from our self-centered sin-nature and restored us as children of the Father--can we unite according to His will with those of another race ("Jew and Gentile"), social class ("slaves and free"), and gender ("men and women"). Without God's *super*-natural intervention in Jesus, our natural differences define us.

The Bible affirms that "there is no difference" precisely because, as the immediately preceding verses declare, "You were baptized into *union with Christ,* and now you are clothed, so to speak, with the life of Christ himself" (Gal. 3:26,27 italics mine). In going underwater and emerging cleansed, the sacrament of baptism celebrates not only birthing out of the amniotic fluid into the world, but in its drowning symbol, the death of Jesus as the avenue to new life. It proclaims the end of our deadly pride and false securities of the flesh, so we can humbly receive God's love and press on into our common destiny as God's children (see Rom. 6:4).

Economically and socially secure white men, however, imagined that human unity was based not upon God's work, but ours. That is, we fancied that we could love people of color, the poor, and even ambitious women, simply by making a conscious decision to renounce and sever ourselves from our racist, class-ist, sexist heritage. "Bring the war home; kill your parents," as 1960's peace activist Jerry Rubin exhorted.

I tried hard and did my best. Desperately, I attacked everything my parents held dear. I now counter-focused my boyhood compliance, and became as dogmatically anti-male, anti-military, anti-white, and anti-business.

Rebellion was much easier then than now. I remember one freshman college classmate in 1960 who was reprimanded by the university Dean because his hair touched the top of his ears. No need in those charmed days to cut, pierce, or otherwise maim your body; just don't go to the barber. For the son of a Navy officer, attending a "peace rally" was especially effective.

Even then, the real issue was relationship, not ideology—which only served as a foil or cover-up for anger at our parents.

The Oldline social-justice congregations, meanwhile, offered me the opportunity to differentiate from my "conservative" parents without having to become anti-church. Our proud self-image in those times as "tolerant and inclusive," however, was belied by the fact that we could not love our conservative Evangelical and Pentecostal brethren, for we were not troubled by our prejudiced, divisive attitude toward them.

RENOUNCING ANCESTORS

Renouncing your parents and ancestors doesn't overcome racism, division, or any other sin. It just disconnects you from your true self. Only Jesus overcomes sin, as you confess it humbly to him.

I'm puzzled, therefore, by the great controversy over "substitutional repentance," by which I as a white male, for example, am called to ask forgiveness from people of color for my ancestors' racism. I don't deny that my ancestors were racist. But asking forgiveness for someone else's sin strikes me as presumptuous.

Worse, it's dishonest.

You don't eat a fish that lives in a polluted stream, because the pollution gets in the fish itself. Our land has been polluted with racism since the first Europeans arrived and encountered Native Americans.

This is my heritage; I have swum in this stream since birth, and thereby carry its pollution myself. If I want sincerely to confess and ask forgiveness for someone's racism, I don't have to look any further back in history than my own life. I and other white Americans have plenty enough racism to repent of in our own selves, right now, without using our ancestors as a foil.

History is clear. People of color know all too well what my white ancestors did with our racism. What remains to be seen is what I and other white folks will do with our racism today.

It's OK if you want to apologize to me for something your grandparents did to my grandparents. But if you really want to win my trust and give me hope for genuine, lasting change, own up to your own sin against me now, and make amends.

By the time I left college in 1964, racism had increasingly been exposed as evil. Therefore, I was determined to prove I had no racism in me, even though I had never even sat down to a meal with anyone who wasn't white and did in fact entertain racist thoughts. How easily youth is seduced by its worldly strength to run from the truth![70]

I joined the Peace Corps and went to black Africa. There, I studied the language diligently, ate *garri* and *fufu*, drank palm wine, wore *agbada* shirts, and took pains to insure that I was not like the "typical white man," anxious to be separate from the inferior "natives." My righteous personal example, I reasoned, would model for Africans that not all Americans were racists. I confess I savored the pride whenever a Nigerian told me, "You're not like other Europeans."

When my two-year Peace Corps tour ended, I returned home to America ashamed of myself and my hidden racism, which threatened the universalistic self-image I had worked so hard to achieve. I decided that graduate school would be a good re-entry cushion, and discovered there an entire, burgeoning academic discipline to accommodate my fear, called "social science." Through courses in anthropology, communications research, sociology, and the like, I could "study" Third World people objectively, and avoid listening to what they were saying about me.

As a further smokescreen, I tried desperately to immerse myself in the "minority struggle." I lived in a Black neighborhood, dated only Black women, taught at a Latino junior high school, spent one summer working on a civil rights project and another studying Spanish in Mexico. I became righteously indignant as only the guilty can, in seeking thereby to dissociate from the racism in my white heritage.

In short, I tried to mask my own provincial prejudices with a universalistic concern for 'the human family' and hide from my shame behind people of color.

FEARFUL OF TRUTH

Thus fearful of the truth, I could allow people of color an identity only in my own terms--the classic racist view. That is, I saw them only as alienated objects of white oppression, not as fellow human beings with their own demanding, here-and-now daily life. I could talk with persons of color about "those awful racists," but not about enduring human concerns—like getting along with your parents, how your job is going, and similar day-to-day, real-life personal issues.

In effect, I withdrew from true friendship with persons of color, even as I desperately sought it, for fear of inadvertently blurting out some racist comment and blowing my cover. I was forever seeking their favor, to save me from the shame of my racist heritage. If they rejected me, the superstructure of my proud self-image would crumble; I would be swept back into the shameful racist dungeon of my white ancestors.

Insofar as I thereby attributed such saving power to persons of color, I idolized them. An African-American's acceptance translated as delivering me from shame—something only Jesus can do. Certainly, my universalistic performance standards commanded that I love all persons. **But ultimately, you can only fear an idol, whose power to give implies power as well to take away**.

It took years for God to break down my pride enough for me to fall on my knees and confess, "Lord, I've got racism in me--the same racism I've fought so righteously in others--and I can't overcome it, no matter how hard I try." In that moment, when I stopped trying to be righteous and confessed instead my hopelessly unrighteous nature, I felt what the Bible calls "grace," even Father God's heart for me. Secure in that truth and grace, I could name and cast the demon of racism out of me.

Indeed, this experience opened me at last to receive His heart for people of all colors. A deep sadness soon filled me, as if I were feeling God's own sadness for all the years of fear and tension I had brought upon myself by striving to hide my shame. At last, I no longer needed to prove "I'm not a racist, like other white people"—especially my ancestors, whose shared DNA chained me organically to them and presumably, their prejudice.

Until I gave my racism to Jesus, I never knew he could save me from it. But when I thereby gave up the struggle to preserve my proud self-image and trusted God's mercy, I knew at last that I was forgiven.

What's more, I felt empowered against racism in a new way. Confronting my own sin added the essential element of grace to the truth I proclaimed. That balance allowed me to welcome a larger truth and see racism in all of us—yes, even in those of color. Indeed, I realized that **in order to see people of color as human beings, I would need to face their own sinful nature as well as my own.**

Energy formerly consumed in covering up my racism was freed now to seek genuine friendships. Issues of character, not race, could now take precedence in my selection of friends.

"Which white persons are qualified to work for civil rights for blacks?" asks Rev. Gregory Johanson in the *United Methodist Journal*.[71] His answer: "The ones who are the most trustworthy and needed are **the ones who know themselves to be racist in their hearts, and who also have the assurance that God has reconciled their hearts, racism and all.**"

Johanson concludes,

> In the field of ministry we don't need heroes, white knights with egos riding high in the saddle. We need healers, namely those who have an assurance that they have been healed. We need to know that healing doesn't take away our dispositions to destructive hatred, jealousy, or power.

> Rather, it grasps us with the knowledge of a graceful power which provides another more realistic, holistic, holy disposition to choose.... We need those who know that the glory of God is incarnated in the ambiguous,

stumbling community which forms under the cross.

BURNING THE CROSS

Even as Satan is a fallen angel, a counterfeit of the Real, the burning cross is therefore a remarkably apt symbol for the evil Ku Klux Klan.[72] The cross defines absolute brokenness and humility before God, where you give up your own self in order for the love of God to flow into and through you to others. In its racist program, the Klan would burn and destroy such a place, in order to proclaim instead the fantasy of their own strength and worthiness before God.

Yet the Klan has no monopoly on that sin, for I've shared it myself. That is, there are other ways to burn the cross than crudely, on someone else's front lawn. You can destroy the witness of Jesus' death in your own life, and thereby forfeit the boons of His resurrection, simply by denying your own brokenness and striving to prove you're righteous--in this case, to prove you have no prejudice.

That's burning the cross without the trouble of pulling a sheet over your head and setting fires at night.

As I therefore began begging God to "search my heart" (Ps. 139:23,24) and surface any racism in me, I could then recognize it, renounce it and and beg the Father to forgive me for it. Certainly, in a polluted stream, even a cleansed fish remains at risk. After this cleansing prayer, you need to monitor yourself regularly and "take every thought captive and make it obey Christ" (2 Corinth. 10:5).

Eventually, I began to experience a freedom in relationships with persons of color. No longer did I idolize or fear them--not because my defenses were at last secure against the charge of racism, but precisely because I'd given up on defending myself and trusted Jesus to free me from it.

Even better, I knew that if someone accused me of racism, I could go humbly to the cross, where Jesus would receive me. By the power of His Spirit, and by the wisdom of others, I could discern whether what I did or said was in fact racist (see 1 Corinth. 12:10; 14:29). If I were guilty, God could heal me yet more deeply and empower me to make proper amends; if not, I could listen to my accuser without lashing back, and invite Jesus to bring us both into a deeper truth and healing.

Only out of "union with Christ Jesus," therefore, did I begin to experience relaxed, friendly "union" with persons of other races. At times, I confess, I relapse and fear what others of color think of me. Yet I learned a foundational lesson: What my own mighty efforts in travel, reading, language study, inner-city teaching, civil rights work and cross-cultural experience could not do, Jesus did. Helpful as those efforts might have been to raise my awareness, **without Jesus they eventually began to hide my racism instead of expunge it.**

In fact, as long as I clung to a political model of unity, I could only abdicate relationship with Jesus to the "conservatives." That is, I could only fear that in turning to Jesus I would be turning away from men and women of color, like the many racially-prejudiced political conservatives who at the same time often promoted "personal relationship with Jesus" so forcefully.

Yet--wonder of wonders!--precisely in turning to Jesus, I received the freedom I had longed for to relate as a fellow human being to persons of color.

Historically, in fact, the very origins of the Pentecostal movement demonstrate dramatically how its witness and that of social justice ministry interrelate.

Few people realize that God's move to restore and release the Third Person of the Trinity in this present age, was spearheaded by African-American pastor William Seymour. A largely unheralded church hero, in 1906 Seymour proclaimed God's vision sovereignly to unite persons of all colors by the power of His Spirit.

With startling myopia, even the black-edited encyclopedic *The African American Century*,[73] in documenting the lives of 100 black Americans who most significantly "have shaped our country" in the 20th century— including religious leaders from Father Divine to Louis Farrakhan—omits William Seymour. Few examples of the world's blindness to God's work can compare to this disregard for arguably the most pivotal move of God on earth since the book of Acts.

AZUSA STREET SABOTAGED

As a young man in the late 1800's, Seymour felt a strong call from God to work for racial reconciliation.[74] In Houston, he had listened to white Methodist Charles Parham's teaching from a segregated outdoor seat. There, he became convinced, like Parham, that the supernatural gifts of Holy Spirit as portrayed in the Scriptures are genuine and available to all believers, even today. In 1906, Seymour moved to pastor a small congregation in the black community of Los Angeles, where eventually those gifts did indeed break out among the people, from glossalalia to healings.

Word of this marvelous outpouring spread like wildfire—wonder of wonders--without any church-growth program, evangelism crusade, or revival preaching. Soon worshippers of all races, nations, and class came as well, and carried back out to the world what God was doing there.

"The people are all melted together," Seymour noted; "made one lump, one bread, all one body in Christ Jesus. There is no Jew or Gentile, bond or free, in the Azusa Street Mission." In what one writer has called "a contribution from the ghetto to the world," this "Azusa Street Revival" continued daily for three years and became "the fountainhead of a worldwide Pentecostal explosion."

As Quaker Richard Foster notes, "The miracle Seymour had been seeking happened: by the power of the Spirit, a revolutionary new type of Christian community was born." A news story from the time rejoiced that **"The 'color line' was washed away in the blood."** Thus, Foster concludes, "Azusa Street was a supernatural work, a Spirit-empowered work, a charismatic work. God freely chose the insignificant, the unimpressive, the foolish to show forth his glory."

Tragically, the glory of God at Azusa Street was sabotaged by racism--betrayed, in fact, by none other than Seymour's early white mentor. Seeking to extend the revival further among whites, Seymour invited Charles Parham to come to Los Angeles. But Parham, who had "maintained close affinities to the Ku Klux Klan," shocked the joyful worshippers when he stood and condemned the Azusa Street Mission in blatantly racist terms.

With Parham's urging, eventually the white leadership among Seymour's congregation were seduced by Parham's rhetoric and broke away to form their own denomination. "They could live with glossalalia but not with the revolutionary interracial fellowship that Seymour insisted flowed from it," Foster declares. "The movement split irreparably along racial lines."

Here, the supernatural-power dimension of God's revelation split from its essential social justice/compassion component. In effect, **the gifts of the Spirit were divorced from the fruits of the Spirit, thereafter**

ensuring among white leadership the all-too-common phenomenon of spiritual gifting without commensurate character. No doubt this has contributed to the "fall" of many of its more celebrated ministry personalities, and of untold others.

Thankfully, however, God may be disgusted with us, but He is not finished with us. Among the most hopeful recent signs of racial reconciliation has been the 1994 "Memphis Miracle," in which leaders of the major racially-separated Pentecostal denominations repented and re-united in the new, multi-ethnic "Pentecostal Fellowship of North America."

Southern Baptists, the largest evangelical denomination in the country, have followed suit. Formed by a north-south split during the Civil War that led to separate white and black Baptist associations, their 1995 national convocation publicly confessed their sin of racism and asked forgiveness of African-American Baptists. Similarly, Evangelical founder Bill McCartney of Promise Keepers men's ministry declared at its opening 1992 football stadium gathering of 25,000 men that God had told him, "If I (God) don't see men of color there, I'm not showing up."

FORGIVENESS NOT ENOUGH

Yet, even as I celebrate and praise God for such breakthroughs, I learned more recently through a local Pastors' Racial Reconciliation group that asking forgiveness is not enough to overcome the awful legacy of racism among us.

"As a rule, we African-Americans tend to be a forgiving people," as Church of God in Christ pastor David Moore declared. "**When whites come and ask us to forgive them, we do—and they take off feeling great, leaving us to clean up the mess they've left us.**

"White churches might better help us if they refused any longer to tolerate the corrupted form of Christianity that tries to absolve them of the guilt feelings that accompany the contempt they hold for blacks, but never erases the contempt."

It's as if I work hard, save my money, and buy a new car and house. You come along and steal my car and destroy my house. Eventually, you feel guilty, come to me and ask my forgiveness. I forgive you—whereupon you turn and drive away in my car, leaving me homeless.

Most whites, that is, have enjoyed considerable privilege in our racist society, from education, job, and housing preferences to unchallenged self-esteem. Is it not appropriate for us whites now to share with others the booty of our privilege—indeed, to give back what we have stolen from people of color and help them rebuild what we've destroyed?

For example, churches could organize tutoring and scholarship programs. White professionals could offer their skills and expertise. We who have access to economic and political power structures could commit to expanding that access to people of color.

Years ago, before realizing this, I received a letter from an African-American church in Norfolk, Virginia, asking if I might consider coming there to speak at a men's conference. Matter-of-factly, I replied with a form letter and schedule of fees. I never heard back from the church.

After listening to my brothers of color in our pastors' group, I felt convicted. Indeed, I remembered being a high school student during the late 1950's in Princess Anne County, Virginia, which borders Norfolk County. When the federal desegregation order hit Norfolk, somehow local politicians conspired to block it in Princess Anne County. Overnight, our high school nearly doubled in size as white students flocked into our district from integrated Norfolk. I remember the gym was converted into classroom space, and packed out with fleeing students.

When my father joined the Navy as an officer in 1942, enjoying both its privilege and salary, few persons of color were allowed such rank. Similarly, my segregated high school and university had afforded me opportunities denied to persons of color.

Clearly, it's time for me to return what my white ancestral culture has plundered from people of color. As an author, I've offered those of color my gifts in editing any articles or books they might write and connecting them to publishers. I've said I'd speak at their churches for whatever honorarium they might be able to afford, or none.

And yes, I wrote back to the church in Norfolk. I asked forgiveness for not being more relational in my dealings, confessed my unwillingness to trust in the Lord for my finances, and offered to come speak there for whatever they felt they could afford.

TODAY'S PIONEERS

In the summer of 1967, I worked for American Friends Service

Committee on a civil rights project in an all-white suburb of Los Angeles. There, a black civic leader urged us to solicit white business and community leaders to lead in renouncing racial barriers—even as years ago, white baseball commissioner Branch Rickey hired Jackie Robinson and opened the sport to black players. **"We had the Jackie Robinsons for years," he declared; "what we didn't have was the Branch Rickeys."**[75]

The "Branch Rickeys" of today are **the white persons who dare not only to seek forgiveness for their racism, but also to build bridges to active reconstruction.** Humble before God in their own brokenness, they're not afraid to recognize it in others; so deeply assured of God's saving power in Jesus that they don't hesitate to engage someone in need—that is, to exercise whatever power God would bring to fulfill that need, from repentance to job training programs.

Here the Christian witness to social justice becomes essential. If God is calling persons of all races together in surrender to Jesus, we're called to overcome racial injustice in the world Jesus died to save. Fair housing, equal employment and educational opportunity, for example, are surely on God's agenda for us. Even as the powers of the world resist, Christians who work for those goals can trust that the God who delivered His ancient people from slavery in Egypt will uphold them today.

As a young man, I believed that racial harmony is rooted in a philosophical ideal of universalism, that is, not about mutual respect and humble confession of sin, but rather, becoming "color blind" and not acknowledging differences. Today, however, I lean humbly on the confession of Peter to the early Church:

> I now realize that it is true that God treats everyone on the same basis. Whoever fears him and does what is right is acceptable to Him, no matter what race (that person) belongs to. You know the message he sent to the people of Israel, proclaiming the Good News of peace through Jesus Christ, who is Lord of all. (Acts 10: 34-36)

The ancient Church received that message of peace from God, in all its terrifying, glorious potential to shatter our racism and transform us into brothers and sisters.

Dare we "Christ"-ians receive it today, too?

TAKEAWAY

A white pastor called to a congregation of color worries how to exercise authority over those who have been oppressed by white racism—and God shows him. Facing honestly your own prejudices is the avenue to the Father's grace and freedom to minister cross-culturally. Jesus came to make us sons and daughters of Father God, so we can thereby recognize each other as brothers and sisters. True repentance for white racism requires not only asking forgiveness from people of color, but acting to overturn its destructive effects. Have you asked God to reveal your own prejudices, and asked His forgiveness? What can you and your church do to overcome its harmful effects on others?

14

Jesus Is Our Peace:

The Alternative to Warmaking

> (Jesus) came closer to the city, and when he saw
> it, he wept over it, saying, "If only you knew today what
> is needed for peace! But now, you cannot see it!" (Luke
> 19:41,42)

Certainly, no human activity undermines God's call to reconciliation and unity more than war. Thus, in the above poignant scene from Scripture, we see Jesus' heartfelt sorrow for his people--who unto today see all too well the division and destruction necessary for war, but can't see what's necessary for peace.

Here, after ministering powerfully in the Galilean countryside--with all the confirming supernatural manifestations promised later upon Pentecost--Jesus is returning at last to Jerusalem to face death before the powers of the world. Where most of us would either withdraw safely or lash back, Jesus comes weeping, even for the very city that will demand his crucifixion.

Clearly, a man who can walk deliberately into the jaws of death and weep for his executioners is centered in vision and power far greater than human. He's either demented or of God—to paraphrase C.S. Lewis.

He's certainly centered beyond what we could see a generation ago, when the polarization among churches crystallized over the Vietnam

War. That season of peace marches and hardhat clashes prompted much divisive rhetoric either against war or for America—but little reference to the heart of Jesus weeping for our blindness to His peace plan.

INTIMATE BLESSING

In the Beatitudes, Jesus announces a variety of human attitudes that God blesses, from mourning to thirsting after righteousness. Yet none beckons a more intimate blessing than that reserved for "those who work for peace," for indeed, "God will call them his children!" (Matt. 5:3-11). Thus peacemaking, in countering the most divisive form of human activity in war, draws its impetus from the most deeply bonded relationship of parent and child. If only we sixties' radicals who cried, "Bring the war home—kill your parents," could have understood that!

Since God called him "son," we can therefore infer that Jesus Himself worked for peace. Indeed, he was the long-awaited "Prince of Peace" (Isa. 9:6), who would blaze the path of healing and reconciliation in a broken and divided world. As Paul declared, "For *he (Christ) is our peace,* who has made us both one, and has broken down the dividing wall of hostility"— whether between nations or denominations (Ephesians 2:14 italics mine).

In the biblical understanding, peace is therefore not about circumstances. Its Hebrew definition, *shalom,* **is not the mere absence of conflict, but rather, the active presence of God, even in the midst of conflict.** That presence—portrayed clearly on the cross--is Jesus. Hence, the name Jesus transliterated from the Hebrew Y'Shua: "God saves/rescues."

Our ancient Jewish forebears in faith saw the coming of the Messiah as an era of light amid darkness, when the great nations of the world "shall beat their swords into plowshares, and their spears into pruning hooks; nation shall not lift up sword against nation, neither shall they learn war anymore" (Isaiah 2:4).

The ministry of Jesus Christ, therefore, promises to turn tools of death into tools of life, as missiles and guns into farm implements. Certainly, the hungry world today needs this power desperately. Estimates of those who suffer from chronic malnutrition range as high as one quarter of the human race. Yet international expenditures on weapons research and production number in trillions of dollars per year.

Insofar as war co-opts resources in a needy world, peace is clearly

a social justice issue.

"Even a gun never fired kills," as WWII General of the Armies and former President Eisenhower warned of the "military-industrial complex":[76]

> Every gun that is made, every warship launched, every rocket fired signifies in the final sense a theft from those who hunger and are not fed, those who are cold and not clothed.

Similarly, a 1976 Vatican report to the United Nations stated that the arms race "is itself an act of aggression which amounts to a crime, for even when they are not used, by their cost alone armaments kill the poor by causing them to starve."

What's more--contrary to popular myth--the arms race has fueled both unemployment and inflation, our worst economic woes. A generation after WWII, the U.S. Department of Labor issued statistics that $1 billion spent for defense creates 78,000 jobs; the same amount spent for goods and services creates 110,000 jobs. Nurses, bus drivers, clerks and police cost less than missile scientists.

Inflation means too much money in circulation and not enough goods to buy, which drives prices up. Money paid to defense industry workers produces no consumer goods or services, thereby increasing the money in circulation without providing more goods to buy with it. Japan and Germany, whose military expenditures have been mandated after WWII as among the world's lowest, have often had the strongest economies; more people want to buy Hondas and Volkswagens than jet fighters.

Many Americans old enough to remember how WWII jump-started a Depression economy back to life, are startled by these realities. As a pastor in the late 1970s, at the height of the Cold War arms race, I decided to educate my congregation on the harmful economic effects of the arms race. All were surprised when I called upon a local labor union official, who spoke forcefully against the armament industry.

BASIC ASSUMPTIONS

These direct and destructive effects of the arms race proceed from its basic assumptions.

For the warrior of the world, death is king: whoever can kill the most and the fastest, rules. For the people of God, however, the Creator of life is king. Whoever dares struggle for peace—to make room for Jesus in their personal lives and in the larger world--is regarded as God's own child. Instruments of death have no place in the Kingdom of God.

God's purposes for humankind, that is, cannot be accomplished with humanly-made weapons. "It is true that we live in the world," as Paul declared,

> but we do not fight from worldly motives. The weapons we use in our fight are not the world's weapons but God's powerful weapons, which we use to destroy strongholds. We destroy false arguments; we pull down every obstacle that is raised against the knowledge of God; we take every thought captive and make it obey Christ. (2 Corinthians 10:3-5)

Guns and atom bombs, as another has noted, are simply not powerful enough to do the transforming work God has called us to do. You can't bomb someone into the Kingdom of God, nor shoot them into the heart of the Father. Only the self-sacrificing love of Jesus can restore a sinful human heart. Indeed, precisely insofar as we refuse that love of Jesus ourselves, we resort to coercion and violence to change others.

Granted, the threat of destruction can make people think more seriously about spiritual matters, and even change their behavior. In that back-handed sense, the devil becomes a servant of God, insofar as evil drives us into the Father's arms for shelter.

But certainly, like any good dad, Father God does not want His children to be so wounded and destroyed. He wants us to come to Him not via the awful threat of evil, but rather, by the promise of His love and power.

The Father will receive us gladly when we turn to Him in desperate need; a "foxhole Christian" is still a Christian. But surely He is more honored— and pleased--when we come to Him at His initiative and not the enemy's, spurred by thanksgiving and praise instead of fear.

More enduring and fruitful than threatening or coercing a child is therefore earning a child's trust—and thereby, changing his/her heart to *want* to obey. This transformation requires self-sacrificing love—which Father God has modeled for us in His son Jesus.

The enemy of God is the Destroyer. It's so hard to create and grow, so easy to destroy. In an instant, a bomb can crumble years of toil, a bullet can destroy decades of life. Could it be that God's power to create, grow, and restore, so threatens us proud and inadequate human beings that we sponsor wars in order to mock God and proclaim instead our own power, albeit destructive?

As Nazi death camp survivor Elie Wiesel declares in an essay, "The Jew and War,"

> In war, man reverts to primary darkness... War has always been a convenient pretext, invoked so as to abolish all laws and give man license to lie, shame, humiliate, and kill. In its name, man feels free to violate social contracts and divine commandments. He thus turns life into a vast simplification: on the one side the good, who must live; on the other, the wicked, who must die. To wage war successfully, man must assume a god-like stance and wear His mask--to be, like Him, above the law. How could Jewish tradition possibly sanction such an attitude?[77]

War-making therefore tempts us into idolatry. "Woe to those who go down to Egypt for help," as the ancient prophet Isaiah warned, "who rely on horses, who trust in the multitude of their chariots and in the great strength of their horsemen, but do not look to the Holy One of Israel, or seek help from the Lord" (Isaiah 31:1 NIV).

Significantly, when this prophecy was proclaimed, the horse and chariot represented state-of-the-art weaponry--so new and terrifying to the common foot soldier legion that its invention upset the balance of power in the Middle East, much as the atomic bomb has done in our own era. The horse and chariot kindled ancient kings' lust for domination. Here, they exalted, was the weapon which would at last place other nations at their feet!

TO PRE-EMPT GOD

Weapon advances tempt sorely our will to power—that is, to pre-empt God. Just as every nation in time developed its own horse and chariot legion, so the spread of nuclear weapons in our time to even the most fanatic regimes is legitimately feared, from North Korea to Iran. The compulsion to build arms is thereby unmasked as not less war, but more; greater casualties, greater fear, greater unemployment and inflation, **greater willingness to reject the difficult path of prayer and negotiation for the seemingly easier path of threat and destruction.**

As Isaiah proclaimed, those who rely on vast military strength—from horse and chariot to nuclear weapons--are doomed. Instead of relying on the Holy God of Life, they look to a vicious cycle of increasing arms. Yet at the height of the nuclear arms race in 1980, a poll conducted by Connecticut Mutual Life Insurance Company showed that 74 percent of Americans believed it is important for the U.S. to have the strongest military force in the world "no matter what the cost"--and that "the most religious and least educated are most likely to believe this."[78]

Religion, that is, often fosters black-and-white, I'm-OK-you're-not-OK thinking, which undergirds the ally-vs-enemy mentality required for war. Such cowboy diplomacy is unfaithful at best and diabolic at worst in an age when a mere computer signal stands between us and total annihilation. "I call heaven and earth to witness against you this day," God proclaimed to our ancient Hebrew ancestors in faith, "that I have set before you life and death, blessing and curse; therefore, choose life, that you and your descendants may live" (Deut. 30:19).

Clearly, "Blessed are the peacemakers" is a radical notion for our time, when glory and honor and power are given to those who put their trust in vast military strength. As peace activist and Catholic priest Daniel Berrigan noted,

> There is no peace because there are no peacemakers. There are no makers of peace because the making of peace is at least as costly as the making of war--at least as exigent, at least as disruptive, at least as liable to bring disgrace and prison and death in its wake.[79]

The hero in the Kingdom of God, according to the Beatitudes, is not the warmaker, but the peacemaker—indeed, the one with battle scars on his hands and feet from trying to love a world hell-bent to turn from Father God. This may explain why even decorated soldiers who return to civilian life talk so little about the horrors of battle. In their God-created hearts they know they have participated in the manifestly unholy program of God's enemy. They have not only seen its ugly fruit in death and destruction, but bear its scars in their hearts—whether their bodies were wounded or not.

Without a church willing to speak with both truth and grace, often veterans either suppress their shame with compulsive-addictive behaviors or displace it on others, even their families in domestic violence. The character traits required to win battles of the world—as solid defenses, punishing offense, and unquestioned authority--neither value feminine grace nor win the hearts of children. **In a severe irony, the traditional warrior of the world often cannot accommodate the very domestic peace he fights for.**

Great soldiers, that is, do not often make great family men. Witness, for example, the renowned warrior King David and his patently dysfunctional family: one son raped his half-sister, was murdered by another son, who set out with his own army to murder their father David himself.

By its very nature, war destroys. The soldier seeks to destroy his enemy, but in that process, often destroys his own heart as well.

I'm not condemning soldiers. In fact, I pray for them even as I weep for their task. But sane men who have seen real combat fight to end war and its horror, not to glorify it. I share their goal. With this book I fight for—indeed, alongside—such soldiers now and in the future.

In the New Covenant sealed by Jesus, the peacemakers are blessed and called God's own children. But on earth, where the power of God is dismissed and seductive powers of death often go unchallenged, peacemakers are often crucified.

"When men go to war," as Wiesel laments, "God is their first victim." That is, from the very first war between brothers Cain and Abel, war to Jews has "always represented absolute evil and chaos... War is an aberration, a denial of God's name, which is...Peace."[80]

Nevertheless, until Jesus comes again and sin is no more, wars and other destruction will remain a threat to God's purposes. In this broken world, we may need to take up arms at times to defend ourselves. We will need those of good intent, both at home as police and abroad as soldiers, to protect us from those of evil intent. This must be seen as a valid, honorable profession.

We cannot, however, simply pay them to do our dirty work. Local law enforcement agencies exist to maintain an order which protects citizens and their free access to resources and accomplishment. We citizens who put them in harm's way must do our part to make their jobs safer. Christians, in particular, must labor deliberately to cover soldiers and police in prayer. In addition, however, **we must combat the personal brokenness and social injustice which often foster the crime and unrest they're called**

to battle.

As Christians, we have a difficult task: to honor our soldiers and police for protecting us even as we abhor the war and violence they're called to engage. The old adage "War is hell" remains apt. Those who participate in destruction and killing--even to defend innocent citizens, even against an evil enemy--must humbly ask the Creator's forgiveness. Otherwise, their hearts become hardened and they forget what they're fighting for.

NO PRAISE OF WAR

Wiesel's distinction, therefore, is essential: "War? Yes, if there is no alternative," he declares. "But praise of war? Never."[81] Indeed, the Midrash, an historic Jewish biblical commentary, "states it explicitly":

Israel's battles are fought in heaven; it is there that their outcome is determined. Or as the Jerusalem Talmud puts it: each time the people of Israel do to war, the celestial tribunal is in session and decides whether that war will end in victory or defeat. **The warriors' courage, power and military virtues are not determining factors; what is important is their faith in God.**[82]

The true enemy, in fact, lies in the spiritual realm. "For we are not fighting against human beings," as the Apostle Paul put it, "but against the wicked spiritual forces in the heavenly world, the rulers, authorities, and cosmic powers of this dark age" (Ephesians 6:12).

For followers of Jesus, the enemy is never the Germans, the Japanese, the Russians, the Vietcong, the Iraqis, Al Qaeda, or any other fellow creatures of God—even though we must at times defend against them appropriately in this fallen world. Thus, Wiesel notes Jewish teaching that God admonished the earliest Jews not to despise the Egyptians who had held them in slavery for hundreds of years: "Are these (Egyptians) not also my children, the work of my hand?"

A new paradigm emerges from Wiesel's view of war: "It is easy to hate war when one is defeated, but Jews have hated war even when they won. We never seem to hate the enemy; it is war we hate, it is war we consider the enemy."[83] Thus, Israelis cheered and danced in the streets when Egyptian President Anwar Sadat visited Jerusalem in 1976, showering blessings on this historic peacemaker whose people only four years before had been in deadly combat with Israel as for thousands of years previous.

To contemplate war is therefore to entertain the powers of darkness and death and miss the mark set for us by the God of life. To participate in war—no matter how "just"--is a sin to be confessed, not a glory to be celebrated. From God's view, war has no winners; all humanity loses. Just ask the soldiers' families—on either side.

Armistice therefore deserves no pompous ceremony in which the vanquished kneel before the victor. Rather, the lasting peace for which Jesus died requires both victor and vanquished to kneel humbly and penitently before God. There, both must ask forgiveness as His children for having together allied themselves with His enemy by fighting each other.

Parents understand this. Suppose you came upon your own children fighting each other with deadly weapons. How would you feel? What would you say if one child explained, "But I didn't start it!" or, "But I'm right!"? **Would you accept *any* excuse if your children were fighting to kill each other?**

More likely, you would seize their weapons and smash them angrily. That's how God looks upon us human beings—no matter what our race, nationality, or religion.

Hence, the famously abused "Be still, and know I am God" scripture—which, contrary to popular sentiment, is no gentle invitation to withdraw from the world and meditate quietly. Rather, it's a Father's fierce command asserting His authority to stop His beloved children from killing each other:

> Come and see what the Lord has done. See what
> amazing things he has done on earth. He stops wars all
> over the world; he breaks bows, destroys spears, and sets
> shields on fire. "Stop fighting," he says, "and know that I
> am God, supreme among the nations, supreme over all
> the world" (Ps. 46:8-10).

To a world seduced by the powers of darkness into a suicidal arms race, "peace" rests upon a faith in the powers of death, that an enemy will not strike you who perceives your response would return equal harm. This foolishness was unmasked by the early official term "Mutually Assured Destruction" and its appropriate acronym, M.A.D. Indeed, even as Satan seeks to counterfeit God, the spiritual source of this premise "Do unto others as they do unto you" is revealed in its seductive distortion of the Bible's "Golden Rule."

NOT AS THE WORLD

In response to warmakers, the world promises Mutually Assured Destruction. But when combatants from both sides surrender to Him, Jesus promises Mutually Assured Restoration. "Peace is what I leave with you," Jesus proclaimed before returning to heaven. However, he declared, "It is my own peace that I give to you; *I do not give it as the world does*" (John 14:27 italics mine). **The world gives peace as cessation of hostilities via dominion of victor over vanquished. Jesus gives peace as surrender to Himself and His dominion over the powers that would divide and destroy us all.**

"Is a nuclear holocaust inevitable if the arms race is not stopped?" asked Billy Graham during the Cold War.[84] He then answered his question with a prophetic edge that speaks to today's terrorists:

Frankly, the answer is almost certainly yes. Now I know that some people feel human beings are so terrified of a nuclear war that no one would dare start one. I wish I could accept that. But neither history nor the Bible gives much reason for optimism. What guarantee is there that the world will never produce another maniacal dictator like Hitler or Amin?

As a Christian, I take sin seriously, and the Christian should be the first to know that the human heart is deceitful and desperately wicked, as Jeremiah says.

"Why all this protest against war?" demanded one man at a retreat I attended during the height of the Vietnam conflict. "Men have always fought wars since the beginning of time. I've lived through World War II, Korea, and Vietnam myself. What makes you think things will ever change?"

As Christians, we answer: The one thing we take more seriously than human sin is God's truth and grace in Jesus Christ. For indeed, He is our peace. We therefore believe things will change because in Jesus Christ God has intervened in human affairs and conquered the powers of sin and death that generate war. What's more, God has called us to partner with Him in that victory, by confessing our complicity with those powers in our awful compulsion to control others--and by at last allowing Him to control us.

History, in fact, records dramatic examples of God's intervening with peace in response to people's heartfelt cries. Here, the Pentecostal ministry of Holy Spirit intersects graphically with the social justice ministry of peacemaking.

In 2 Chronicles 20, Israel is threatened by a large Edomite army far more powerful than Israel's natural ability to overcome. King Jehosophat calls the nation to humble prayer and fasting, and the choir leads the army of God's people into battle singing "His love is eternal" (Ps. 118). At that, God stirs the enemy troops into a panic and they disperse.

Similarly, when in 1756 French forces prepared to invade England, the English King proclaimed a "day of solemn prayer and fasting." [85] In his journal, John Wesley declared that "the fast day was a glorious day, such as London has scarce seen since the Restoration. Every church in the city was more than full, and a solemn seriousness sat on every face. Surely God heareth prayer, and there will yet be a lengthening of our tranquility." Wesley added in a footnote, "Humility was turned into national rejoicing for the threatened invasion by the French was averted."

Centuries later, when Nazi forces blazed across Europe in 1940 and stood poised to invade England, a small contingent of students at the Bible College of Wales was not only holding fast, but counter-attacking. [86] Led by former coal-miner Rees Howells, these persevering prayer warriors blazed a trail for us today, when hideous acts of religiously motivated terrorism are at last revealing **the truth: not only that we battle a spiritual enemy, but that the world's weapons--from atomic bombs to spy satellites--are not powerful enough to destroy terrorist strongholds.**

When the Nazis came to power in 1936, these determined men and women in Wales began interceding tirelessly for God's victory. As Christians, they were not confused about who the enemy was—and it was neither the nation Germany nor the man Hitler. "In fighting Hitler," Howells declared early in 1940 after war broke out, "we have always said that we were not up against man, but the devil. Mussolini is a man, but Hitler is different. He can tell the day when this 'spirit' came into him."

VISIBLE AND INVISIBLE WAR

By no means does this spiritual view of warfare imply passivity. "We are going up to battle," as Howells declared in May of 1940, when Nazi forces had overrun France. "God gets at the enemy visibly and invisibly, through the army and through us." As Nazi bombing of civilian England intensified later that year in the Battle of Britain, God's spiritual warriors in Wales fought back harder.

"We have bound the devil over and over again," Howells declared. "If you can believe that you have been delivered from hell, why can't you believe that you have been delivered from air raids?...Don't allow those men at the Front to do more than you do here."

On September 8, the Government declared a National Day of Prayer, which prompted a breakthrough for the forces of God. At the Bible College of Wales, the day began with repentance. "Our country has only the outward form of religion," Howells confessed in his journal, "neither cold nor hot, like the church at Laodicea. May God bring the nation back" (see Rev. 3:16).

That afternoon, when he rose to speak at the College chapel, sirens wailed and *Luftwaffe* bombs blasted outside. Yet, as he preached, a profound sense of release fell upon everyone. "What victory!...What joy! What praise!" he recalled. "How the Holy ghost came down this morning in the communion service and told us of His victory!... We had never been in such victory before, carrying on exactly as if there was no war. How could we get victory for the world, unless we had first believed it for ourselves?"

Emboldened, on September 11 the College began to pray that "London would be defended and that the enemy would fail to break through." Indeed, Howells concluded, "Unless God can get hold of this devil and bind him, no man is safe."

That very week, the Lord honored these prayers dramatically. In fact, in his *War Memoirs*, Prime Minister Churchill noted September 15, 1940, as "the culminating date" in the Battle of Britain. Visiting the Royal Air Force Operations Room that afternoon, he stood stunned as wave after wave of *Luftwaffe* bombers and fighters poured over the Channel toward the vastly outnumbered British airmen.

"What other reserves have we?" he asked the Air Marshal anxiously.

"There are none," was the terse reply.

After grave moments of silence, something very strange happened. "It appeared that the enemy was going home," Churchill recalled. "The shifting of the discs on the table showed a continuous eastward movement of German bombers and fighters. No new attack appeared. In another ten minutes, the action was ended."

"Even during the battle," Battle of Britain Air Chief Marshal Lord Dowding declared shortly after the war, "one realized from day to day how much external support was coming in. **At the end of the battle one had the sort of feeling that there had been some special Divine intervention to alter some sequence of events which would otherwise have occurred."**

I do not believe that God wanted or caused tragedies like WWII or the 9/11 terrorist attacks. In this fallen world, the enemy yet lives. In Jesus, however, God has offered us not only an open door to our destiny, but power and protection to fulfill it.

As a good Father, God has respectfully given us free will to walk victoriously through that door with Him. But to mature us in faith and fit us for His larger, Kingdom purposes, God has placed us in community—as families, churches, nations, even citizens of this ever-shrinking planet--bound together for better or worse by His common destiny.

In a world where deceptive powers of darkness and destruction lurk, nations that by consensus choose not God but their own desires and strength will suffer the consequences of disengaging from the Almighty Savior. Even the passionately faithful in that nation will suffer—as Jesus, indeed *with* Jesus—often, like the ancient prophet Jeremiah, precisely in order to bear that suffering to God in behalf of the nation, and intercede for its redemption.

Whether the Prime Ministers and Presidents, Commanders and Air Marshals of the world see it or not—indeed, whether the very people saved see it or not—Father God is present among men and women who humbly confess they have turned away from Him and cry out for His saving power in war.

A century and a half before Hitler, Napoleon ran roughshod over Europe and boasted of his victories. When the Pope warned him to cease his destruction, the French emperor scoffed, "How many divisions does the Pope have?"

Similarly, Christians condemn today's acts of terrorism. And the ageless Enemy at work in the terrorists sneers, "How many explosives and suicidal slaves do the Christians have?"

NOT THE WORLD'S WEAPONS

To this, we affirm clearly and boldly: "We have none. For the weapons we use in our fight are not the world's weapons--which can intimidate and destroy, but cannot free human hearts from fear, overcome our proud separation from God, and draw us back into our created purpose as His sons and daughters. And so, rather, we wield the mighty super-natural weapons of God, poured out through Jesus in His Holy Spirit—even now, to bind you, to reveal and destroy your strongholds!"

In response to the 2001 terrorist attacks, President Bush announced, "We are at war." Christians, however, know that this battle did not explode suddenly on September 11, 2001. Rather, it began long, long ago in the spirit realm and is waged on earth unto today in the hearts of men and women who long to see God's rule restored to earth.

This is the battle Jesus came to win, and through His life, death, and resurrection He has poured out upon us His Spirit to engage us in that victory. As surely as He turned Hitler's bombers away from Britain, the God who split the Red Sea, informed Elijah of the enemy's every planned move (see 2 Kings 6:8-23), and raised His Son from death can locate terrorists and deliver them into the hands of justice.

Even when God has promised victory, however, war often requires suffering and loss until that victory manifests. Many were killed in WWII after D-Day, even though that victory insured Hitler's defeat. Christians know that someday Jesus will return to claim the earth wholly for the Father, but meanwhile, "all of creation groans with pain, like the pain of childbirth" (Rom. 8:22).

Those who groan and grieve faithfully will come to know not only God's comfort, but also the Father's Spirit of anger toward any who would harm His children (see 1 Samuel 11:1-6). Memorial flowers, flag-waving, and candle-lighting, that is, may be necessary to comfort the afflicted, but will not suffice to subdue the afflictor.

When the lamb in us has wept faithfully the tears of God, it's time for the lion in us to roar His victory—that is, together to engage fiercely in deliberate spiritual warfare with Jesus' authority and Holy Spirit's power. Thus, like Reese Howell's WWII prayer battalion, we move from hospital to barracks and discover that the healing Great Physician is none other than the conquering "Commander in Chief of the Lord's Army" (Joshua 5:14).

Evil, flamboyantly destructive, has performed before us. As TV spectators of the 9/11 horrors, we watched helplessly and trembled. But what if the Great Playwright of human destiny would use this drama in order to induct us into God's Story as actors, even warriors, with a definitive role in its outcome? The battle against the evil in terrorism was not finished when our capacity to grieve waned and the 24-hour newscasts once again yielded to commercials and ball games.

After 9/11, the focus of national protection shifted from natural disaster, whose destruction is eventually contained and remedied by human effort, to deliberate acts sponsored by an elusive and aggressive religious community. No natural borders insure protection today for any country. As Howells declared, unless God can get hold of this devil and bind him, none of us is safe.

COMFORTABLE NORM

We're engaged in war, and 9/11 was only an opening salvo. We dare not succumb to the seductive call for "back to normal." Our comfortable norm literally crumbled into a 10-story pile of dust. We must let God use the awful pain of this cataclysm to recall us to His norm, lest in a complacent stupor we leave ourselves yet more vulnerable to future attacks.

Amid the rubble, Americans discovered among us a heart to feel and hands to help. But as Howells' prayer warriors in the Battle of Britain, we must discover among us as well the Spirit to discern and overcome the Evil celebrity who has too long dominated the stage of world attention. Let it not be said of Americans simply that we grieve and rebuild well, but indeed, that we battle and overcome faithfully, wielding every powerful weapon Jesus died to give us.

Mere patriotism, even moral support, will not sustain our political or military leaders in the battle ahead. Today we must ask, as Howells' biographer--Is there anywhere in America or the whole of the world among God's people a committed battalion of intercessors willing to stand in the gap against demonic acts of terrorism?

It's too late to hide either in lukewarm religion as tolerant cowards, or behind inflammatory politics as blind avengers. Like the early Pilgrim settlers who fled the then-repressive Church of England, we Americans seek not vengeance, but freedom for God to fulfill His created purposes in, among, and through us. At times, this victory may require restraint, and at other times, armed conflict. **But its fountainhead is a passionate and committed relationship with the living, acting God revealed in Jesus.**

This relationship and its crown of victory is born in surrender--not to the enemy or worldly circumstance, but to Jesus. Without that surrender to Jesus, ultimately we will comply unwittingly with the enemy and go AWOL.

Submitted to God, we can walk in His victory. Like the prophets of ancient Israel, the Apostle Paul in the early Church, and the Wales intercessors, first we confess that as a nation we have fostered the outward form of religion, but not genuine relationship with God.

Because the destructive consequences are unbearably painful, like Jesus before Jerusalem, we cry. And cry we must, for indeed, this is the Spirit of a loving, grieving Father crying in us for the pain we have tried to bear without Him. Our tears re-open relationship with Him, allowing Him access once again to our hearts.

Facing both the frightful limits of our own power and the limitless mercy of our Father, we then beg God to receive us again and restore His covering. We renounce our natural vision, so hopelessly clouded by our human fears and desires. We ask God to fill us with His Spirit, so we might receive His super-natural vision "to see what God is doing" and join Him in it, neither by vengeful aggression nor ideological passivity.

Until our materialistic Western society can become so humble before God, we can bear no boldness to the world for its redemption.

In a diabolic irony, the same spirit of religion which has historically dominated the European Church is the driving force behind the terrorists and their faith. Naively, European culture has displaced the spirit of religion with its polar opposite spirit of philosophic universalism—which has left Europe spiritually disarmed.

Thus, the militant terrorists' religion spreads largely unchallenged in a militantly secularized Europe. Invested wholly in politically correct ideology, Europeans "are trying to fight religion with non-religion," as one commentator lamented. Without Jesus as a credible third option, Europe may be seduced by this new, religious invasion into retreating to the degradation of its nativistic, racist past.

The primary Christian ministry of peacemaking is neither bombing the enemy nor denouncing armed conflict, but rather, identifying the spiritual root of genuine evil and equipping the world with God's power to overcome it. (see my book *No Small Snakes: A Journey into Spiritual Warfare* for a more complete treatment of this subject).

To that end, we receive at last His blessing, from that ancient warrior in the Spirit, the Apostle Paul:

> I ask the God of our Lord Jesus Christ, the glorious
> Father, to give you the Spirit, who will make you wise
> and reveal God to you, so that you will know Him. I ask
> that your minds may be opened to see His light, so that
> you will know what is the hope to which He has called
> you, how rich are the wonderful blessings He promises
> His people, and how very great is his power at work in
> us who believe. This power working in us is the same
> as the mighty strength which He used when He raised
> Christ from death, and seated Him at His right side in the
> heavenly world. (Ephes. 1:15-20)

TAKEAWAY

No human behavior strikes more deeply against unity than warmaking. The popular myth that war increases jobs and stimulates the economy is a lie from the enemy of God. Guns and bombs are not powerful enough to do the job God has called us to do, but Holy Spirit enables the true peace Jesus bears.

How is the peace Jesus gives "not as the world gives"? Paul declared that Jesus "is our peace." What does it mean for Jesus to be your peace? Have you ever prayed over an argument or disagreement, asking Jesus to lead you into His reconciliation and peace? How could your church learn more about Jesus' ministry of peace? How He might want to use you in that effort?

Healed by God:

From Religion to Relationship

Instead, by speaking the truth in a spirit of love, we must grow up in every way to Christ, who is the head. Under his control all the different parts of the body fit together, and the whole body is held together by every joint with which it is provided. So when each separate part works as it should, the whole body grows and builds itself up through love. (Ephes. 4:15,16)

15

Blackmailed by Shame,

Freed by Grace and Truth

God gave the Law through Moses, but grace and truth came through Jesus Christ. (John 1:17)

We've seen here four major revelations by which Jesus makes Himself known to and through His Church, and how Christians have largely divided ourselves accordingly. We've seen how each faction has often seized upon its own, preferred revelation to discount and disparage that of the others.

Because these divisions stem from authentic, biblically-based revelations of Jesus, however, neither one camp can be wholly misled. Indeed, this dogmatic fragmentation of God's larger purpose, embraced with such scandalous complicity within the entire Body of Christ, can only point to the spiritual enemy of God as its orchestrator.

This is no "devil-made-me-do-it" whitewash to deny our guilt. As Adam and Eve were suckered by the Snake, we've chosen to comply with the enemy and separate from each other. The good news is, if we own our sin, we can choose instead to let God unite us.

Each of the four factions can fall on their faces together before Jesus—perhaps at a national conference for leaders, or even in local congregations. In that humility before Him, we can recognize ourselves and each other as equally guilty accomplices in this debilitating charade. We can beg Jesus to forgive us all for breaking and wounding His Body, ask each other's forgiveness for judging one another, and pledge to respect His witness in us each. We can commit ourselves to pool our giftings toward overcoming our common enemy and together restoring God's Kingdom on earth as it is in heaven.

Only as we thereby renounce enmity and division among ourselves can we overcome it in the world.

Our world today—from religion vs. religion and sect vs. sect to race vs. race and nation vs. nation unto husband vs. wife and parent vs. child--groans desperately for the Body of Christ to lead in this reconciliation. We're all tired of serving the enemy, wasting our energy and resources in accusing and shunning each other.

Humanity, in fact, is forever homesick for Paradise, where Father God reigns. Unto our very Genesis, we long to feast again on the Tree of Life, that is, to surrender to Jesus and be animated by His Spirit. We want to let Father God do the judging and trust Him meanwhile, as Jesus prayed, to keep us safe even as He makes us one.

ENEMY STRATEGY

When we surrender to Jesus as the source of our common identity, the Father fulfills His Son's prayer and makes us one. That is, we thereby engage His Spirit's vision and power so deeply that we forget about our petty squabbles. Indeed, we see the enemy's strategy to divide and destroy the Body of Christ, so evil can proceed not only unhindered, but in fact, with our help. Penitently, hopefully, we can covenant together no longer to surrender to the Accuser, but rather, to Jesus.

Secure in that vision, we can now return at last to Francis MacNutt's pivotal question in Chapter One, namely, What is that "something in us that wants to narrow things down and block ourselves off"—which thereby fuels the crippling division today in the Body of Christ?

Our spiritual enemy's goal is to separate us from God, leaving us vulnerable to deception, division, and destruction. The Snake accomplished that in the Garden by misrepresenting God. The resulting gap between us and God may properly be called sin, that is, a natural propensity to distrust God and thereby miss His mark or plan for us.

How did sin become embedded so irrevocably into our human nature?

Even as Adam and Eve covered themselves with fig leaves after eating from the Tree of Knowledge, missing God's mark stirs shame. It's a bowling-ball-in-your-gut conviction not simply that I've *done* something wrong, but that by nature I *am* something wrong. Its immeasurable power over the human heart lies in its threat, "You can't measure up, and when others find out, they'll banish you forever into outer darkness!"

It's true that in our sinful human nature, we *are* something wrong. We don't measure up to God's standard. What's more, we can't (see Rom. 7:18). The shame from that inability is therefore intrinsic to humanity. From a biblical perspective, in fact, shame precedes and prompts sin; indeed, Adam and Eve fell to sin only after the Snake stirred shame by intimating that they were inferior to God (see Gen. 3:1-5).

Even as Jesus came to overturn the consequences of sin, therefore, His deliverance and healing focus on overcoming shame. To do that, He had to bear our shame Himself, on the cross, so we could thereafter go unburdened to the Father, know His blessing of son/daughtership, be filled with His Spirit and thereby, receive power to measure up to His calling.

Jesus therefore came not to promote religion, but to promote the Father (see John 14). Specifically, He demonstrated on the cross that, even though our sin nature turns us away from the Father in shame, God still loves us and will do anything to overcome that gap between us. To prove it, He has not only sacrificed Jesus to blaze the trail back to Him, but indeed, poured out His Holy Spirit to empower us to get there—that is, to do in and through us what we can't do for ourselves.

That's called "grace."

Moses came to tell us what to do; Jesus came to show us Who does it.

If you're wondering, I'll give you a clue: it's not you.

Until you trust your Father enough to discover that, you'll struggle, strive, and work to cover your shame and prove you're OK. Eventually, you'll either crumble under the weight of your fruitless efforts—from depression to compulsive-addictive behaviors, unto suicide itself—or displace it shame-less-ly onto others, as in racism, sexism, or denominationalism.

Indeed, if our natural human talent and energy could measure us up to God, why did Jesus have to suffer on the cross? We could simply try harder and have saved Him all that pain. Rather, the Father wants us to surrender to Him, to cry out that we can't make ourselves acceptable, and trust His grace to do that. But instead--even as the Snake misrepresented

God as a vengeful egotist (see Gen. 3:1-5)--we hide fearfully from Him, like Adam and Eve.

Since our common Genesis, all division in this world stems from the enemy's efforts thereby to separate us from God and from each other. **It grows from the natural human impulse to hide the shame of our inadequacy, which arises when we distrust the Father's heart for us and fear His punishment.**

The impulse to cover your shame is therefore the primary indication of separation from God, for it belies His saving act in Jesus.

NO CONDEMNATION

When we realize that we can't overcome the shame of our innate "un-measure-up-able-ness," we become frantic to cover it up. Distrusting the Father, we dismiss His saving work in Jesus and try to measure up ourselves. The Good News is that the Father has already sent Jesus not merely to cover our shame, but to remove it altogether on the cross. "There is no condemnation now for *those who live in union with Christ Jesus*," as Paul proclaimed (Rom. 8:1, italics mine).

The enemy, however, wants to make sure we do *not* live in union with Christ Jesus, to divide and weaken His Body via fear of condemnation. Clearly, religious posing offers the most acceptable covering, as its veneer of holiness makes you appear righteous and therefore, beyond reproach.

Lacking the substance of righteousness, we thereby fabricate its appearance. The Apostle Paul decried this mere "outward form of religion," (2 Tim. 3:5) even as Jesus scorned the Pharisees. In fact, such performance-oriented religion only hardens your heart and separates you from others for fear they'll discover your inadequacy.

Sooner or later, that is, you discover that you can't make yourself OK, that you can't achieve all the goals and standards God has said are true and best for you. In desperation, you judge others to divert attention from your shame. You contrive a relative dignity by dumping your "not OK" shame onto others, as, "You're not OK. So that makes me OK, because I'm not you."

Thus, we divide.

Shame thrives in darkness, in cover-up—and thereby, serves as diabolic manna from the Prince of Darkness, even the father of Lies.

"The Gospel tells us...what is of paramount importance," as radio personality Garrison Keillor counters: "To lead an honest life. To be able to walk anywhere without fear, without self-consciousness, and **without worry that your lies will be discovered.**"[87]

Here, at last, we have flushed out our prey, the root culprit that fuels not only religious sectarianism--found in virtually every organized religion--but indeed, all humanly-contrived division and factions.

It is shame.

BLACKMAILED SINCE CREATION

Since Creation itself, our common enemy has blackmailed humanity with shame, threatening to reveal our sin nature if we dare to bond with one another and serve God openly. Jesus, meanwhile, has removed our shame on the cross and paved the way with His grace and truth to unite us in our common destiny.

In the Beginning, that is, Adam separated from God when the Snake played upon his inability to measure up. The Tree of the Knowledge of Good and Evil promised falsely to bridge the gap between Adam's weakness and God's power, and thereby, eliminate the shame which Adam's lesser knowledge stirred in him. Inasmuch as what divides us from God thereby defines the very source of division itself, **all human division arises from this common impulse to hide our shame.**

After eating from the Tree of Knowledge, Adam and Eve are catapulted beyond their innocent childlike trust into the tempting draw of Good and Evil. Having fallen to evil, they now experience both the knowledge of sin and the desire to be good, with its subsequent compulsion to please God—*whose love they already enjoyed.*

That new polarizing awareness does not allow them to trust and rest in the Father. Instead, the desire to please God stirs a fear of His judgment and punishment—a recipe for self-deception and pretension.

Hence, the performance-oriented dimension of religion.

The Tree of the Knowledge of Good and Evil is religion. It not only sponsored our exit from Paradise, but short-circuits our return unto today. Jesus is the Tree of Life, who overcomes the power of sin and death and thereby enables God's Kingdom to be restored on earth as it is in heaven. In that sense, religion tries to bring us to heaven; Jesus brings heaven to us.

The legacy of Adam's shame, meanwhile, is not mere disobedience, but the awful knowing that you're flatly incapable of obeying. Thereby cut off from God—knowing the good thing to do but unable to do it, fearing inevitable judgment and punishment with no advocate--Adam panics. "Who will rescue me from this body that is taking me to death?" as Paul agonized (Rom. 7:24).

At this pivotal point, Adam could've trusted Father God and openly confessed his sinful act. But instead, he bows to shame and tries to hide it: "I was afraid and hid from you, because I was naked" (Gen. 3:10).

The rest is history.

This shame-inspired impulse to distrust the Father's grace and hide from the truth terrorizes humanity and truncates an individual's destiny. It does the same to the divided Body of Christ today.

Indeed, from Genesis to Revelation, from its inception to its resolution, life on earth is framed by the threat of and deliverance from shame. Thus, the New Covenant promises end-time deliverance from its debilitating condemnation: "Yes, my children," John exhorts the Jesus-believers, "remain in union with him, so that when he appears we may be full of courage and *need not hide in shame from him on the Day he comes* (1 John 2:28 italics mine).

Here at last, John clearly identifies shame as "that something which wants to narrow things down and block ourselves off."

REAL AND SAFE

Shame beckons the root sensation not only of disappointing Dad and Mom, but indeed, of never being able to please Definitive Authority and thereby escape condemnation and punishment. "I don't measure up, and never will," portrays the crime, sentencing you to a vicious cycle of forever striving and failing—which stirs shame, which stirs yet more striving.

Shame, therefore, is born out of Adam's fear that you can't be both real and safe with the Father. Naturally, this fear often germinates in a childhood fear of your earthly parents. It manifests as you hide not only from God, but from other people as well, never daring to reveal your inadequacies.

Thus, division.

Patently unable to bear the eternal weight of such shame, we need a Savior. Indeed, we need the One who can bear it for us, and thereby, deliver us into the grace of receiving unconditional love from God, the "parent who is immortal, not mortal" (1 Peter 1:23). That's why Jesus came, and why he had to bear our "stripes" on the cross (Isaiah 53:1-6).

Even as Adam was kicked out of the Garden, the fruitless effort to hide the truth of your inadequacy and bear its shame consumes you and sabotages your destiny. When all your energies focus on avoiding an enemy, that is, you have no energy or vision left to focus on discerning and fulfilling God's call in your life (see Ephes. 2:8-10).

The enemy thereby begins to command your responses, and in that sense, to define you. "I'm no good," you can only conclude, and therefore, "I'm not worthy to be loved, nor capable of accomplishing anything worthwhile."

Hell could aptly be described as "the state of trying to bear your shame." It's living a lie, forever sandbagging against the rising tide of truth--an eternally exhausting distraction from your holy destiny. It cuts you off from the One sent explicitly to bear your shame and thereby free you in spite of it to pursue that destiny.

GRACE AND DIS-GRACE

Another word for shame is dis-grace. Its polar opposite, therefore, is grace. Thus, Paul agonizes over his dis-grace-ful dilemma, "even though the desire to do good is in me, I am not able to do it" (Rom. 7:18).

When sooner or later, like Paul, you realize you can't bear your shame, two voices contend for your heart.

The enemy of God is evil but not stupid. He starts with the truth, in order to sucker you into the later lie, always based on a distorted image of God. "You don't measure up to God's standard," he whispers. "What's more, you can't. Since we all know *the Father will punish and turn away from you when inevitably you disobey*, don't dare go to Him.

"You can't rid yourself of shame, but you can do the next best thing and cover it, like Adam's fig leaf, by pretending you measure up to God. You can deny your inadequacy, look good, and bear its shame inside you.

"If that's too hard, we can always make others bear your shame by displacing it onto them. We'll find people to belittle—maybe another race, gender, or denomination--so you'll feel better compared to them. If none of that works, just drink this, eat that, check out this pornographic website, smoke that, and/or sit in front of the TV for hours until you forget all about it. After all, you're just trying to be righteous, so you deserve a little reward!"

Significantly, Jesus also begins with the truth—but uses it instead to draw you to Himself and set you free from shame. "It's true you don't measure up," Jesus says. "And it's true that you can't. **That's why the Father sent me.**

"Stop trying to do it right and start being real. Come to me, fall on your face and cry out your shame, and I'll bear it. I'll welcome you just as you are, pour my Holy Spirit into you, and adopt you into God's beloved family (see Rom. 8:14-16). Then, together, we'll go to Father God to receive His blessing of son/daughtership, and His Spirit will empower you to do it right" (see Ezek. 36:26,27).

In attempting to bear your shame, you can only repress it below consciousness and eventually, disconnect from your honest feelings—which sabotages trusting relationship with Father God and breeds performance religion. If you're not helped to re-connect with your heart, depression beckons, and the ultimate depression of vitality itself in suicide.

To "depress" the brake pedal means to press it down. When a person tells me "I'm depressed," the first question I ask is, "What are you depressing?" That is, "What unacceptable feeling are you pressing down below conscious level in an effort to avoid the shame of facing it?" Certainly, clinical depression has a chemical dimension which may need to be addressed, but no medication can eliminate your shame. That's Jesus' job.

EXTERNAL HELP

When we can no longer hold down shameful feelings, we often enlist external "help" to do so. Thus, addictive behaviors--from drugs and alcohol to compulsive sex and overeating--are all designed to distract from shame and numb its accompanying fear of punishment.

Addictions counterfeit the ministry of Jesus by promising to overcome your shame. Unable to satisfy the true and underlying deficiency that fuels shame, addictions prey upon our distrust and fear of being naked before God. In thereby distorting God's image as a shaming punisher, their source is revealed as the enemy of God. Addictions indicate graphically that shame stirs sin.

From this perspective, the ultimate addiction is religion, that is, a system of beliefs and practices designed to earn your Father's approval and thereby save yourself from shame. It's the ultimate seduction: from "principles of godly manhood" and "steps to biblical womanhood" to "marks of a spiritual champion" and a host of "sacrifices" in energy and resources "serving the Lord."

What's missing here is simply what's essential, namely, not performance and sacrifice, but rather, "a broken and contrite heart" surrendered to Jesus and confessing your absolute need for Him to serve you (see Ps. 51:17, Matt. 9:13).

Eventually, an alcoholic becomes seized by the lie and cannot will him/herself to stop drinking. In that sense, centuries of division in the Church reflect not simply a temporary misunderstanding, but rather, a spirit of addiction in the Body of Christ. Indeed, even as alcoholism destroys the alcoholic's home and destiny, so religious addiction destroys a church family and sabotages its calling.

God is therefore not satisfied with temporary, substitutionary offerings, but rather, wants the real thing, namely, your entire being. "Offer yourselves as a living sacrifice, dedicated to his service and pleasing to him," as Paul urged (Rom. 12:1,2). On the cross, God has modeled the way by yielding Himself to us. **He saves us by offering not a substance or achievement to cover our shame, but rather, His own self to remove it.**

We remember and appropriate this reality in the sacrament of communion.

Religion, after all, focuses on God, the greatest of powers, who created the standards and therefore, to whom we must ultimately measure up. By its very nature, religion promises Absolute Truth and its Unassailable Righteousness--the ultimate refuge from shame, the place we're literally dying to be.

In our human hearts, we know the awful punishment we deserve for turning away from God. What our human hearts don't know, what the enemy is hell-bent to efface, and what Jesus has come to demonstrate, is the grace of the Father—and His heart not to destroy but to save us from our sin and restore us to our created purpose. "For God did not send his Son into the world to be its judge, but to be its savior," as John declared (John 3:17).

Often, God uses the brokenness of this world and its pain to surface the shameful truth of our inadequacy, otherwise hidden by our efforts to appear in control. From divorce and parenting failures to illness and death, such awe-ful grace cracks your hard shell of pride, in order that the seed of your destiny can at last germinate (see John 12:24).

Death to the shell means life to the seed. Until we drop our defenses and get real with each other--that is, become "naked but not ashamed" (Gen. 2:25)--we remain divided and can't grow together into God's purposes for us.

If you're real, God can make you right. But if you're right, the Enemy of God will make you real. When all your material resources for hiding are exhausted and the pain bears down, you either surrender to the darkness, accept its condemnation, and withdraw from life, or you surrender to Jesus and discover the grace of "full life in union with Him" (Col. 2:10).

The Good News is not that you have to be right, but that you get to be real. That's the promise of grace.

If your eyes have been used to darkness, the light hurts. But plants do not grow in darkness. As you learn to trust the Father's grace amid the onslaught of life's pain and brokenness, you adjust to the light of His truth, and learn not to fear but to welcome it as the avenue to freedom (see John 8:32). In that annealing fire, you surrender to God's purposes, beg Him to root out your lies, and shape you at last for His calling (see 2 Corinth. 1:1-5).

Thus, He promises to take away "your stubborn heart of stone and give you a heart of flesh" (Ezekiel 36:26NIV).

CREATURES OF SURRENDER

It's simple, but not easy. If our self-centered human nature yielded so readily to God, Jesus would never have needed to suffer our shame for us on the cross.

Resurrection, that is, requires crucifixion, even as being born again requires death to the self. Those who understand this enough to surrender their own agendas discover that we human beings are creatures of surrender. It's organic, hard-wired into us. The question is not whether we will surrender, but rather, to whom or to what? Either we surrender to the God who saves us through His grace and truth, or we surrender to the gods we make and burn out sacrificing to cover the shame and lies they require.

God's antidote for shame is grace, that is, not just mercy, but blessing—not just forgiving our individual sins, but pouring out His Spirit to overcome our sinful nature and empower our destiny.

Apart from God's grace, when we realize we can't perform, we lose hope. "I don't deserve it," we despair; "therefore, I can never have it." **We're more impressed by our unworthiness than by God's grace.** Therefore, we either try to mask our sin and convince ourselves that we *do* deserve God's blessing, or we make our own gods, from sports teams and movie stars to pastors and denominations, and fabricate a counterfeit grace-by-association: "I'm OK because my church preaches correct doctrine, my ball team wins, my favorite musician is popular, etc."

Jesus, meanwhile, is not about what we deserve, but about what the Father gives. If you want to demand, "Father, give me what I deserve," let me first put some distance between us. I don't want to get toasted by the lightning.

In the theater of religion, the script calls for correct performance, and therefore values obedience over trust. It sounds so holy; what could possibly be more righteous than trying to do what God wants?

Just this: letting God do what we need.

Religion focuses on me and what I do, thereby re-enforcing my sense of control and saving me from the awful risk of trusting God. "If I do it right, I get the blessing; if I don't, I pay." It's me-centered, cash-and-carry spirituality, tailor made for "modern," self-reliant men and women.

Sadly, churches today are filled with people trying to do God's will--who have never confessed they can't. Until we confess what we can't do, we'll never experience what God can do. This humility is the first step in allowing Him to unite His Church.

In the theater of God's Kingdom, that is, the script calls first and foremost for surrender to the Father. Jesus is not about what I do but rather, what the Father does. "I can do nothing on my own authority," Jesus Himself declared; "I judge only as God tells me" (John 5:30). Thus, He tells His disciples then as now, "You can do nothing (that bears fruit for God's Kingdom) without me" (John 15:5).

This means you have to trust that God will love you even when you can't do it right, that indeed, when you finally confess the shame of your inadequacy, God will not only embrace you as a true son/daughter, but His Spirit will empower you to do it right (see Ezek. 36:26,27).

That's grace.

As another has said, religion is our reaching to God; Jesus is God's reaching to us.

We all want to please the Father by doing what He says, to "measure up" to His standard, and so by implication, be counted among His beloved. If the Father's favor depends upon our obeying a written law, our efforts determine who's in and who's out.

But if it's literally impossible to obey the law, if none of us sin-addicted human beings can do what God has shown us leads to life, then we're doomed. There's literally no way in this world we can expunge our shame and save ourselves. "Who will save me from this body that is taking me to death?" as Paul cried out (Rom. 7:24).

If you don't surrender in this state to God, you surrender to the world and must wait until its brokenness intrudes—as through divorce, severe illness, or other painful loss--convincingly enough for you at last to confess the truth: "I'm dying and can't save myself."

Then, at last, you're exposed and vulnerable, like an infant. You're ready to be born again—indeed, to embrace Paul's conclusion, "Thanks be to God, who (saves us) through our Lord Jesus Christ" (Rom. 7:25).

BOUNDARIES FOR PROTECTION

Like the Snake in Paradise, however, shame is poised to strike when you're most vulnerable, with his patented "distortion-of-God" defense: "God sets those standards just because He's a tight-fisted Father who doesn't want you to have any pleasure."

In fact, He's a loving Father who sets boundaries like freeway lane hashmarks, in order to protect His children from accident and pain and guide them into their destiny. Our fear of shame, however, has led all of us to trust the Snake and not the Father.

The classic "liberal" response to shame is simply to change what God wants, by twisting or eliminating the Scriptures to accommodate our inadequacy. "God commanded those behaviors thousands of years ago only because folks then weren't as educated and sophisticated as we are today," goes the argument.

Such universalists promote grace at the expense of truth. **They proclaim "tolerance" and "inclusiveness," with little truth by which to distinguish harmful from helpful action.** This mindset is dangerous because it cannot accommodate the reality of evil. Furthermore, it promotes an unbalanced, and therefore, false femininity, in which by scorning truth men are discounted and women are exalted. Goddess worship is beckoned here.

The classic "conservative" defense to shame, on the other hand, is to inflate our own performance rating and make it appear that we actually *are* doing what God wants--unlike those sinners over there. "If the rest of you proclaimed the truth and worked as hard as us at being good," goes this argument, "you'd be as righteous as we are."

Such religion-ists promote truth at the expense of grace. **They proclaim standards of "biblical morality" and exclusiveness, with little grace by which a merciful God overcomes our deadly sin and causes us to act faithfully.** This mindset is dangerous because it often becomes obsessed with evil, focusing exclusively on shame, sin, and punishment.

Furthermore, it promotes an unbalanced, and therefore false masculinity, in which by excluding grace, women are discounted and men are exalted. Harsh and punitive war-gods are beckoned here.

LIBERAL/CONSERVATIVE FARCE

While liberals focus on "who's in" and conservatives focus on "who's out," nobody focuses on Jesus. Both pretenses provoke division as each preempts God and presumes to define righteousness. The Tree of Knowledge hosts this farce.

"The religious fundamentalists and the secular fundamentalists make the same mistake," as another has put it. "They separate truth from freedom. For Osama bin Laden, freedom must be sacrificed for the sake of truth. For our secular fundamentalists, any claims of truth must be abandoned in the interest of freedom."[88]

Jesus is not about morality, as "conservatives" often claim, by which they're in and others are out. But neither is He about ideology, as "liberals" counter, by which everybody's in and nobody's out.

Rather, Jesus is about reality. His ministry among us today through His Spirit focuses on rescuing the Father's beloved children in a dangerously fallen world and empowering our destiny. He's struggling to unmask the shame that has blinded us not only to our hopeless condition, but to the Father' saving hand.

As any parent of a teenager knows, this is no easy task.

Jesus defines relationship with the living God, Who loves us as a good

Father and therefore wants the best for us. **His Law is designed not to deprive us of pleasure, but to save us from pain.**

The Scriptures are God's gift to us, as the Manufacturer's Manual that reveal how the world has been designed, and accordingly, how we function best in it. When God says, "Don't do that," He speaks not, as the Snake charged, as a totalitarian egomaniac who wants to boost His inflated image at our cost. Rather, he pleads as a loving dad, who wants to save His children from harm for their created purpose.

That's the marriage of grace and truth—which can only be celebrated by those who know both the reality of evil and the Father's heart to deliver us from it.

Similarly, parents might tell their children, "The Law of Gravity says that in this world, unsupported things fall. I love you so much, so please don't step off that high tree branch, or you'll get hurt."[89]That's neither condemnation nor tolerance, but simply speaking the truth of harmful consequences, with the caring grace to warn and save. It's how God breaks down the walls we erect between ourselves to cover our shame.

Children who grow up in homes where it's not safe to be real and express themselves openly, do not experience authority as a caring effort to save them from harm. Instead, they learn through punishment to fear authority and shut down their hearts. Later, as adults, they seek refuge from the risks of relationship in ideology--whether "politically correct" or "religiously correct."

Jesus did not come to determine who's correct, but to save those who know they're hopelessly incorrect.

The Old Covenant commandments and Law grow from the Tree of Knowledge, not the Tree of Life. **The path to unity therefore begins not with obeying the Law, but with trusting the Father.** As Paul exhorted,

> For Christ himself has brought us peace by making Jews and Gentiles one people. With his own body he broke down the wall that separated them and kept them enemies. He abolished the Jewish Law with its commandments and rules, in order to create out of the two races one new people in union with himself, in this way making peace. (Ephes. 2:14-15)

The "Law with its commandments and rules" is the Tree of the Knowledge of Good and Evil—the very fountainhead of division as it co-opts relationship with the Father, fortifies shame, and promotes division.

Most of us, meanwhile, have been wounded in our closest relationships, often by family members. We thereby try to control others in order not to be hurt by them. The great problem for human nature, however, is that in a loving relationship you can't control or coerce other people. Even God gave us freewill to turn away from Him, and in that sense, released control over us.

NEW COVENANT TRUTH

Here, therefore, lies the great New Covenant truth that our human nature is incapable of grasping: Jesus is not Moses. He comes to us bearing not the Law, but the Father's heart. **Jesus does not command us to control our lives, but rather, invites us to trust God's control.**

Until we're broken enough to risk trusting God, we say "No" to His invitation—or at least, "No, thank you," if we're religious.

Confident that we can control ourselves just fine, we ask instead, "What aspect of God's will can I attempt to fulfill with the greatest chance of appearing successful, and therefore, righteous?" The rub, of course, is that building God's Kingdom requires many tasks, and others will do some of those things better than you--thereby exposing your inadequacy and deepening your shame.

Human nature's "solution" is to declare that your thing is the one and only right thing—that in fact, all the others are at best insignificant, and at worst--when they threaten to expose your deficiency—diabolic. Thus, for example, among some social-justice Reformers, the sacraments are discarded altogether; among some Evangelicals, the Pentecostal gifts of Holy Spirit are regarded as demonic.

The most *di-abolic* act is that which separates us from God, thus leaving us vulnerable to destructive powers. Our natural human ability, that is, cannot discern and overcome the powers of evil. Out of love for him, God therefore told Adam not to eat from the Tree of the Knowledge of Good and Evil--as if to say, "You can't handle this. It will open you to pride and deception far beyond your ability to control, and thereby, mislead you unto destruction."

The Snake however, tells Adam what our flesh thrills to hear: that we are wholly capable of good, and God's kill-joy commands are just a power trip, designed to make God look great at our expense (see Genesis 3:5). The Snake thereby sows the seeds of division between us and God by distorting the character of God and playing upon our inadequacies and shame.

Thus, shame breeds sin.

OBEDIENCE OR TRUST?

Religion says that sin is about disobeying God. To overcome sin, therefore, you must pull up your moral bootstraps and obey. Jesus, however, has come because our sin-nature makes us incapable of obeying God.

Thus, religion leaves us between a rock and a hard place.

The Snake "rescued" Adam and Eve from this dilemma by charging that God is a self-centered tyrant who demands obedience to shore up his otherwise flimsy self-esteem. This deceit fosters a counterfeit salvation in grasping after religion to cover your shame, instead of surrendering to Jesus.

God, however, is a loving Father who calls us in Jesus to trust Him in order to be saved from the world's evil for our created destiny. **From this New Covenant view, sin is not about disobedience, but rather, eating from the Tree of Knowledge--which leaves humanity at the world's mercy unto division and death.**

Any loving parent understands this essential distinction.

Suppose you tell your child to wear a helmet when riding a bike. The other kids scoff, "Your parents just don't want you to have the freedom they have!" So your child disobeys you and pedals away with no helmet—then falls and cracks a skull on the sidewalk. As your child lies there bleeding and crying, how do you respond?

Angrily, as the voice of religion: "You disobeyed me! I'm going to punish you severely for that!"?

Or compassionately, as the voice of the Father: "Oh, my child! Let me carry you to the hospital!"?

The extent to which you affirm either of these responses indicates the extent to which you're invested either in religion or in the Father. A father who seeks vindication for himself above his child's welfare has disconnected from "the Father from whom all fatherhood in heaven and on earth receives its true name" (Ephes. 3:14 NIV footnote).

Too often, we're afraid God is an exacting, punishing Parent who will destroy us for not measuring up. We don't trust the Father loves us, so we don't trust that what He tells us to do is for our own good. "So then, love has not been made perfect in anyone who is afraid," as John put it, "because fear has to do with punishment" (1 John 4:18).

Insofar as I refuse to accept the grace of God in Jesus, I'm hostage to shame, unaware that both my wrong-doing and my wrong-being have been covered on the cross. I don't know that I'm loved, valued, and empowered to fulfill my unique calling in this world. Therefore, I cannot love, value, and empower others in their calling. Their giftings threaten me, instead of beckoning my own gifts to join with theirs in God's common purpose for us both (see 1 Corinth. 12:12-31).

Welcome to the broken Body of Christ.

Fear of shame is the genesis of pride, and the preface to a fall—unless you fall helplessly into the arms of the Father.

When we're all on our faces humbly begging God to "search my heart," that is, we may trust Holy Spirit will come and "lead you into all truth" (Psalm 139:23-24; John 15:13). We will not then rise divided. As all in the Body honor Jesus' call to be born again, to celebrate His victory in the Eucharist, to receive the baptism of Holy Spirit, and to go forth in His power to heal this broken world, the cry of our self-centered flesh fades.

NO STANDARDS

On the cross, God proclaimed, "Both sin and shame are real and must be faced. But I send my son to set you free from both, so you can fulfill the purpose for which I created you." In the late 1960's, a brave, new Boomer generation upended this reality. Fleeing the judgment and shame of their parents' religion--fearing truth and desperate for grace--they proclaimed instead, "Let there be no standards!"

This new dispensation counterfeited God's New Covenant to "abolish the Law with its commandments," and replaced them not with Jesus, but rather, with humanly generated "tolerance" and "inclusiveness."

Amid such adolescent escapism, where no good or evil can be measured beyond your own perception, danger goes unrecognized. No one can hold another person accountable to any standard, not even to warn against harmful consequences. Sin cannot be acknowledged, and therefore, its destructive effects cannot be overcome.

From this view, to speak truth is to cause shame; only grace is permissible. The way to overcome your shame and appear righteous is therefore not to hurt anyone else or suggest any fault. Righteousness lies in not "oppressing" others—a goal which can be achieved by simply pulling the covers over your head in the morning, or indeed, by similar escape via drugs.

True righteousness, however, is not about what you don't do, nor even about what others have done to you, but rather, what God has done for you in Jesus. Thus, to my generation of "flower children" desperate to escape the pain of a shame-based upbringing, life's highest goal became not to hurt anyone else.

It's a good thing surgeons don't share that goal.

VIRTUAL RIGHTEOUSNESS

Under this new, politically-correct dispensation, to exercise a specific gift, calling, and thereby, commensurate authority, is branded as "exclusive" and "intolerant." Righteousness--the ticket out of shame—becomes relative, and is conferred by default upon those treated "unjustly."

A culture which regards all truth as relative can only proclaim a virtual righteousness in being treated unjustly by others.

You're justified, that is, by being treated unjustly; becoming an innocent victim confers righteousness and frees you from shame. If I can feel treated unjustly, I can feel righteous with respect to those who mistreat me.

And what child does not feel treated unjustly by his or her parents?

Hence, an entire generation of affluent white youth sought to escape our innate human shame by embalming ourselves in adolescence.

To achieve righteousness in this mindset, you must cause others to oppress you, or otherwise reject you unjustly. You can't harm others, of course, since that would warrant their rejecting you. But you must challenge the culture sharply enough to make others in authority over-react, in order to expose their shameful "intolerance." Thereby, you become by contrast a "righteous" victim.

In the early sixties, for example, we discovered that just letting your hair grow could stir such offense in "the establishment"--a.k.a., Mom and

Dad. Clearly, it's safer for insecure youth to fabricate an oppression with "outrageous" lifestyle choices. That way, you don't have to risk genuine failure and incur your own unrighteousness. In portraying yourself as a victim, your righteousness is ensured. You never have to face your shame—and you never experience the saving power of God to fulfill His call.

BOUNDARIES OF ACCEPTANCE

This bogus deliverance, however, gets harder as every generation pushes back the boundaries of rejection. Now that long hair is commonly accepted, you need to dye it purple and spike it technicolored in order to be judged. Patched bell-bottoms no longer do the job; now, you have to cut your skin permanently with offensive tattoos and puncture your nose, ears, lips, tongue, and eyebrows. The ultimate limit is already here in punk songs urging suicide and rap music about beating women.

It's just not that hard. We don't need either to cover our shame with high self-achievements or preclude it with low victim-hood. When we all fall humbly on our faces before Jesus, in truth He will show us our sin, and in grace give us what we need to overcome its effects.

Our shame-saturated culture cries out for this ministry of freedom—which God has entrusted to His Church.

The broken Body of Christ today therefore reflects our unwillingness to trust God, bring the full truth of our sin to Jesus, and rely upon Him to overcome its shame with grace. Every division in the Church today can be traced back to those who decided, "We're right, and in order to stay pure in our right-ness, we must dissociate from others--who by definition, are wrong."

The "conservative" legalists, that is, fear grace. They have forgotten that self-control is a fruit of the Spirit (Gal. 5:23), gained not by punishing sin but rather, by trusting God's grace and surrendering your sin to Jesus.

The "liberal" universalists, on the other hand, fear truth. They have forgotten that love and peace are fruits of the Spirit (Gal. 5:22), gained not by denying sin, but by facing the truth of your sin and surrendering it to Jesus.

As another has said, grace without truth becomes sentimentality; truth without grace becomes cruelty.

We need each other.

And therefore, we need Jesus, who mediates the essential balance of grace and truth that precludes shame and draws us together to save not only ourselves, but a dying world.

Shame, therefore, is born out of Adam's fear that you can't be both real and safe with the Father. Naturally, this fear often germinates in a childhood fear of your earthly parents. It manifests as you hide not only from God, but from other people as well, never daring to reveal your inadequacies.

Thus, division.

Today, our distrust of God and efforts to hide our shame have paved a boulevard of division into the Body of Christ, rendering it not only divided, but worse, irrelevant. As children, the Boomer generation suffered truth without grace, and rebelled to rear a generation in grace without truth. Neither generation can now confess either the truth of its human sin-nature or Father God's grace in Jesus to overcome it.

With no apparent avenues to overcome its shame, the younger generation today faces an alarming despair. More often than their parents, they're real enough to know they don't measure up, but like their parents, don't know what to do with the shame that generates. And so they try to cover it with drugs and alcohol, pornography, impersonal sex, media entertainment, virtual online relationships, and other diversions.

As children, many youth today experienced division unto emotional death in their parents' divorce. Many have feasted on material prosperity yet remain starved for love and significance. Many outside the social mainstream are mired in poverty and see little hope for change.

None, however, can tolerate the divisive religious games which Christians insist on playing while their world falls deeper into alienation and destruction. **That's why youth dismiss church: not because they're so immature but because the Church is so immature.** They want desperately to get real and overcome shame, but too often in the Church they see people who are using religion to avoid facing it.

If shame fuels division and Jesus bore our shame on the cross, then His Body is commissioned not to accommodate but rather, to overcome the shame in this world. To do this, we must begin at home, not just in our churches but in our own hearts.

"The greatest persecution of the Church doesn't come from enemies on the outside," as Pope Benedict XVI declared, "but is born from the sin within the Church."[90] Similarly, Elie Wiesel declares that "man's true victory is not contingent on an enemy's defeat. Man's true victory is always over himself."[91]

The battle we face, from external terrorists to internal sin, is manifestly spiritual, and the ultimate victory belongs to Jesus. Our enemy may well be evil, and our doctrine correct. **But as long as Christians ourselves keep striving to do it right when we've never trusted our Father enough to confess we can't, the spirit of religion will divide us from one another and sabotage our efforts to battle its shame and alienation in others.**

The very Story of Jesus' coming—from dirty manger and nondescript shepherds to Mary's conceiving apart from her husband--proclaims that our faith is not about doing it right, but about being real before God. When Jesus is born in your heart, that is, you can go to your Father just as you are, broken and needy, like a child.

You don't have to burn yourself out any more trying to hide your shame from not measuring up to some standard, no matter how "biblical," "moral," or "tolerant." You can trust your Father and cry out, like Paul. "even though the desire to do good is in me, I am not able to do it!" (Rom. 7:18). You can fall at Jesus' feet, and give it all to Him.

"Hit bottom and cry your eyes out," as James put it (James 4:9TMB).

From this genuinely humble foundation, you can learn again to surrender and trust. You can go restored and open before your Father—like an excited child on Christmas morning, ready to receive the gifts you need to let Him do it right. (see Luke 11:9-13).

ACHIEVING OR RECEIVING?

Yes, God has a plan for each of us in His Church. But to walk it out we must be equipped. Thus, when the very first disciples were energized by Jesus' resurrection and chafing to rush out and tell the world, the Risen Lord urged,

> Do not leave Jerusalem, but wait for the gift I told you about, the gift my Father promised. John baptized with water, but in a few days you will be baptized with the Holy Spirit...You will be filled with power, and you will be witnesses for me...to the ends of the earth. (Acts 1:4,5,8)

Jesus is not about what we do for God, but what God has done for us (see 1 John 4:10). His plan for us and for His Church therefore grows not out of *achieving,* but *receiving.* Thus, when the deceptive and destructive powers of the world have broken us open enough to confess at last we can't save ourselves, the Father pours His Spirit into us through that wound.

That's how He makes us into His sons and daughters (see Rom. 8:15-16), animated no longer by our misguided natural desires, but rather, by His supernatural power to save us for our created destiny (see I Peter 1:23; John 1:13; John 3:6). Becoming a "real Jew"--that is, a true man or woman of God--is therefore "the work of God's Spirit, not of the written Law" (Romans 2:28-29).

It's a good thing. Because all my life I've tried, really hard, and I just can't come up with enough discipline, talent, energy, and perseverance to overcome the thoughts and behaviors that God has clearly warned will sabotage my destiny.

As a young man, in fact, I went to church regularly and never once heard a sermon about grace nor experienced it in my own life. Diligently, desperately, I tried to model religion and do it right.

It didn't work. Striving to cover my shame only heightened the fear that my faults would be discovered and punished.

Two thousand years ago, the Apostle Paul reminded the church at Ephesus that "we are not fighting against human beings, but against the wicked spiritual forces in the heavenly world" (Ephes. 6:12). In today's post-9/11 world, Christians must recognize that we are fighting neither against those of another faith nor other denomination in which Christians meet Jesus differently from our way.

Our common enemy is the spirit of religion, of which the 9/11 perpetrators were but a manifestation—even as the Pharisees who engineered Jesus' death and the crippling division which would destroy His Body unto today.

Shame fuels that spirit. The religion in which that shame metastasizes seduces us from facing our sin and impels us instead to displace it onto others. Such religion denies the saving work of Jesus, and in that profound sense, serves the enemy of God.

Jesus, that is, has overcome our shame on the cross so we can become fit vessels for His Spirit to transform this world on earth as it is in heaven. He calls us even now to let Him do that in our personal lives and, indeed, in His Church.

If we refuse Him, we not only abandon the world Jesus died to save, but we become accomplices with its Destroyer. **If, however, we receive the Father's truth and grace in Jesus, we can minister it not only to one another, but to this fallen world--and thereby, become His partners in its salvation.**

Some years ago, I was enjoying lunch with an African pastor friend in a Los Angeles cafe, and the conversation turned to division in the Church around the world. At one point, we both declared vehemently that the world's brokenness cries out for a model of Christian unity.

Suddenly, a booming voice broke in.

"Would you gentlemen please tell me," snapped a large man turning to face us from the booth beside, eyes blazing, "why is the Church so split into denominations instead of being one and together, the way God wants it?"

Startled, my friend and I drew back as the man glared at us. "I guess because we're all still sinners," I offered, shrugging my shoulders helplessly, "--hopelessly proud and scared to get real."

Clearly poised to attack if we defended the Church, the man was thrown off balance by my reply. "Well, I guess so!" he huffed with face-saving indignity, and returned with a vengeance to his burger.

Even as we continued our conversation in hushed tones, my friend and I were startled by how widely shared is our dismay over the division among churches today. Clearly, this was not just a theological issue reserved for clergy elite. The man in the café booth beside us was furious. Very likely, he'd been badly wounded personally by this division in the Body, and none of the apparent perpetrators had listened to his hurt with compassion.

How many others in our world today, like my coffee shop inquisitor, are longing for healing only the Body of Christ can provide, yet fear to embrace so broken a Body itself?

Frankly, I must raise my own hand here.

SETTLE QUICKLY

I had not then, nor do I now have, any desire to condemn the Body of Christ--nor to defend it against wounded and sincerely disillusioned

Believers. The world harbors plenty enough condemnation toward the Church. And indeed, when you're accused of a genuine sin, to defend yourself is like struggling in the quicksand; you just go down faster. As Jesus urged, the more quickly you "settle your dispute" with your accuser "on the way to court" by owning up to your sin, the more quickly you can experience God's grace, and get on with His plan for your life (Matt. 5:25).

I'm not anti-church. I am now and have always been an active church member. I'm anti-religion, which has infected the Body of Christ with its crippling shame and performance orientation.

Jesus did not come to start yet another religion, but to preempt religion altogether. I'm therefore cautious of any belief system which allows that we can measure up to God's call apart from wholesale surrender to Jesus and hospitality to Holy Spirit--not because it's incorrect, but because it's inadequate to heal the fundamental brokenness of life on this planet.

I'm not advocating cookie-cutter churches which all reflect the same full commitment to every way of meeting Jesus. I want to see churches surrendered to Jesus—deeply enough to discern and pursue His ordained gifting for themselves, to appreciate and learn from His other giftings in other churches. "Christ is like a single body that has many parts," as Paul declared; "it is still one body, even though it is made up of different parts" (1 Corinth. 12:12).

I'm not anti-Christianity. I bless a faith which preserves the story of God's activity, reveals His character, empowers us to recognize and overcome destructive behavior, and mediates God's power to deliver us from evil into our ordained destiny.

I'm not saying here that we shouldn't try to meet the standard Father God has set for us. I'm saying not only that we must meet God's standard, but that we can't—indeed, that until we confess this truth, fall on our faces before Jesus, and receive His Spirit, our efforts only ensconce the lie and insure our Fall yet again.

Meanwhile, even as the Pharisees engineered Jesus' death, the shame-based spirit of religion is killing the Body of Christ today.

It's time to heal His Body. It's time for Christians to fight together against the common enemy of humankind and that enemy's deception in our very midst. It's time to confess the truth of our divisive sin, surrender its shame to the Father's grace, and experience together His family embrace.

That simple process paves the way for God to enter not only His

Church, but the world through it.

God's antidote to religion is neither secularism nor piety. It's Jesus. Victory in the battle at hand today therefore requires the fullest possible manifestation of His presence and power. Can we Christians therefore welcome Jesus among us all in being born again, in the sacrament, in the baptism of the Holy Spirit, and in social justice ministries?

A broken and dying world awaits our answer.

TAKEAWAY

The awful gap between what God calls us to do and what we're humanly able to do fills with shame. The root/Genesis of all human division lies in our natural human impulse, as Adam, to hide our shame, often behind religious posturing, instead of surrendering it to God. Unable to make ourselves OK, we can only fabricate a dignity by displacing our shame onto others and believing "You're not OK, so that means I'm OK by comparison." Thus, we divide. On the cross, Jesus has invited us to exchange the illusion of our control for the reality of God's power.

Where in your life is Jesus calling you to confess you can't control someone or some situation? What would it take for you to surrender it all to Him? Has your church cast shame onto another church or denomination because they're different from you? Who would dare lead your church to repent of that and in fact learn from those other churches?

Epilog

Rise and Jog

Some years ago, while jogging one evening around my regular neighborhood circuit, I began to tire and noted an approaching side-street cutoff that would put me back home in a hot shower straightaway. "Lord," I complained out loud, "do I have to run the whole way tonight?"

"No." Clear and matter-of-fact, the simple word entered my mind.

Sighing in relief, I bypassed confirmation and turned toward the shortcut corner with a self-satisfied smile. After a few strides, I was drawn up abruptly by three added words:

"You get to."

Startled, I slowed my pace. Sighing again—this time in dismay—I tossed out a prayer of thanks. As I re-focused dutifully on the full-circuit path, I flashed on a plate of lima beans and a boyhood voice admonishing, "The starving people in the world would be happy to eat that!"

Right.

A year later found me sitting on an orthopedist's table with a badly aching right knee. The bottom line: either no-guarantees surgery or no more jogging. Whether by faith or fear—it's a fine line sometimes—I chose to throw away my running shoes. Tough call for an old Peace Corps Volunteer who began running on Nigerian bush paths in canvas Keds.

After five years of surrendering, praying, stationary-cycling, and fast-walking, I began to sense it might be OK to jog again. One day, I asked the Father about it and heard no words—but a bright sensation of openness filled me.

Haleluia! sprang forth in my spirit—followed immediately by a pause.

Was that the Father's green light, or just my own magical thinking?

I waited several weeks with no pain, sought out prayer partners, and the sense persisted. Hesitantly, almost secretively, I began shopping for new running shoes. With a glance over my shoulder, I bought a pair that fit well and hid them in the back of my closet.

And then, one bright and crisp February afternoon, I knelt beside a dirt path near home and laced up my new jogging shoes. Standing slowly, I rocked tentatively from one foot to the other.

No pain.

OK, Father, I whispered, *let's go.*

And then, I was stepping ahead, then walking, now faster, loping gingerly, and with a deep breath, lifting my knees at last and the wind patting me on the back and the tall bush leaves high-fiving me alongside and the tree branches hailing me in the breeze and my arms raised in praise and my voice crying out *Haleluia to the Living God! My Father, my Savior, King of Kings and Lord of Lords!*

I was jogging again!

What a Daddy I got!

Can I have another helping of lima beans—please?

BLESSING OF FREEDOM

This story is not about the rewards of striving harder. Plenty of injured people have suffered and worked more than me, yet never been restored. I don't know why the Father healed me; I only know that my own restoration has led me to pray harder and with greater faith for those He hasn't.

Rather, this story is about the blessing of freedom God has given us in Jesus. It's about our true and gracious Father, Who "wanted us to enter into the celebration of his lavish gift-giving by the hand of his beloved Son" (Ephes. 1:6TMB) —and the Father of Lies, who steals the joy in those gifts by distorting them rather as obligations, duties, and religious tasks.

This seductive spirit urges Christians to believe "You must meet Jesus in a particular way or you're not a real Christian"—and implies not-so-incidentally, "That particular way is mine."

Certainly, any avenue to meeting Jesus should be verified by Scripture. But within biblical boundaries, several avenues are clearly validated, each of which contributes to a fuller experience of God.

Who wouldn't want that?

The answer: **Those who use religion to cover their shame.** For these truncated souls, faith is about who's a real Christian; for those who long to be saved from sin and fulfill their destiny, however, it's about who's the real God.

For the latter, the issue was settled when Jesus declared that he did not come for those who are well, "but only those who are sick" (Matt. 9:12,13). Those who fancy that they're well—who, in the language of Alcoholics Anonymous, hide their brokenness behind addictive "denial"—will see only that portion of life which their myopic, shame-colored lens allows them. Those who know they're sick unto death, on the other hand, will cry out for Jesus to deliver them from their shame, and thereby experience the freedom and resurrection power of His grace (see Ephes. 1:15-20).

Religion is about what you must do in order to be acceptable to God; Jesus is about what Father God has done to make you acceptable to Him. When churches distrust the Father's work in Jesus, we foster a competitive, zero-sum religion--like jealous siblings for whom Dad has only so much time and love, and if you get yours, I lose mine.

It's the Father of Lies' blueprint for division and destruction.

Father God, meanwhile, knows that your greatest desire is for Him and wants to fulfill it in ongoing relationship with Himself. That's why He sent Jesus. **Those who want the fullness of that relationship will embrace Jesus fully. Those who fear Jesus and the truth He bears, however, will tailor His image to fit their own.**

WE GET TO

Evangelicals, for example, may require others to cite the date and time when they were born again. Anyone who lives in this broken world, however, will sooner or later run out of natural resources—if only on their deathbed--and face that the path he or she has chosen to live leads to a dead end. When you finally realize that hiding your sinful nature and need to be saved from it only consumes you, who wouldn't want a new life, complete with the power to restore you to your intended destiny, even unto heaven?

We don't have to be born again.

We get to.

Likewise, some Sacramentalists insist, "True Christians must take communion." But when you realize that the blood of Jesus makes the power of death pass over you, no matter how grievous your sin or painful your predicament—who wouldn't want that?

When the brokenness of this sin-sick world infects you, whether through illness, loss, family strife, financial problems, or however your life is missing God's mark—**who wouldn't want a transfusion of Jesus' blood and the substance of His life in yours?**

We don't have to take the sacrament.

We get to.

In the Pentecostal tradition, some have vowed, "You must speak in tongues, or you're not a real Christian." In the Trinity, however, Jesus is one with Father God and Holy Spirit. If Jesus is in your heart, then Holy Spirit with this, His supernatural gift, is also within you, awaiting only your desire to open it.

When you don't know how to pray, when your natural human intelligence and sensitivity have brought you to a dead end, when the Enemy is closing in and you have no idea what to do, you can break out in *super*-natural prayer that circumvents your human limitation and takes you right to your Almighty Father's heart.

We don't have to speak in tongues.

We get to.

Similarly, some Oldine social justice advocates maintain that "You must serve the poor and oppressed" in order to follow Jesus. But those who have faced unto death the oppression of their own sinful nature know the abject poverty of their own natural resources to overcome it. If you let Jesus deliver you from that oppression, you want to share the boons of His freedom. You're not threatened by the plight of others, but are motivated to do something about it—because you've seen Jesus do something about it in your own life.

Having received the compassionate heart of the Father in your own journey of healing, you're strengthened, encouraged, and uplifted by the privilege of giving to others what the Father has so graciously given to you. "He helps us in all our troubles," as the Apostle Paul declared, "so that we are able to help others who have all kinds of troubles, using the same help that we ourselves have received from God" (2 Cor. 1:4).

We don't have to serve the poor and oppressed.

We get to.

Yes, I can hear the protest—not only in my readers' hearts, but in my own. "But Scripture says you must...," "But the Church has always held that...," "But the Spirit told me...," "But justice requires..." I respect such misgivings, but do not bow to them.

It's truth—but not grace. In fact, it's good—but not the best.

It's Moses, but not Jesus (see John 1:17).

It's eating from the Tree of Knowledge, not the Tree of Life.

Truth is embraced and effective when it's balanced with grace. To function as the Body of Christ, therefore, we must let our judgments yield to God's promise: Release at the Cross your need to be right and face your need to get real. Confess your sinful nature and any act which manifests it, ask Him to forgive you for displacing its shame onto others, and give Him a chance to show you what He can do—not only through you in others, but through others in you.

If your distrust of God and fear of losing control compels you to fortify your own "revelation corner," I have some advice: Hunker down and keep struggling to be right as long as you can. But when at last you realize you can't do what needs most to be done in your life--when you're literally fed up from gorging yourself at the Tree of Knowledge—savor the Tree of Life.

Give up to Jesus and fall into your Father's arms. Rest, and let His Spirit lead and empower you (see Hebrews 4). Trust that God has created you for a task and will—in His timing—reveal that and provide what you need to fulfill it.

Under New Testament grace, that is, God's commandments become promises, as Argentine pastor/author Juan Carlos Ortiz has noted. When we listen to Jesus, we no longer hear a Lawmaker's threat: "Thou shalt not do this or you die," but rather, a Father's promise: "Doing that will harm you badly, and your human willpower is not sufficient to stop yourself from doing it. Please, surrender to me. Let me put my Spirit within you, and I promise you—you won't do it." (see Ezek. 36:27; Philip. 2:13; Ephes. 3:20).

That's eating from the Tree of Life.

COUNTERFEIT FRUIT

Ah, "but will the Son of Man find faith on earth when He comes?"

as Jesus wondered in dismay (Luke 18:8). No doubt, He'll find plenty of religion: people striving to cover their shame by trying harder, to reap blessings by "applying biblical principles" and to gain God's favor by being good and doing it right.

Very likely, He'll find Christians fabricating the fruit of the Spirit with dramatic "love," happy-face "joy," tolerant "peace," simmering "patience," overweening "kindness," wimpy "goodness," name-it-claim-it "faithfulness," self-righteous "humility," and teeth-gritting "self control" (Galat. 5:22).

If anything blasphemes the Holy Spirit, it's working like this to counterfeit His fruits.

God does not need us to fulfill His promises for Him or manufacture the fruit of His Spirit. Indeed, we can't. **That's why the Father sent Jesus: not as a courtesy to save us the effort, but to free His children from the deadly grip of this sin-infected world so He could do in us what we can't do for ourselves.**

The truth is, we're dead without Jesus.

The grace is, the sooner we realize and confess that, the sooner we become born again, infused with His body and blood, able to receive His Spirit, and ready to minister His justice to a needy and oppressed world.

"Answer this question," as Paul challenges an earlier generation of Christians—even as our own today:

> Does the God who lavishly provides you with his own presence, his Holy Spirit, working things in your lives you could never do for yourselves, does he do these things because of your strenuous moral striving or because you trust him to do them in you? (Gal. 3: 5 TMB).

For those who don't know the answer, here's a clue: A woman I know was utterly drained and exhausted as a new mother by nighttime feedings and baby-care demands. Night after sleepless night, she cried out to Jesus to provide what her baby needed from her. Years later, after watching her infant grow up into a bright and engaging youth, she shakes her head in wonder. "It was so hard," she says, brushing away a tear, "but you know, I miss it, and would do it all over again in a minute."

I wonder: How would our lives be different if we dared to trust these words of Jesus:

> Are you tired? Worn out? Burned out on religion?
> Come to me. Get away with me and you'll recover your

life. I'll show you how to take a real rest. Walk with me and work with me—watch how I do it. Learn the unforced rhythms of grace. I won't lay anything heavy or ill-fitting on you. Keep company with me and you'll learn how to live freely and lightly. (Matt 11:27-30TMB).

All I know is this: I once was tired, but now I'm free.

I don't have to eat from the Tree of Life.

I get to.

TAKEAWAY

Father God sets boundaries on your behavior in order to protect you, not to punish you. Shame crushes your heart, blinds you to Father God's grace, and pre-empts His love with religious duties and "shoulds." Grace means not that we *must* meet Jesus in the four ways described, but that we *get to*.

Where in your life are you doing something out of duty when in fact, it's a privilege? What new gift from among the four Christian traditions would you especially like to try or have?

Notes

Introduction

1   Thomas Paine, *Common Sense* (New York: Meridian Books, 1984), 24.

2   Francis MacNutt, A Christian Manifesto, www.christianhealingmin.org, 2006, p. 1,2

3   Harvey Cox, *Many Mansions* (Boston: Beacon Press, 1988), 4.

Chapter One: Are You A Christian

4   Charles Albert Tindley, "I'll Overcome Someday," in *Songs of Zion* (Nashville, Tennessee: Abingdon Press, 1981), 25.

5   Harvey Cox, ibid., 8-9.

6   Ibid., 9.

7   Ernest Falardeau, "Spiritual Ecumenism," *New Covenant* magazine, 1/86, 13-14.

Chapter Two: A Platypus Christian

8   Cornish R. Rogers, "Black Church Experience," (Letter to the editor) *The Christian Century*, 9/19-26/90, p.851.

9   The late healing prayer pioneer Agnes Sanford said this, but I do not remember where.

10   At Mt. Soledad Prestbyerian Church, San Diego, CA.

Chapter Three: From Blah to Aha!

11   quoted in Stephen E. Strang, "A Call for Cooperation," *Charisma* Magazine, 9/85, 8.

12   John Dart, "Baptist Professor Absolved of 'Heresy' by Evangelical Panel," *Los Angeles Times*, 12/14/85, B6.

13   Jim Wallis, Editor, *Peacemakers* (San Francisco: Harper & Row, 1983), 4-5

14   Billy Graham, "A Change of Heart," *Sojourners* Magazine, 9/79, 13-14.

15   *Time* Magazine, 1989.

16   Richard Lovelace, "Is There Hope for the WCC?" *Charisma* Magazine, 9/85, 21.

17   C. Peter Wagner, *Spiritual Power and Church Growth* (Altamonte Springs, Florida: Strang Publishing, 1986).

18   Robert C. Girard, *Brethren, Hang Loose* (Grand Rapids, Michigan: Zondervan, 1972), 112.

19   Gayle D. Erwin, *The Jesus Style* (Palm Springs, California: Ronald N. Haynes Publishers, Inc., 1983), 181-3.

Chapter Four: A Time to Die, A Time to Be Born--Again

20   Paul Tillich, *The Shaking of the Foundations* (New York: Charles Scribner's Sons, 1948), 154.

21   Michael Kaplan, "He Doesn't Do Tricks: Interview with Ricky Jay," *American Way* magazine, 97.

22   *The Heidelberg Catechism with Commentary* (New York: The Pilgrim Press, 1962), 27.

23   Paul C. Vitz, "Was Jesus Self-Actualized?" *New Covenant*, 7/80, 7-8.

24   Ibid., 9.

25   interview with Garrison Keillor, *Wittenburg Door*, 12/84-1/85, 19-20.

Chapter Six: A Protestant Confession: From Symbol to Power

26   William H. Gardner, "Letters to the Editor," *The Christian Century*, 9/25/85, 845.

27   Madeleine L'Engle, "The Possible Human," *Cross Currents,* vol. XXXVIII, 387.

28   *Heidelberg Catechism*, 117.

29   Bob Slosser, *Miracle in Darien* (Plainfield, New Jer4sey: Logos International, 1979), 43-44.

30   John Sandford, "Freedom from the Pit and the Past," Elijah House Ministries, Post Falls, Idaho.

31   William H. Cleary, "Undocumented Protestants," *The Christian Century*, 8/14-21/85, 737.

32   *Heidelberg Catechism*, 134.

33   Ibid., 131.

34   Aimee Semple MacPherson, "The Great 'I Am' or 'I Was'?," in Vinson Synan, *The Century of the Holy Spirit* (Nashville: Thomas Nelson, 2001), 134.

35   James Gaughan, "How Ecumenical Are We?" *The Christian Century*, 1/16/85, 77-79.

36   Stanley Hauerwas and William H. Willimon, "Embarrassed by the Church: Congregations and the   Seminary," *The Christian Century*, 2/5-12/86, 117-119.

37   Rick Casey, "In Praise of Bad Sermons," *National Catholic Reporter*

Chapter Seven: Faith Encounters of the Third Kind

38 Interview with Ronald M. Enroth and J. Gordon Melton, "Why Cults Succeed Where the Church Fails," *Christianity Today*, March 16, 1984, 15-18.

39 Abraham H. Maslow, Religions, *Values, and Peak-Experiences* (New York: The Viking Press, 1970), viii.

40 Interview in *Leadership* magazine,

41 Loc.Cit..

42 Maslow, 42.

43 Loc. cit.

44 Ibid., 43.

45 from Mere Christianity, quoted in Philip Yancey, *Rumors of Another World* (Grand Rapids: Zondervan, 2003), 227.

46 Maslow, xxi.

Chapter Eight: Who is Holy Spirit?

47 C. Brandon Rimmer & Bill Brown, *The Unpredictable Wind* (Glendale, California: Aragorn Books, Inc, 1972), 1.

48 Don Basham, *Ministering the Baptism in the Holy Spirit* (Monroeville, Pennsylvania: Whitaker Books, 1971), 17.

49 Ibid., 20.

50 Robert Rensing, "Thoughts on the Universality of Christianity," *Friends Journal*, 2/1/84, 4-5.

Chapter Nine: Healing Past Emotional Wounds

51 Hugh Missildine, *Your Inner Child of the Past* (New York: Simon & Schuster, 1963).

52 Ruth Carter Stapleton, *The Gift of Inner Healing* (Waco, Texas: Word, Inc., 1976). Though I do not endorse all the teaching in this book, it did awaken me to the Spirit's work of emotional healing.

53 Ann Barry, "What To Do When You're Red-Hot Mad," *Redbook*, 7/82, 71.

54 This text is cited in a chapter titled "Inner Healing," in John Wimber, *Kingdom Warfare* (Anaheim: Mercy Publishing, 1993), 206.

Chapter Eleven: From Pier to Ocean

55 I have searched but cannot find a reference for this story.

Chapter Twelve: Of Jogging and Cat Food

56   This story first appeared as an opinion editorial in the *Los Angeles Times*, "Jogger Fails to Cross the Culture Gap," 6/4/81, B8.

57   Larry N. Lorenzoni, SDB, "Marcos' Faith," Letters to the Editor, *Los Angeles Times*. I saved this clipping, but failed to record the date.

58   Gabriel Fackre, *Word in Deed* (Grand Rapids, MI: Eerdmans, 1975), 9.

59   Larry Christenson, "Charismatics Shake Hands with Social Activists," *PRRM Renewal News*, May-June, 1988, 7.

60   John Wimber of the Vineyard churches coined this phrase.

61   Mary Andrews-Dalbey, *The REST of Your Life: Finding God's Rest in a Driven, Demanding, Distressful World* (Atlanta, GA: CarePoint Ministries, 2007).

62   Ibid.

63   The cat food story appeared in my article, "Material comfort, security, shouldn't make rich Christians insensitive to suffering," *The United Methodist Reporter*, 3/1/85.

64   Gordon Dalbey, "Why I Am Giving Up Something for Lent," *New World Outlook*, 3/81, 15.

65   Elie Wiesel, *Souls on Fire* (New York: Random House, 1972), 73.

66   Dalbey, 15-16.

67   Archbishop Krill, "Renewal of Humanity, Unity of the Church, and New Thinking," *Cross Currents*, Summer, 1988, 196.

68   Christenson, 7.

Chapter Thirteen: The Mirror of Prejudice

69   Charles Barkley, *I May Be Wrong—but I Doubt It* (New York: Random House, 2005).

70   See my chapter "Battling Racism" in *Fight like a Man*.

71   Gregory J. Johanson, "An Assurance Doctrine of the Cross," *Challenge to Evangelism Today*, summer '89, vol. 22 #2, 8.

72   This point is developed further in my article, "Cross-Burning at Home," *The Christian Ministry*, 7/80, vol X #4, 33.

73   Henry Lois Gates, Jr., and Cornel West, *The African American Century*, (New York: The Free Press, 2000).

74   All quotes referring to the Azusa Street Revival are from Richard Foster, *Streams of Living Water*, (New York: HarperCollins, 1998), 112-125.

75 G. Dalbey, "Brotherhood and the Marshmallow Wall," *Motive*, summer/1968, 14.

Chapter Fourteen: Jesus Is Our Peace

76 Dalbey, "War: The Real Enemy," *The Church Herald*, 9/4/81, 3-6.

77 Elie Wiesel, *A Jew Today* (New York: Random House, 1978), 173.

78 *Los Angeles Times*, 4/11/81.

79 I have been unable to find the source of this quote.

80 Wiesel, loc. cit.

81 Ibid, 178.

82 Ibid., 177.

83 Ibid., 171

84 Rev. Dr. Billy Graham, "A Change of Heart," *Sojourners*, 9/79, 14.

85 Quoted in Richard Foster, *Celebration of Discipline* (New York: Harper & Row, 1978), 44.

86 All quotations are from Norman Grubb, *Rees Howells, Intercessor*, (Fort Washington, PA: Christian Literature Crusade, 1980), 246-262.

Chapter Fifteen: Blackmailed by Shame

87 Keillor, op. cit., 21

88 Kevin J. Hasson, Becket Fund for Religious Liberty, www.becketfund.org

89 I heard John Sandford (Elijah House Ministries) say this some years ago at a conference.

90 *Time* Magazine, 12/27/10, 20.

91 Wiesel, p. 205.

ABOUT THE AUTHOR

Gordon Dalbey's widely acclaimed classic *Healing the Masculine Soul* helped pioneer the men's movement in 1988 and is still a bestseller today, with French and Italian translations. A popular speaker at conferences and retreats around the US and world, he has ministered in England, Hong Kong, Australia, New Zealand, Italy, France, Switzerland, Canada, and South Africa. A former news reporter (Charlotte NC), Peace Corps Volunteer (Nigeria), high school teacher (Chicago, San Jose CA) and pastor (Los Angeles), he holds an M.Div. from Harvard Divinity School, an M.A. in journalism from Stanford, and a B.A. from Duke.

Gordon has appeared on many radio and TV programs, including Focus on the Family. He lives in Santa Barbara, CA, and may be reached at www.abbafather.com.

Other Gordon Dalbey Books

paperbacks, audio cd/mp3 at www.abbafather.com

ebooks at www.kindle.com

> Both refreshing and upending, Gordon Dalbey's men's books take us to depths of authentic manhood where we're humbled by its mystery and engaged by its call. Apart from either violence or lust, his books restore courage and passion to manhood. Here's a masculinity you can trust—and the Father who makes it happen.

Healing the Masculine Soul

Today, politically correct voices cry out for men to be more sensitive, to tame our masculine nature. Meanwhile, the media bombards us with "macho" images of violence and lust. Is it any wonder men today are left bewildered about what manhood really is?

This pioneering, bestselling classic gives men hope for restoration by showing how Jesus enables us to get real with ourselves, with Him, and with other men. Its refreshing journey into the masculine soul dares men to break free from deceptive stereotypes and discover the power and blessing of authentic manhood.

Sons of the Father
Healing the Father-Wound in Men Today

"When you became a dad for the first time, did your own dad reach out to you with support, encouragement, or helpful advice?" Out of 350 Christian fathers, only 5 hands went up. "When you were 11 or 12, did your father talk to you about sex and relating to women?" I asked another gathering of 150 Christian men. Two hands.

Men today suffer a deep father-wound, which has left us unequipped for manhood. The father of Lies capitalizes on its shame and blackmails us into isolation, denial, and a host of bogus cover-ups—from money and guns to alcohol, sex, and performance religion.

The true Father of all men has come in Jesus to draw us back to Himself and to the man He created you to be. Here's the map to get you there.

Fight like a Man:
A New Manhood for a New Warfare

9/11 revealed the enemy of God and humanity as rooted in shame-based religion. The focus of warfare has now shifted dramatically from military battles to the hearts of men.

This trail-blazing book focuses on the crippling byproduct of fatherlessness in men today, namely, shame—too often fostered by religion, always overcome by Jesus. It's not about how to be a man, but knowing the Father who rescues and restores men. It's not even about how to be a warrior, but surrendering to the Commander of the Lord's Army.

Here, you won't be exhorted to obey, but invited to trust. You won't be commanded to do it right, but freed to be real. You won't be warned to be strong, but promised your Father's strength as you experience the grace and dignity of being His son.

> The awful wounding of our times, from family breakups and sexual confusion to drugs and violence, has left us hungry for a faith that embraces reality as graphically as we're forced to in this increasingly lost and broken world.

No Small Snakes
A Journey into Spiritual Warfare

This is my upending personal story of meeting and learning to overcome the powers of evil as portrayed in the Bible.

The problem in confronting spiritual reality, I discovered, is not that our childish imagination gets hooked into foolish fears, but that something real is evil and we can't control it. This humbling truth stirs shame in our Western, control-oriented culture and we deny the reality of supernatural evil. But pretending there's no thief in your house doesn't protect you from being robbed; it only gives thieves free rein to steal whatever they want.

In Jesus, God has invited us to exchange the illusion of our control for the reality of His power. This book extends that invitation to you.

Gordon Dalbey's books will stir you to a faith both passionate about its truth and compassionate in its grace. Here's freedom from universal tolerance on the one hand and narrow condemnation on the other—and Jesus at work today as God's vital Third Option to the world's self-defeating enmity.

Religion vs Reality
Facing the Home Front in Spiritual Warfare
Go figure out what this scripture means:

'I'm after mercy, not religion. I'm here to invite outsiders, not to coddle insiders'. (Matt. 9:13,14TMB)

Since Jesus, religion is obsolete. Religion is our human effort to cover the shame of our sin-nature. Honest human beings know it doesn't work. That's why Jesus came—and thereby, revealed religion as a tool of the enemy to distract us from His work.

And so our sophisticated, materialistic Western worldview denies the reality of evil because it reminds us we're not in control; we thereby forfeit the power to overcome it. Chapters focus on works of the enemy often hidden by popular culture and religious denial. Titles include 9/11 and the Spirit of Religion, Ball Games and the Battle for Men's Souls, Homosexuality and the Father Wound, White Racism and Spiritual Imperialism, Unmasking Halloween, Overcoming Depression, and Delivered from Abortion.

Pure Sex
The Spirituality of Desire
There's more to sex than mere skin on skin. Sex is as much spiritual mystery as physical fact. (1 Corinth. 6:16,17TMB)

Today's quest for "sexual freedom" has misled us into a vast wilderness of options where we've forgotten what sexual desire is, where it comes from, how it was designed to function, and where the power comes from to fulfill it.

Christians, meanwhile, have banned sexuality from church, leaving a vacuum which the world is literally hell-bent to fill. "Sex is dirty and immoral," as the culture confounds, "so save it for marriage and the one you love most!"

Here's the trailhead to authentic sexual freedom: not the absence of restrictions, but the presence of Father God, who enables its authentic fulfillment.

Chapters include Sex as Holy Nostalgia, The Genesis of Modesty, Homosexuality and History: A Perfect Storm, Spiritual Consequences of Sexual Union, Sexuality and Religion: A Marriage Made in Hell, Controlling Uncontrollable Desire, Was It Good for You (Too)? Sexual Bonding and a Woman's Heart (Mary Andrews-Dalbey PhD).

Loving to Fight, or Fighting to Love
Winning the Spiritual Battle for Your Marriage
with **Mary Andrews-Dalbey, PhD**

Our spiritual enemy's most deliberate efforts to distort the image of God focus on His most fundamental reflection in this world—namely, on the union of "male and female." The enemy of God is therefore attacking marriages today with a vengeance. The divorce rate among Christians, however, is the same as among others, at about 33%. Clearly, the overcoming power God has given to His church is not being widely received and exercised by Christian couples.

"They say marriages are made in heaven," actor Clint Eastwood once commented. "So are thunder and lightning."

In this fallen world, storms come to every honest couple. Those who fight in the power of the flesh think the question is, Who's right? But for those who fight in the power of the Spirit, the question is, What's God trying to teach us?

It's not about how to make your marriage work, but how to let God work in your marriage. Chapters include Never Waste a Good Fight, Leaving Father and Mother: The Trailhead to Marriage, For Better or Worse: A Woman's View (Mary), When You're Hot You're Hot; When You're not It's Time to Talk about Sex, Fire Prevention: How to Stop a Fight before It Starts, and A Couple's Guide to Spiritual Warfare.

88174777R00154

Made in the USA
Columbia, SC
01 February 2018